Springer Series on International Justice and Human Rights

Series Editor

George J. Andreopoulos
City University of New York
John Jay College of Criminal Justice
New York, NY, USA

The Springer Series on International Justice and Human Rights aims to document the ongoing international criminalization of human rights violations, focusing on the processes associated with the pursuit of justice in international society, the key actors and institutions involved, and the normative as well as policy considerations that shape their actions. Titles in this series critically examine the effectiveness of current justice systems, new opportunities for addressing longstanding challenges, the interplay between domestic and international justice options, the role of social justice movements and non-judicial initiatives, and the collective impact of all entities involved in creating a more humane and peaceful world. Contributions are invited from scholars in the humanities, social sciences, legal, and interdisciplinary fields. This series aims both at showcasing cutting-edge research in this critical issue area.

More information about this series at http://www.springer.com/series/10641

George J. Andreopoulos • Rosemary L. Barberet
Mahesh K. Nalla
Editors

The Rule of Law in an Era of Change

Responses to Transnational Challenges and Threats

Springer

Editors
George J. Andreopoulos
Department of Political Science
John Jay College of Criminal Justice
and the Graduate Center
City University of New York
New York, NY, USA

Rosemary L. Barberet
Department of Sociology
John Jay College of Criminal Justice
City University of New York
New York, NY, USA

Mahesh K. Nalla
School of Criminal Justice
Michigan State University
East Lansing, MI, USA

Springer Series on International Justice and Human Rights
ISBN 978-3-030-07892-8 ISBN 978-3-319-89908-4 (eBook)
https://doi.org/10.1007/978-3-319-89908-4

Printed on acid-free paper

This Springer imprint is published by the registered company Springer International Publishing AG part of Springer Nature.
The registered company address is: Gewerbestrasse 11, 6330 Cham, Switzerland

Preface

This volume is based on papers initially presented at John Jay College's 11th Biennial International Conference on *The Rule of Law in an Era of Change: Security, Social Justice and Inclusive Governance* held in Athens, Greece, June 11–14, 2014. This conference was organized in collaboration with the Center for Security Studies (KEMEA) of the Greek Ministry of Public Order and Citizen Protection. It was funded by a generous grant from the Stavros Niarchos Foundation (SNF), whose commitment to and support of this project is gratefully acknowledged.

There are many people who made the conference and the resulting publication possible. More specifically, the Conference Organizing Committee composed of George Andreopoulos (chair), Jana Arsovska, Rosemary Barberet, Rosemarie Maldonado, Mayra Nieves, Katherine Stavrianopoulos, and Patricia Tovar worked diligently to ensure the conference's success. The Organizing Committee was very ably assisted in this task by Aferdita Hakaj, its Executive Assistant. At KEMEA, former President Michalis Tsinisizelis, Vasilis Grizis, Irene Kolevri, and Nikos Petropoulos provided invaluable support and assistance in all aspects of this undertaking. The conference proved to be a forum for very informative exchanges and insightful deliberations made possible by the very engaged presenters and participants. The contributors to this volume deserve a special note of thanks: they had to initially revise their papers and turn them into book chapters and then address the extensive comments and suggested revisions offered during the editorial process. Last, but not least, I would like to thank Katie Chabalko, Hana Nagdimov, Menas Donald Kiran, and Lavanya Venkatesan at Springer for all their assistance throughout the process of turning this manuscript into a book.

I hope that the end result will live up to the expectations of all those who were part of this project.

New York, NY, USA George J. Andreopoulos

Acknowledgment

ΙΔΡΥΜΑ ΣΤΑΥΡΟΣ ΝΙΑΡΧΟΣ
STAVROS NIARCHOS FOUNDATION

This volume is based on papers presented at John Jay College's 11th Biennial International Conference on *The Rule of Law in an Era of Change: Security, Social Justice and Inclusive Governance* held in Athens, Greece, June 11–14, 2014. This conference was organized in collaboration with the Center for Security Studies (KEMEA) of the Greek Ministry of Public Order and Citizen Protection. It was funded by a generous grant from the Stavros Niarchos Foundation (SNF), whose commitment to and support of this project are gratefully acknowledged.

Contents

1 **Introduction: Rule of Law in an Era of Change – Challenges and Prospects** 1
George J. Andreopoulos, Rosemary L. Barberet, and Mahesh K. Nalla

2 **Drones, Distance, and Death** 15
Tziporah Kasachkoff and John Kleinig

3 **War as Play, War as Slaughter, and the Laws of War** 47
Karsten J. Struhl

4 **The Quest for Accountability: The Resolution 1373 Process at the United Nations Security Council** 73
George J. Andreopoulos

5 **Victims of Terrorism Associations After September 11th and March 11th: Claims, Demands, and Responses** 103
Rosemary L. Barberet and Cristina Flesher Fominaya

6 **The Relationship Between the International Criminal Court (ICC) and Truth Commissions** 125
Kate Louise Mc Eleney

7 **Legal Assumptions and Unintended Meanings Before International and Hybrid Criminal Courts: Effects on Trial Proceedings and Defense Rights** 151
Dragana Spencer

Index 177

About the Editors

George J. Andreopoulos is Professor of Political Science and Criminal Justice at City University of New York (CUNY), and Founding Director of Center for International Human Rights at the John Jay College of Criminal Justice, CUNY. He has written extensively on international organizations, international human rights, and humanitarian law issues. He has lectured widely in the USA and abroad and has served as consultant for the United Nations and nongovernmental organizations. He is President of the Interdisciplinary Studies Section (IDSS) of the International Studies Association (ISA) and past President of the Human Rights Section of the American Political Science Association (APSA).

Rosemary L. Barberet is Professor in the Sociology Department at John Jay College of Criminal Justice who teaches in the MA and BA programs in International Criminal Justice. Dr. Barberet's research interests include the use of criminal justice data and research in policymaking, crime indicators, victimization, gender and crime and cross-cultural methodology. Dr. Barberet was awarded the Herbert Bloch Award of the American Society of Criminology for service to the society and to the professional interests of criminology, as well as the Rafael Salillas Award of the Sociedad Española de Investigación Criminológica. Her most recent book, *Women, Crime and Criminal Justice: A Global Enquiry*, won awards from both the Division of International Criminology of the American Society of Criminology and the International Section of the Academy of Criminal Justice Sciences.

Mahesh K. Nalla is Professor of Criminal Justice at Michigan State University in East Lansing, Michigan, USA. His current research projects are focused on two areas in emerging and transitional democracies: *governance, legitimacy, and social regulation (public and private policing); and gendered spaces, victimization, and public health.* He had coordinated and led a global project, firearm-related violence prevention programs, for the United Nations that covered over 180 countries. His research appeared in leading journals that include the *Journal of Research and Crime and Delinquency*, *Justice Quarterly*, and *European Journal of Criminology*, among others.

Contributors

Kate Louise Mc Eleney is a former Mc Cabe Fellow at John Jay College of Criminal Justice (2013–2014), New York. She holds a Bachelor of Civil Law (B.C.L.) and an LL.M. in International Human Rights Law from the National University of Ireland, Galway, in addition to an M.A. in Criminal Justice (Terrorism Studies) from John Jay College of Criminal Justice. Kate is a diplomat in Ireland's diplomatic service having previously served as a police officer with An Garda Síochána (Ireland's National Police Force).

Cristina Flesher Fominaya is an Editor of *Social Movement Studies*, a Founding Editor of *Interface Journal,* and author of *Social Movements and Globalization* (Palgrave). As of April 2018, she is a Reader in Social Politics and Media at Loughborough University, UK. She publishes widely on European and global social movements, hybrid parties, digital politics and media, collective identity, democracy, civil society, and political participation.

Tziporah Kasachkoff is Professor Emerita of Philosophy at Ben Gurion University and the Graduate Center, City University of New York. She is coeditor of the American Philosophical Association's *Newsletter on Teaching Philosophy* and specializes in moral, social, and political philosophy, topics on which she has published in various philosophy and law journals.

John Kleinig is Professor Emeritus of Philosophy at John Jay College of Criminal Justice and the Graduate Center, City University of New York. He is also an Adjunct Professor of Philosophy at Charles Sturt University, Australia. He is author/coeditor of 22 books on moral, social, and political philosophy.

Dragana Spencer is Senior Lecturer in Law at the School of Law and the Centre for Criminology, University of Greenwich. She holds a PhD in International Criminal Law and her interests and areas of expertise are in procedures and practices of international criminal courts and tribunals with a focus on defense rights and sentencing practices.

Karsten J. Struhl teaches political philosophy, philosophy of religion, and cross-cultural philosophy at John Jay College of Criminal Justice (CUNY) and the New School for Public Engagement. He has coedited *Philosophy Now*, *Ethics in Perspective*, *The Philosophical Quest: A Cross-Cultural Reader*, and *When Young People Break the Law: Debating Issues on Punishment for Juveniles*. He writes about human nature, just war theory, problems of revenge and punishment, global ethics, visions of communism, ecology, Marxism, and Buddhist philosophy. His articles have appeared in a variety of journals, books, and encyclopedias.

Chapter 1
Introduction: Rule of Law in an Era of Change – Challenges and Prospects

George J. Andreopoulos, Rosemary L. Barberet, and Mahesh K. Nalla

A Contentious Revival

The rule of law (RoL) is a concept that has undergone several transformations in its long and turbulent history.[1] With the end of the cold war, RoL has witnessed a major revival[2]; a revival that has proven to be a mixed blessing at best. On the one hand, it has become an indispensable component in the efforts to build well-ordered societies, particularly in the aftermath of conflict situations. It is ritualistically invoked by leaders of regimes all over the world, whether democratic, illiberal democratic, transitioning, or authoritarian, as well as by international agencies. Its alleged reach though is global and goes beyond merely assisting in broad democratization and peacebuilding efforts. Its proponents claim that it can contribute to the cure of major domestic and international societal ills that include poverty, gross, and systematic human rights violations, as well as intra- and interstate violence.[3] This core belief is best reflected in the United Nations General Assembly Resolution 67/1, which reaffirmed the concept's "fundamental importance…for the further development of the three main pillars upon which the United Nations is built: international peace and security, human rights and development."[4] In addition to such official

---

[1] For a useful overview, see Brian Z. Tamanaha (2004).

[2] Thomas Carothers (1998).

[3] David Marshall (2014), p. xiv.

[4] United Nations General Assembly Resolution 67/1 (2012).

G. J. Andreopoulos (✉) · R. L. Barberet
Political Science Department, John Jay College of Criminal Justice,
City University of New York, New York, NY, USA
e-mail: gandreopoulos@jjay.cuny.edu

M. K. Nalla
School of Criminal Justice, Michigan State University, East Lansing, MI, USA

G. J. Andreopoulos et al. (eds.), *The Rule of Law in an Era of Change*,
Springer Series on International Justice and Human Rights,
https://doi.org/10.1007/978-3-319-89908-4_1

pronouncements, many studies have joined the chorus of extolling the RoL's virtues.[5] In a certain sense, the moral appeal of the RoL resembles that of human rights: everybody is in favor even – or, some may say, particularly – when they routinely violate them.

On the other hand, this focus on RoL's indispensability and alleged promise have elicited much critical scrutiny and skepticism, when examined in light of the record of massive RoL reform projects undertaken during the last 25 years or so. Some analysts, while sympathetic to the relevance of RoL assistance programs, do question the facile attributions of beneficial causal effects resulting from RoL interventions and reform efforts that are often unsupported by the available empirical evidence.[6] Other analysts, writing from a critical theoretical perspective, point to a lot of wishful thinking about the RoL's achievements, primarily manifested through narratives that portray a rather "harmonious and mutually reinforcing relationship between development, human rights, and security."[7] Such narratives, according to these critics, are premised on the misplaced assumption that the RoL is "technical, legal, and apolitical"[8] and fail to capture the tensions among the three main pillars of the UN system; tensions that the invocation of the RoL, regardless of definitional variations, cannot fully resolve.[9]

Notwithstanding the merit of some of these criticisms, it is important to distinguish the argument about the misplaced optimism generated by the RoL as a panacea for the world's ills, from the argument about the irrelevance of the concept's content. To be sure, there is a growing consensus among analysts that the "cure for all ills" invocation of the concept is reflective of a form of wishful thinking normally associated with fierce advocacy unconstrained by critical examination. At the same time, few would argue against the proposition that the concept's content is determinative of the way in which issues of security, development, and human rights are approached, even if the resulting policies often fall well below the expectations of their proponents and, more importantly, of their intended beneficiaries.

While debates about the content and reach of the RoL are ongoing, there is no serious dispute about the concept's central role in global conversations on critical world order issues, such as inclusive governance, sustainable development, peace/security, and human protection. Why does the RoL matter in these discussions? And what are some of the challenges facing its implementation in an era of rising expectations about its relevance?

---

[5] See, among others, Jane Stromseth et al. (2006); Agnes Hurwitz and Kaysie Studdard, *RULE OF LAW PROGRAMS IN PEACE OPERATIONS.* Policy Paper, International Peace Academy, August 2005, https://www.ipinst.org/wp-content/uploads/publications/ipa_e_report_rule_of_law.pdf; and Jennifer A. Widner 2001.

[6] On the RoL and development, see Michael Trebilcock and Ronald Daniels (2008); and James J. Heckman et al. (2010). On the sequencing between democratic transition and the development of an independent court system, see Tom Ginsburg (2010).

[7] Balakrishnan Rajagopal (2008, p. 1375).

[8] Rajagopal, p. 1349.

[9] Ibid.

The Relevance of the RoL: Challenges and Prospects

Any examination of the RoL must begin by addressing contending theoretical formulations of the concept. Most analyses identify two broad categories: "formal" and "substantive" versions with a range of accounts in each version that, depending on the content requirements, span a continuum from "thin" to "thick."[10] To begin with, both versions view the RoL as a principle aimed at preventing the arbitrary exercise of governmental powers. Formal versions focus on the manner in which the law is promulgated (by proper authority) and the extent to which the law is general, clear, precise, and prospective. The latter attribute relates to the degree to which the legal rules offer guidance to those affected by it, so that they know what to expect and plan their actions accordingly; here the nonretroactive character of rules is of vital importance since it acts as a safeguard against unpredictability.

According to Hayek, one of the most prominent theorists of the formal conception of the rule of law, the three key attributes of the RoL are generality, certainty, and equality (absence of arbitrary distinctions).[11] In this understanding of the RoL, no allowance is made for specific requirements with respect to the content of legal rules. Any attempt to the contrary, that is, render the RoL an instrument in the service of a specific social agenda – for example, in the context of efforts to advance the cause of social justice – would promote the adoption of partial (as opposed to general) measures and privilege particular individuals and/or groups with adverse impact on the RoL and the cause of liberty.[12] In its extreme formal version, devoid of any substantive content, the RoL can accommodate very repressive regimes, as Joseph Raz has noted: "A non-democratic legal system, based on the denial of human rights, on extensive poverty, on racial segregation, sexual inequalities and religious persecution…will be an immeasurably worse legal system, but it will excel in one respect: in its conformity to the rule of law."[13] History is not short of examples of formal RoL-oriented regimes that exhibited massive and systematic cruelty against those under their jurisdiction and control: Nazi Germany, South Africa during apartheid, and Southern Rhodesia come prominently to mind.

In fact, it was the Nazi regime's blend of extreme formalism and cruelty that led to the revival of natural law on the aftermath of the World War II. This was reflected in the preamble to the Universal Declaration of Human Rights (UDHR) with its affirmation that "disregard and contempt for human rights have resulted in barbarous acts which have outraged the conscience of mankind." This reference

---

[10] Tamanaha, *On the Rule of Law,* note 1, p. 91.

[11] F. A. Hayek (1978). Hayek discusses extensively these principles in Chapter 14, *The Safeguards of Individual Liberty*, pp. 205–219.

[12] Hayek is very emphatic on this point: "Law was meant to prevent unjust conduct. Justice referred to principles equally applicable to all and was contrasted to all specific commands or privileges referring to particular individuals and groups.…Yet to break the principle of *equal treatment under the law* even for charity's sake inevitably opened the floodgates to arbitrariness. To disguise it the pretence of the formula of 'social justice' was resorted to"; F.A. Hayek (1979).

[13] Joseph Raz (2009, p. 211).

constituted a repudiation of extreme formalism and an acknowledgment of the need to ground all rule-oriented action on a firm commitment to "fundamental human rights" and to "the dignity and worth of the human person." While the relationship between human rights and the RoL was clearly undeveloped in the UDHR, the reference to the RoL in this foundational document signaled the long process of reorienting the international community's efforts toward the advancement of substantive versions of the RoL concept.[14] The aspirational nature of this foundational document notwithstanding, it demarcates a pathway that increasingly associates membership in the international community with adherence to certain fundamental norms and standards.

An emphasis on rule content firmly juxtaposes substantive with formal versions of the RoL. And while huge debates have raged around the successes and failures of the post-World War II human rights era, few would question the centrality of human rights in any conceptualization of substantive RoL versions. The widely shared view that human rights norms and rules constitute a source of legitimacy[15] has firmly anchored such versions within the human rights orbit.

This conceptualization is reflected in the UN definition of the RoL. The UN Secretary-General's Report on the RoL defines the concept as:

> a principle of governance in which all persons, institutions and entities, public and private, including the State itself, are accountable to laws that are publicly promulgated, equally enforced and independently adjudicated, and which are consistent with international human rights norms and standards. It requires, as well, measures to ensure adherence to the principles of supremacy of law, equality before the law, accountability to the law, fairness in the application of the law, separation of powers, participation in decision-making, legal certainty, avoidance of arbitrariness and procedural and legal transparency.[16]

This is a hybrid definition that combines formal and substantive elements with due attention to the requirement of consistency "with international human rights norms and standards."[17] While substantive RoL versions that incorporate adherence to such norms and standards can avoid the aforementioned pitfalls of purely formal versions, they confront their own set of challenges. This volume takes the UN definition and associated narratives (declarations, resolutions) as its starting point of reference and critically examines certain key issue areas relevant to the implementation of the RoL at the national and international levels. In this vein, the remainder of this introductory chapter will briefly address, due to space limitations, two of these issue areas and the related expectations and challenges, as well as their potential impact on the RoL's relevance.

---

[14] The only reference to the RoL in the UDHR is in the preamble: "Whereas it is essential, if man is not to be compelled to have recourse, as a last resort, to rebellion against tyranny and oppression, that human rights should be protected by the rule of law." For the full text of the UDHR, see http://www.ohchr.org/EN/UDHR/Documents/UDHR_Translations/eng.pdf. United Nations (1948).

[15] Ruth W. Grant and Robert O. Keohane (2005, p. 35).

[16] United Nations Security Council (2004, 23, p. 4).

[17] Ibid.

The starting point for this brief enquiry can be stated as follows: the reach and relevance of the concept automatically generate a plethora of expectations which cannot be easily or fully realized. The abovementioned United Nations General Assembly Declaration on the rule of law[18] is instructive here: the rule of law is nothing short of "the foundation of friendly and equitable relations between States and the basis on which just and fair societies are built."[19] At the national/domestic level, the Declaration points to the importance of "fair, stable, and predictable legal frameworks" for inclusive social orders and equitable development. At the international level, it points to "the resolution of disputes by peaceful means and in conformity with the principles of justice and international law." Notions of predictability, justice, equality, and legitimacy are relevant to both levels and converge on the presumed necessity of adherence to human rights norms and standards: inclusive social orders can only be built on respect for human dignity and nondiscrimination; and peaceful international orders can only be built on upholding the sovereign equality/self-determination of states and advancing the quest for self-determination of those "peoples" who remain under foreign occupation and colonial domination.[20]

In this context, we will examine two issues that underscore key narratives of the UN's conceptualization of the RoL: the alignment of *predictability* and *legitimacy* and the relationship between the RoL and security, human rights, and development, the three main pillars of the UN system.

The sweeping language of resolution 67/1 affirms that *predictability* and *legitimacy*, two key terms associated with the hybrid UN definition, must be closely aligned. In fact, the resolution is quite categorical on this point: "respect for …the rule of law and justice should guide all of their (i.e. States and international organizations) activities and accord predictability and legitimacy to their actions." To be sure, there are situations in which the exigencies of predictability and the quest for legitimacy are aligned, for example, when faced with the challenge posed by the unequal distribution of power. Expectations of rule-following and the concomitant consistency and predictability in the application of the relevant rules invariably clash with power considerations. The centuries-long effort aimed at curbing the arbitrary power of rulers and other authority structures in the domestic arena, let alone the continuing challenge of subjecting them to effective human rights scrutiny, is a testament to such an alignment.

Needless to say, this challenge is even more pronounced once the focus shifts to the international arena where the absence of an overarching authority and extreme power differentials have often undermined consistency in the application of rules and produced outcomes inimical to rudimentary notions of legitimacy. The "international rule of law," meaning the application of RoL principles and standards to

[18] See note 4.

[19] Ibid.

[20] In the context of our discussion, the self-determination of states in the international arena is manifested in the juridical equality of states and its corollary, noninterference by external actors in domestic affairs. For a brief discussion of these two types of sovereignty, see Stephen Krasner (1999, pp. 14–25).

interstate relations and to "other subjects and objects of international law," undoubtedly adds another layer of complexity.[21] The emphasis placed by international law on the maintenance of international peace and security is telling here. The traditional (and rather inadequate) definition of international law as the body of rules that "governs relations between independent states"[22]/or "which are binding upon civilized states in their relations with one another"[23] invariably privileges, in its quest for compromise,[24] the orderly conduct of interstate relations over general rules, rules which can also be consistent with the pursuit of a legitimate social purpose, like the promotion and protection of internationally recognized human rights standards. To be sure, the universe of international law has become infinitely more complex with the growth and legal reach of international organizations and other nongovernmental entities whose actions have often sought to minimize this challenge.[25] However, even in issue areas such as accountability for human rights/humanitarian law violations where the rule of law is supposed to have registered great progress, we still see provisions that reinforce it. A telling example here is Article 16 of the Rome Statute of the International Criminal Court which provides for the United Nations Security Council (UNSC) to request, in a resolution adopted under Chapter VII, deferral of an investigation or a prosecution by the International Criminal Court (ICC). Presumably, the UNSC would issue such a request if it was to determine that the said investigation or prosecution could constitute a threat to international peace and security. Given the wide discretion that the UNSC has in making such determinations, it came as no surprise to see this provision invoked by the Council shortly after the entering into force of the Rome Statute.[26]

---

[21] United Nations General Assembly-Security Council (2008, p. 4).

[22] Permanent Court of International Justice, *The Case of the S.S. Lotus. France v. Turkey. Judgment;* http://www.worldcourts.com/pcij/eng/decisions/1927.09.07_lotus.htm para.44.

[23] J. L. Brierly (1963, p.1).

[24] See on this Tamanaha, *On the Rule of Law,* note 1, 132–133.

[25] On the contribution of international organizations to international law-making, see Jose Alvarez (2005). The growth and reach of international organizations and the concomitant expansion of transborder agreements have contributed to what some analysts have called "international regime complexity," namely, parallel, nested, and partially overlapping international regimes in a particular issue area which affect implementation since they reduce the clarity/certainty "of legal obligation by introducing overlapping sets of legal rules and jurisdictions" governing the said issue area. On this, see Karen J. Alter and Sophie Meunier (2009). A good example of such regime complexity would be in the area of human rights for European countries. Human rights are addressed by the partially overlapping regimes of the Council of Europe and the European Union that include their respective legal instruments (the European Convention for the Protection of Human Rights and Fundamental Freedoms, the Charter of Fundamental Rights of the European Union, and their Social Charters), as well as their corresponding judicial organs (the European Court of Human Rights and the Court of Justice of the European Union). It is beyond the scope of this introductory chapter to address this issue.

[26] We are referring of course to the back-to-back resolutions (1422 in 2002 and 1487 in 2003) adopted by the UNSC, at the insistence of the USA, exempting peacekeepers from countries not parties to the Rome Statute from possible ICC prosecution. After the second annual adoption in 2003, the UN Secretary-General noted that its continuation could undermine the ICC.

There are situations though in which predictability and legitimacy are in tension. A telling example is offered by the growth of international human rights law and its shift from universal rights expressed in the earlier instruments[27] toward targeted protections for specific groups (e.g., children, women, indigenous peoples, and persons with disabilities). This development together with the proliferation of transborder agreements and platforms from which coalitions of national, transnational, and international actors can advance these groups' claims works against the exigencies of predictability which is premised on the adoption of general rules applied across the board. In this context, the requirements of legitimacy point to the adoption of particularistic protective regimes that cannot easily be subsumed under general rules, if they are to advance their key object and purpose of overcoming discriminatory/exclusionary treatment. Some analysts have argued that the shift toward greater protections for specific groups does not mark a qualitatively different turn but is simply another manifestation of the "vocabulary" and "institutional practice of human rights promotion"[28] which tends to focus "on discrete and insular right-holding identities" that undermine "awareness of diversity, of the continuity of human experience, of overlapping identities."[29] Such a focus undermines articulations of alternative expressions reflective of a shared, communal experience informed by general, as opposed to specific, rule-making.

Likewise, a more complex picture emerges once the connections between the RoL and the three pillars of the UN system are subjected to closer examination.[30] Resolution 67/1 not only reaffirmed the centrality of the RoL in the UN system but also emphasized the collective decision "to develop further the linkages between the rule of law and the three main pillars of the United Nations." To be sure, no one expected the inclusion of a critical perspective in a celebratory document adopted at the conclusion of a UN General Assembly High-Level Meeting. Yet, it is precisely the mantra-style invocation of seemingly unproblematic compatibilities that invites scrutiny.

The main problem with this image of harmonious convergence is that *human rights* have invariably followed quite a distinct trajectory as a discourse of resistance and social emancipation, a path that did not easily fit within the "technocratic ambiance" surrounding traditional/formal RoL initiatives. This does not mean that human rights have been immune to the embrace of technocratic expertise in the service of power-wielders. On the contrary, the growing corpus of international human rights law, one of the seminal developments in the international legal order, is a key indicator of both the professionalization of human rights advocacy and the

[27] Namely, the UDHR, the International Covenant on Civil and Political Rights (ICCPR), and the International Covenant on Economic, Social and Cultural Rights (ICESCR), collectively known as the International Bill of Rights (IBR) United Nations (1948, 1966a, b).

[28] Terms used by David Kennedy (2004, p. 13).

[29] Ibid, pp. 15–16.

[30] Space does not allow for an exhaustive treatment of these linkages. Our introduction seeks to identify some key problematic aspects of these linkages so as to set the stage for the chapters that follow.

co-optation of the human rights discourse by actors that focus on the consequences, as opposed to the causes of human rights violations.[31] A key manifestation of this development is the privileging of political and civil rights whose protection can be achieved by judicial means, as opposed to socioeconomic rights whose protection can be primarily advanced in the context of challenging dominant political and socioeconomic structures and forces. The fact that, for several advocates, justiciability remains a key criterion for the distinction between "rights" and "aspirations,"[32] is an indication of the extent of the human rights predicament. Yet, human rights have constituted in the past, and continue to this very day, a discourse for mobilizing the vulnerable, the persecuted, and the marginal, irrespective of the nature of the cause of the violation. While success in the quest for socioeconomic justice has often proved to be elusive, human rights have tended to monopolize the emancipation narrative at the expense of competing discourses.[33] Grassroots mobilizations and resistance around issues of corporate accountability, environmental protection, and indigenous peoples' rights to their lands are indicative of the continuing appeal of and belief in the human rights discourse's transformative potential. To phrase it in another way, human rights have maintained, despite their co-optation by powerwielders, an interactive dualism: a discourse of accommodation and resistance.

The same could not be said about *development* or *security*, which have been invariably amenable to pragmatic narratives of cost/benefit calculations that often belie the "established" political premises underscoring their policy prescriptions. More specifically, in the case of development, the RoL emphasis on formal rules has reinforced, especially in the post-Cold War era, the emphasis on institutions and procedures that ensured the smooth functioning of the free market at the exclusion of considerations about the distributional outcomes of free market policies.[34] To be sure, the "formalization of legal entitlements"[35]as a precondition for development is not a new notion; it dates back at least to the nineteenth century.[36] What ties together different perceptions on the relation between formal rules and development is not the particular outcome – which in its most recent incarnation is associated with the neoliberal paradigm – but the belief that hard political choices can be kept out of policy making. This approach presents a picture of the RoL as manifested in

---

[31] For more on this, see Tony Evans (2005), especially pp. 1066–1068.

[32] Aryeh Neier is a typical advocate of this approach: ..."the justiciability of questions involving rights and their judicial enforcement seems crucial to making rights a reality. It is hard to imagine how rights could be upheld in practice without a body that is insulated from the regular political process playing a decisive role." *The International Human Rights Movement. A History.* Princeton University Press, 2012, p. 68. Other analysts are critical of this view:"...the human rights movement fetishizes the judge as someone who functions as an instrument of the law rather than as a political actor. This is simply not possible ...given the porous legal vocabulary with which judges must work and the likely political context within which judges are asked to act"; Kennedy, *The Dark Sides of Virtue,* note 28, p. 22.

[33] For example, discourses drawn from religious traditions and local social resistance practices.

[34] Rajagopal, note 7, pp. 1363–1364.

[35] Expression used by Kennedy, note 28, p. 158.

[36] Ibid; and Rajagopal, note 7, p. 1363.

arrangements such as clear property rules, enforcement of contracts, and a secure environment for investment that can best thrive in a milieu that reduces discretion and political choice.[37] For example, a society in which clear property rules are adopted in order to minimize uncertainty on titles could witness a growth in foreign investment on land at the expense of local ownership.[38] This may be the desired and achievable outcome of a specific governmental/societal policy aimed at benefiting a particular group of foreign investors at the expense of local property owners. However, invoking the RoL transforms, what is clearly a political choice, into the only possible outcome. As one analyst, writing about the formalization of the law as a requirement for development, put it: it "heightens the sense both that the rule of law can be injected without political choice, and that its implementation is a precondition to economic growth rather than a choice among alternative theories of development."[39] In a nutshell, the RoL should be viewed as a terrain of contestation for the adoption of specific developmental strategies and policies with corresponding distributional outcomes; it constitutes an integral part of the "engagement with the politics and economics of development policy making"[40] not a substitute for it. This is in sharp contrast to the imagery of "harmonious convergence," premised on a perception of the RoL as *exogenous* to such policy making.

If the discourse on development can be criticized for sidelining politics and distributional outcomes, the discourse on security can be criticized for sidelining legitimacy and accountability outcomes. This is particularly troubling in light of the new era in security that supposedly dawned at the end of the Cold War. Invocations of a "New World Order," "a world in which freedom and respect for human rights find a home among all nations"[41] were to demarcate the beginnings of a period characterized by multilateral approaches to peace and security, a period in which international organizations like the UN would finally realize their potential as envisaged by their founders. Nothing exemplified better this "new era" than the growing activism of the UNSC and its expansive determinations on issues that could constitute "threats to international peace and security." More specifically, while between 1946 and 1989 the UNSC adopted 646 resolutions, it adopted 638 resolutions only in the period between 1989 and 1999.[42] In addition, many of these resolutions determined that a variety of situations that included violations of human rights and international humanitarian law, terrorist attacks, and the overthrow of democratic governments

---

[37] Kennedy, p. 158.

[38] On this, see Eve Darian-Smith (2013, p. 296).

[39] Kennedy, p. 157. This is not the only criticism. Other studies have questioned the extent to which RoL institutions have been consequential to growth and development by pointing to, among others, the example of the East Asian Tigers; see Erik G. Jensen (2014), "Postscript: An Immodest Reflection," in Marshall, note 3, pp. 296–297.

[40] Kennedy, p. 167.

[41] George Bush 1991; http://www.presidency.ucsb.edu/ws/?pid=19364

[42] *The UN Security Council and the Rule of Law*, note 21 at 1.

constituted threats to international peace and security.[43] Last but not least, the UNSC established two ad hoc international tribunals (ICTY and ICTR) to hold accountable those responsible for these violations.[44]

This expanding universe of "threats to the peace," manifested through the proliferation of potential triggers for action, paved the way for a variety of interventionary activities ranging from selective/targeted/comprehensive sanctions to military interventions, ostensibly geared toward human protection purposes, and post-conflict peace building experiments.[45] Yet, the move toward the broadening of our understanding of security, and of the nature of the threats that seek to undermine it, did not generate a corresponding call for more robust adherence to RoL standards by those entities undertaking such actions (whether states or international organizations). On many occasions, the multilateral nature of such activities was used as a proxy for legitimacy, instead of as an entry point to greater transparency and accountability.

Once again, the record of the UNSC and its member states is instructive here. There is a wide range of activities authorized and/or initiated by the UNSC, including the abovementioned criminal tribunals and military interventions. Concerning the latter, the 2005 World Summit endorsed, under certain circumstances, the idea of collective action through the UNSC.[46] The adoption of the Responsibility to Protect (RtoP) was to signal the end of impunity and the pursuit of accountability for the most egregious human rights violations: genocide, war crimes, crimes against humanity, and ethnic cleansing. While a lot of attention understandably focused on the targeted entities, the conduct of those actors authorizing and enforcing the applicable RoL standards was not subjected to commensurate scrutiny. More specifically, it was somewhat ironic to have the UNSC leading the charge for accountability in the former Yugoslavia and Rwanda, or insisting on adherence to the RoL within UN-administered territories (Kosovo and Timor Leste), while being less responsive to the relevance of these standards in the behavior of UN peacekeeping troops,[47] or to the manner in which individuals may be selected for inclusion in sanctions lists and to the due process challenges confronting de-listing requests.[48]

To be sure, the application of the international rule of law is, as noted earlier, an infinitely more complex issue. This, however, does not mean that the way forward is to paper over these difficulties by simplistic overgeneralizations about "harmonious

[43] Such violations of human rights and humanitarian law included obstacles to the delivery of humanitarian assistance, internal as well as cross-border population displacement, targeting of civilians, abuse of detainees in conflict situations, and overthrow of democratic government, among others. See, for example, UNSCR 688 (Iraq), UNSCR 770 (Bosnia-Herzegovina), UNSCR 794 (Somalia), UNSCR 940 (Haiti), UNSCR 1199 (Kosovo), UNSCR 1272 (East Timor), and UNSCR 1778 (Chad, CAR and Sudan-border region).

[44] UNSCR 827 (ICTY-for the former Yugoslavia) and UNSCR 955 (ICTR-for Rwanda).

[45] See, among others, Anne Orford (2003); Anthony Anghie (2005); and Michael Barnett (2011).

[46] United Nations General Assembly Resolution 60/1. *2005 World Summit Outcome;* A/RES/60/1, 24 October 2005, paras 138 and 139.

[47] See, among others, United Nations General Assembly (2005).

[48] Post (2012).

and mutually reinforcing" relationships. On the contrary, these difficulties should be acknowledged as a precondition for the establishment of certain fundamental baselines on which necessary and sustainable improvements can be pursued. In this context, a key baseline is the reaffirmation that international legal rules apply to all the members (whether state or non-state) of the international community. Any concerns about the challenges posed by partially overlapping legal regimes and the fragmentation of the international legal order do not negate the fact that, despite concerns about the clarity and specificity of particular rules, the way forward is not to sideline them, but to further develop/refine them so as to address existing ambiguities and tensions. A corollary to this reaffirmation is that there is a particular onus for rule adherence on those entities, whether at the national or international level, that are considered guardians of fundamental principles and have a supervisory and/or enforcement role. In order to be effective in the capacity of guardian/supervisor/enforcer, these entities must possess legitimacy; an attribute that stems from adherence to the rules and standards that they seek, by word and deed, to promote. The customary international law maxim *venire contra factum proprium non valet*[49] is a powerful reminder that, even in the absence of effective supervisory mechanisms to "guard the guardians," the guardians' credibility rests on their ability to act in manner consistent with the expectations that they have about, and the demands that they place on, the conduct of others.

In this vein, the contributions to this volume, while acknowledging the importance of a substantive conceptualization of the RoL, are reflective of the moral and legal challenges facing rule-based conduct and of the evolving tensions between the RoL and two of the main pillars of the United Nations system: security and human rights. Whether addressing the moral relevance of distance in drone warfare, assessing the implications of the revival of the play motive in modern warfare, critically examining the UNSC's accountability challenges in the "war on terror," focusing on the needs of victims of terrorism and on the role of their advocacy groups, reconsidering the role of truth and reconciliation commissions within the context of the Rome Statute, and dissecting the effects of both linguistic and paralinguistic misinterpretations on the effectiveness of the international criminal process, a key overarching theme emerges: while there are no magic bullets here, the exigencies of an international system based on rules demarcate the terrain on which the pursuit of legitimate domestic and international justice options must proceed.

Several of the contributions address a range of issues relating to modern warfare and, in particular, the ongoing "global war on terror;" more specifically, these contributions deal with moral questions raised by the use of specific weapons (drones), the continuing relevance of the expanding corpus of the laws of war, the legitimacy and accountability deficits in UNSC's counter-terrorism, and the important role of civil society organizations created to assist and advocate for the victims of terrorism.

Tziporah Kasachkoff and John Kleinig kick off this part with a critical look at drone use through the lens of the moral relevance (if any) of distance. The authors

---

[49] One may not set one's self in contradiction to one's own previous conduct; http://www.oxfordreference.com/view/10.1093/acref/9780195369380.001.0001/acref-9780195369380-e-2077

examine two key dimensions to this question: the moral relevance of distance to our *actual* moral obligations and the effect of distance on the way we *perceive* our moral obligations and permissions. They argue that though drone use does not constitute a distinctive moral wrong, it does present distinctive moral risks. The main challenge, according to the authors, "is to be able employ the available modern technologies that allow us …to carry out our justified military missions, while leaving intact and even further developing the moral acuity necessary for us to both fully grasp the moral enormity of our actions and effectively sharpen the moral sensibility … to appreciate the full measure of that enormity."

Karsten Struhl takes Huizinga's notion of *Homo Ludens* (man the player) as the starting point of his enquiry into just war theory and modern warfare, with particular emphasis on the "global war on terror." The author argues that the play motive of war is both bound up with just war theory and functions, in tandem with that theory, as a restraint and, more disturbingly, as a partial cover for the slaughter that is characteristic of all wars. According to him, new visual technologies and robotics are only making things worse, since they are constructing, conjoined with the war on terrorism, "war as a video game without limits." He concludes that the way out of this impasse necessitates a radical approach that would render war obsolete, a development unlikely to materialize any time soon.

George Andreopoulos undertakes a critical examination of the role of the UNSC in counter-terrorism by focusing on the process launched by Resolution 1373, adopted in response to the 9/11 attacks. The author argues that the 1373 process has reinforced measures adopted by states in the areas of legislation and administration of justice, conferring on them a degree of legitimacy despite their failure to adhere to fundamental human rights norms and standards. This process has also reignited the debate on the human rights obligations of the UNSC. According to the author, the UNSC is bound at least by *jus cogens* norms, and this perspective demarcates the contours of what he calls the accountability gap in UNSC counter-terrorism, a gap that has developed as a result of the fact that the human rights obligations of the UNSC are underspecified, and this deficit is rendered more acute in the context of a situation of global emergency ("war on terror").

Rosemary Barberet and Cristina Flesher Fominaya examine the role of advocacy groups for victims of terrorism, looking at those created after 9/11 in New York with a brief comparison to those created in Spain after the March 11, 2004, Atocha train bombings in Madrid. The "thick" definition of the rule of law includes the human rights of the victims of crime: repeated mentions of victims and civil society organizations that advocate for their interests appear in the Secretary-General's 2004 report on the rule of law and transitional justice in conflict and post-conflict societies, and subsequent international legal documents recognize the rights and needs of victims of terrorism. Barberet and Flesher Fominaya's chapter reviews the missions and activities of the organizations that were created to advocate for the victims of terrorism of these two attacks. Their research shows how the needs of victims of terrorism change over time and also highlights how civil society organizations learn transferable skills that are useful to other types of victims and tragic events.

The remaining chapters of this volume address accountability challenges in the context of international criminal justice mechanisms and processes. Kate McEleney investigates the complex relationship between the International Criminal Court (ICC) and Truth Commissions. The author challenges the view that questions the potential for coexistence between the ICC and Truth Commissions. By analyzing the provisions of the ICC Statute on complementarity, admissibility, and prosecutorial discretion and dissecting the concept of justice in the context of the said Statute, the author concludes that its conceptualization cannot be confined to retributive justice; "it thus provides adequate space for Truth Commissions to exist alongside the ICC."

The volume concludes with a critical yet understudied facet of the international criminal justice process: the issues of interpretation and translation in international proceedings and their effects on the quality and procedural fairness of trials. Dragana Spencer takes a critical look at the right to seek and expect effective language services from international criminal courts. The author argues that the protection and further development of these rights are essential for, among others, procedural fairness and the right to a fair trial. What is at stake, according to the author, is "the integrity, independence, and transparency of international criminal courts," values that are undermined if all aspects of the courts' operations do not adhere to fundamental human rights standards. The key task at hand, the author claims, is for judges and interpreters to "engage in the process of quantifiable and verifiable professional development."

As noted earlier, the examination of RoL challenges discussed in this volume is by no means exhaustive. What we do hope though is that this volume will contribute to the ongoing global conversation about the reach and limitations of the RoL and to ways of rendering existing mechanisms and processes more effective in advancing it. Notwithstanding problems of coherence and harmony, a "thick" understanding of the RoL offers a promising entry point to a whole array of world order issues that merit the urgent attention and constructive engagement of the international community.

References

Alter, K. J., & Meunier, S. (2009). The politics of international regime complexity. *Perspectives on Politics, 7*(1), 13–24.

Alvarez, J. (2005). *International organizations as law-makers*. New York: Oxford University Press.

Anghie, A. (2005). *Imperialism, sovereignty and the making of international law*. New York: Cambridge University Press.

Barnett, M. (2011). *Empire of humanity. A history of humanitarianism*. Ithaca: Cornell University Press.

Brierly, J. L. (1963). In H. Waldock (Ed.), *The law of nations* (6th ed.). Oxford: Oxford University Press.

Bush, G. (1991). *Address Before a Joint Session of the Congress on the Cessation of the Persian Gulf Conflict*; http://www.presidency.ucsb.edu/ws/?pid=19364

Carothers, T. (1998). The rule of law revival. *Foreign Affairs, 77*(2), 95–106.

Darian-Smith, E. (2013). *Laws and societies in global contexts: Contemporary approaches*. Cambridge University Press.

Evans, T. (2005). International human rights law as power/knowledge. *Human Rights Quarterly, 27*, 1046–1068.

Ginsburg, T. (2010). The politics of courts in democratization. In M. Trebilcock & R. Daniels (Eds.), *Rule of law reform and development: Charting the fragile path of progress* (pp. 175–191). Northampton, MA: Edward Elgar.

Grant, R. W., & Keohane, R. O. (2005). Accountability and abuses of power in world politics. *American Political Science Review, 99*(1), 29–43.
Hayek, F. A. (1978). *The constitution of liberty*. Chicago: University of Chicago Press.
Hayek, F.A. (1979). Law, legislation and liberty. Volume 3. The political order of a free people (pp. 100–101, 103). Chicago: Routledge & Kegan Paul.
Heckman, J. J., Nelson, R. L., & Cabatingan, L. (Eds.). (2010). *Global perspectives on the rule of law*. New York: Routledge.
Jensen, E. G. (2014). Postscript: An immodest reflection. In D. Marshall (Ed.), *The International Rule of Law Movement. A Crisis of Legitimacy and the Way Forward* (pp. 296–305). Human Rights Program Series, Harvard Law School.
Kennedy, D. (2004). *The dark sides of virtue. Reassessing international humanitarianism*. Princeton: Princeton University Press.
Krasner, S. (1999). *Sovereignty. Organized Hypocricy*. Princeton: Princeton University Press.
Marshall, D. (2014). Introduction. In D. Marshall (Ed.), *The international rule of law movement. A crisis of legitimacy and the way forward*. Cambridge, MA: Human Rights Program Series, Harvard Law School.
Neier, A. (2012). *The international human rights movement. A history*. Princeton: Princeton University Press.
Orford, A. (2003). *Reading humanitarian intervention*. New York: Cambridge University Press.
Permanent Court of International Justice., *The Case of the S.S. Lotus. France v. Turkey. Judgment;* http://www.worldcourts.com/pcij/eng/decisions/1927.09.07_lotus.htm
Post, K. (2012). Fair process and the security council: A case for the Office of the Ombudsperson. In A. M. Ana Salinas De Frias, K. Samuel, & N. White (Eds.), *Counter-terrorism. International law and practice* (pp. 409–423). New York: Oxford University Press.
Rajagopal, B. (2008). Invoking the rule of law in post-conflict rebuilding: A critical examination. *William & Mary Law Review, 49*(4), 1347–1376.
Raz, J. (2009). *The authority of law: Essays on law and morality*. Oxford: Oxford University Press.
Stromseth, J., Wippman, D., & Brooks, R. (2006). *Can might make rights? Building the rule of law after military interventions*. New York: Cambridge University Press.
Tamanaha, B. Z. (2004). *On the rule of law. History, politics, theory*. New York: Cambridge University Press.
Trebilcock, M. and Daniels, R. (2008). *Rule of Law Reform and Development: Charting the Fragile Path of Progress*. Northampton, MA: Edward Elgar.
United Nations (1948). *Universal Declaration of Human Rights;* http://www.ohchr.org/EN/UDHR/Documents/UDHR_Translations/eng.pdf
United Nations (1966a). *International Covenant on Civil and Political Rights;* http://www.ohchr.org/en/professionalinterest/pages/ccpr.aspx
United Nations (1966b). *International Covenant on Economic, Social and Cultural Rights*; http://www.ohchr.org/EN/ProfessionalInterest/Pages/CESCR.aspx
United Nations General Assembly (2005). *A comprehensive strategy to eliminate future sexual exploitation and abuse in United Nations peacekeeping operations*; A/59/710.
United Nations General Assembly Resolution 60/1. (2005). *2005 World Summit Outcome;* A/RES/60/1.
United Nations General Assembly Resolution 67/1. (2012). *Declaration of the High-level Meeting of the General Assembly on the Rule of Law at the National and International Levels*. A/RES/67/1.
United Nations General Assembly-Security Council. (2008). *The UN Security Council and the Rule of Law. The Role of the Security Council in Strengthening a Rules-based International System. Final Report and Recommendations from the Austrian Initiative, 2004–2008;* A/63/69-S/2008/270.
United Nations Security Council. (2004). *The rule of law and transitional justice in conflict and post-conflict societies. Report of the Secretary-General*. S/2004/616.
Widner, J. A. (2001). *Building the rule of law*. New York: Norton.

Chapter 2
Drones, Distance, and Death

Tziporah Kasachkoff and John Kleinig

Introduction

The development and deployment of armed unmanned aerial vehicles (UAVs), popularly known as drones,[1] have been accompanied by strongly conflicting responses: on the one hand, support for what are claimed to be relatively economical precision weapon use that does not place employing personnel at risk and, on the other hand, opposition to what is claimed to be an unreliable and alienating military strategy that deflects attention from the horror of war and war-like measures undertaken to counter terrorism.

There are many angles from which we may evaluate the post-9/11 introduction of drone warfare. We may view it through the lens of an emergent technology (such as the development of heart transplant technology, problematic at first, but getting

[1]There has been much debate about using the terminology of "drones." Sometimes they are referred to, inter alia, as remotely piloted aircraft/vehicles (RPA/Vs). For convenience we will stick with "drones." In this paper we will confine ourselves to issues raised by armed drones that are under the direct control of human operators. So-called autonomous drones raise additional problems. For background, see Sifton (2012); see also, more generally, Blom (2010). Many countries now possess drones, including weaponized drones (loaded with remotely guided Hellfire missiles). To date, the major drone manufacturers have been Israel and the United States, though China is now moving into the rapidly developing market. See Wong (2013).

T. Kasachkoff (✉)
Philosophy Program, Graduate Center, CUNY, New York City, NY, USA

Department of Philosophy, Ben Gurion University of the Negev, Beersheba, Israel

J. Kleinig
Department of Criminal Justice, John Jay College, New York City, NY, USA

School of Humanities, Charles Sturt University, Wagga Wagga, NSW, Australia
e-mail: jkleinig@jjay.cuny.edu

G. J. Andreopoulos et al. (eds.), *The Rule of Law in an Era of Change*, Springer Series on International Justice and Human Rights,
https://doi.org/10.1007/978-3-319-89908-4_2

better[2]); we may look at it in sociological terms (the effects that drones have on the people against or among whom they are deployed or on the institutional practices of the military[3]); we may view drones in terms of military strategy (whether and how well they succeed in promoting military goals[4]); and we may view them in the context of military ethics (say, just war theory[5]). No doubt there are other perspectives from which we may assess them (economic,[6] political,[7] and legal[8]).

The present paper does not take up any of these approaches, except incidentally, but will address the topic of drone use via some larger discussions about *the moral relevance, if any, of distance*. One of the notable features of much current drone use, and one that is often associated with both support for and uneasiness about such use, is the fact that the "cockpits" (as they are called) of those who deploy drones are often situated many thousands of miles from where the drone-based lethal action is taking place.[9] Someone at an air force base in Nevada or New Mexico triggers a weaponized drone that is hovering in the deserts or above a village in Afghanistan, Pakistan, Somalia, or Yemen.[10] We shall ask whether the fact of this distance between the agent(s) of harm and the harm(s) caused has any moral relevance, and, if so, what and how?

---

[2]A critical difference, though, is that medical technologies are directed at saving lives, not terminating them. One might allow greater ethical latitude for failure in the former case than in the latter. See note 44.

[3]The audible or visible presence of drones may create a sense of communal dread, and drone mistakes may do more to alienate those among whom they are used than conventional military actions. See, e.g., Wyler (2013), Kilcullen, and Exum (2009).

[4]Basically, that is likely to be a matter of a "resources/damage" ratio, discounted by so-called collateral damage. See, e.g., Raskin and West (2008). For statistics, see Bureau of Investigative Journalism.

[5]See, e.g., O'Hara (2010), Brunstetter (2012), Freiberger (2013), Enemark (2013).

[6]For example, drones cost substantially less than conventional fighter jets, though, when other factors are taken into account, the financial advantage is not as great as often suggested. See Boyle (2012).

[7]For example, by virtue of not endangering one's own soldiers, drones are easier to sell politically. Or, on the other side, the public outrage in communities that experience drone targeting may undercut their political value. Also included may be issues of transparency/secrecy and whether drones might lower the threshold for entry into war. These claims are given extended discussion in the section on "Asymmetric Unfairness" (5) and (7).

[8]For example, whether the use of drones by the CIA violates international law (O'Connell 2012). In the United States, despite a presidential initiative (under Obama) to do so, Congress has been reluctant to shift responsibility for the CIA's drone program to the military, thus shielding much drone use from public scrutiny.

[9]Apparently there are approximately 64 bases distributed across the United States, some of which control drones in other parts of the world. Of these bases, 12 are used to operate Predator and Reaper drones, the armed UAVs with which this essay is concerned (Public Intelligence 2012). Of course, not all drones are operated from the United States. Some are operated from much closer sites, such as Djibouti and Saudi Arabia.

[10]We will refer to the pairs of people who sit in cockpits as "operators," though they comprise a pilot (on the left) and a sensor operator (on the right). The pilot controls the drone and fires the weapon; the sensor operator handles the visuals, including zoom and infrared capabilities.

There are two dimensions to this question. One concerns the moral relevance of distance to our *actual* moral obligations: Does geographical distance per se affect what we are morally obligated or morally permitted to do? The second concerns the effect of distance on the way we *perceive* our moral obligations and permissions: Does geographical distance, either per se or in conjunction with other factors, affect how we *view* our moral situation? Does distance influence how we think or feel about what we are morally required and/or permitted to do?

Both of these dimensions run through the debate about drones and both will occupy us. We should note at the outset, however, that though we do not presume a lack of connection between what, on the one hand, we feel that, morally, we ought or are allowed to do and what, on the other hand, our actual moral obligations and permissions are, we believe that our moral feelings and perceptions do not *straightforwardly* determine the morality of our conduct. If they did, there would be no room for mistaken moral perceptions – for our mistakenly believing or feeling that we ought not to do what, in fact, we ought to do, or our mistakenly having no moral qualms about doing what is, in fact, wrong. What we wish to say at this point is that our moral perceptions, though they do not determine the morality of our actions, *do* have normative implications. At the very least, our moral perceptions reflect the moral character of our motives and attitudes even if not the moral character of our actions.

In choosing to approach the use of drones via the issue of distance, we recognize that we will be bracketing other (perhaps more basic and important) ethical questions raised by drone use. For one thing, and perhaps most fundamentally, we will not be discussing the morality of killing a fellow human being and, as a subsidiary consideration, the morality of militarily based killing. We will also be bracketing a debate about the particular military circumstances in which drones are currently being employed whether it is war or something "short of war" (Ford 2013).[11] Furthermore, we will not be discussing ethical questions regarding the legitimacy both of drone killing in the countries in which such killing currently takes place such as Afghanistan, Pakistan, Yemen, and Somalia (if we limit ourselves mostly to US drone strikes) or the very important issues of targeted killing generally, the construction of "hit lists," and the moral legitimacy of killings conducted by the CIA (rather than by authorization of Congress). These issues are of great significance and, depending on the conclusions we reach about them, could render our discussion about the moral implications of distance almost beside the point.

Nevertheless, without presuming a particular position on these other questions, we believe there is merit in exploring the moral significance (if any) of distance. Inter alia, the merit consists in discerning the worth of the claim, made by some, that warfare and anti-terrorism strikes conducted by means of drones reduce them to something akin to games played on an arcade-game console except, of course, that real people are being killed. Drone use is alleged to be morally distorting (Sharkey

[11] The phrase "lethal force short of war" is somewhat vague, but Ford (2013) provides a working account of the territory over which it ranges.

2012; Bumiller 2012). There is also merit in considering the worth of the claim that the distance enabled by drone use secures the important minimization principle of not putting one's own troops at unnecessary risk (Strawser 2010).

For the most part, we will also forgo discussion of an old and even ancient debate about the moral relevance of distance. In some form, the moral relevance of distance was already raised by Aristotle (1386a, 1388a10)[12] and then later taken up by David Hume (1896: Bk. II. Pt. 3.7–8, et al.), Denis Diderot (1749; 1966: 17),[13] and Adam Smith (1790), before finding a contemporary and somewhat different expression in Peter Singer's much discussed article on whether distance is relevant to our obligations to humans in need (1972; rev. 2011; cf. Unger 1996).

We will proceed as follows. In "The *Kinds* of Distance That Might Be of Ethical Concern" we consider the different kinds of distance that might be involved in discussions of moral relevance. In "Distance and Obligation" we review the ways in which different *kinds* of distance might be seen as morally relevant to actions in which distance is a significant feature. "Obligations to the Distant Needy" focuses on spatial distance and reviews the role that it may have in the very different debates about, on the one hand, appropriate moral responses to the needy and, on the other hand, appropriate use of drones to monitor and/or kill the enemy. "Drones and Depersonalization" picks up on (what is claimed to be) one broad commonality – depersonalization – and considers how that may play out in the case of drone use. In "The Significance of Face" and "The Psychological Effects of Spatial Distance", we review two additional explications of the claim that use of drones leads to depersonalization. So, in "The Significance of Face", we briefly consider Emmanuel Lévinas's claims about the significance of seeing the other's face in human encounters. In "The Psychological Effects of Spatial Distance" we review the argument that drone use reduces warfare or counterterrorism, at least in the eyes of the operators, to no more than an arcade game. In "Asymmetric Unfairness" we look at a group of arguments that purport to show that, because of distance, drone use is asymmetrically unfair. In "The Charge of Cowardice or Lack of Courage" we review the argument that drone use betrays cowardice. "Fragmenting Responsibility" considers the argument that in drone use moral responsibility for killing is fragmented and therefore seemingly diffused. We offer some summary remarks in "In Summary".

[12] There is an insightful discussion of Aristotle, Hume, and Diderot in Ginzburg (1994).

[13] "What difference is there to a blind person between a man urinating and a man bleeding to death without speaking? Do we ourselves not cease to feel compassion when distance or the smallness of the object produces the same effect on us as lack of sight does on the blind. Thus do all our virtues depend on our way of apprehending things and on the degree to which external objects affect us! I feel quite sure that were it not for fear of punishment, many people would have fewer qualms at killing a man who was far enough away to appear no larger than a swallow than in butchering a steer with their own hands." For Diderot, the relevance of distance is a matter of visualization rather than distance per se, though his point is that insofar as distance affects what we see, it also affects our moral perceptions.

The *Kinds* of Distance that Might Be of Ethical Concern

One obvious and perhaps the most basic kind of distance is *spatial distance*. This is the distance that immediately comes to mind when thinking about drones. Alan and Alice, in their Nevada cockpit, are at a great spatial distance from Abdul in the borderlands of Pakistan.

But spatial distance is only one of many kinds of distance, several of which may be simultaneously applicable in a given case. Consideration of some of these other kinds of distance may explain the worry that is often said to be associated with spatial distance.

Consider, for example, *sensory distance*. Imagine that Abdul, though spatially distant, is visually presented to Alan/Alice via a transmitted camera image. Abdul's presence is manifested to Alan/Alice, however, not as a three-dimensional person who may be touched, smelled, and heard but only as a two-dimensional visual image on a screen. Not merely spatially distant, Abdul is presented in a way that fails to convey the full impact of his personhood, the likeness that we associate with flesh-and-blood persons. Whether and to what extent this sort of distance has emotional and other ramifications depend very much on context.[14]

A further important but overlapping sort of distance is *epistemic distance*. This is the distance between what takes place as a result of what we do and how much we know of what takes place as a result of what we do. How much knowledge do we have of the activity in which we are engaged, and how much knowledge do we have of the ramifications of that activity? There is an intimate, indeed a conceptual, connection between our awareness of what we are doing to others and the responsibility we bear both for what we do to them and for what happens to them as a result of what we do.[15] In the case of drones, this is obviously important. To what extent do Alan and Alice fully appreciate the fact that flesh-and-blood human beings such as themselves with beliefs, emotions, families, loved ones, and anticipated futures are in their sights and are not just targets at which they are aiming? To be sure, Alan and Alice know that their actions will result in the death of another human being: after all, that is the point of their taking those actions. But some have wondered whether what appears on their screens when they act is sufficiently detailed and clear to allow them to grasp fully the moral gravity of their conduct. Sensory and epistemic distances tend to be interconnected.

---

[14] Sometimes, in some contexts and to some extent in those contexts, photographs, though they depict humans or animals only visually, *may* have visceral effects. (That is why photographs of abused animals and children are often used by charitable organizations in their written and televised solicitations of funds to prevent and/or treat such abuse. The photographs trade on the emotional resonance that certain photographs are likely to have in those who view them. Sometimes, however, again, depending on context, photographs may leave one emotionally unaffected.) This may have some relevance to Lévinas's claims about the importance of the eyes and face. See the section on "The Significance of Face".

[15] Compare Diderot's remark about the blind person's inability to appreciate the moral difference between the nearby person who is urinating and the one who is bleeding to death, which draws on the importance of vision to knowledge and hence to the moral sentiments that are triggered and the responsibility we bear. We need, in addition, to keep in mind the difference between epistemic distance over which we have no control and culpable ignorance.

Cultural distance is another sort of distance that may have an effect on our perceptions. Alan and Alice are not only spatially distant from Abdul, they are culturally distant from him by virtue of their upbringing, beliefs, way of life, and vision of their future and of what is important to it. "Cultural" is of course a vaguely defined and context-dependent term; it may or may not include religious, moral, and political beliefs along with social customs and mores. Alan/Alice and Abdul may be culturally distinct in some ways but not in others: they may share relevantly similar family connections and feelings even as they differ greatly in their moral, religious, and political beliefs, beliefs that, not surprisingly, often determine the contours of and significance of family life. (This is but to note that cultural similarities and dissimilarities are not always to be neatly categorized.) Someone piloting a bomber flying directly over Abdul may be equally culturally distant as Alice/Alan piloting a drone thousands of miles away.

Another kind of distance is *associative distance*, most often cultural but sometimes geographical, between what we recognize as, in some sense, "ours" and what we consider as "not ours." My next-door neighbor may be very different from me in his ethnic identity and lifestyle (and in that sense culturally removed from me), but I may nevertheless recognize him as a *fellow American* or a *fellow New Yorker*. On the other hand, those who share my culture may not share my national or other group affiliations and so in that way may be associatively distant from me. Here too we are dealing in probabilities rather than rigid categories: associative distance may be only more likely, but not always inevitably, associated with spatial distance.

A further, albeit overlapping, kind of distance is *psychic or emotional distance*. Where people are culturally, or in other ways associatively connected, they are also (to some degree) more likely to be psychically or emotionally drawn, as well as sensitive, to one another. As an empirical fact, we are more likely to warm to, as well as feel obligated to, those with whom we identify.[16]

Finally, we can think in terms of *temporal distance*.[17] We can appreciate the emotional force of temporal distance by noting that we tend to feel less obligated to

[16] This is not to say that associative nearness constitutes a necessary condition for positive emotional affect. Those who run foreign charities are well aware of – indeed, they count on – the extent to which most of us are emotionally drawn to the plight of children, however distant their origin, place of residence, or foreign their ethnicity. (The vulnerability and guilelessness of children move us in a way that has little parallel with our response to adults to whom we are not related by blood, country, tradition, or custom.) This is evident in the many references made to the number of children who are killed, injured, or traumatized by drone strikes (as well as by other calamities that befall them).

[17] Hume notes, problematically: "Our servant, if diligent and faithful, may excite stronger sentiments of love and kindness than Marcus Brutus, as represented in history." However, he immediately continues: "we say not upon that account, that the former character is more laudable than the latter. We know, that were we to approach equally near to that renown'd patriot, he would command a much higher degree of affection and admiration. Such corrections are common with regard to all the senses; and indeed 'twere impossible we cou'd ever make use of language, or communicate our sentiments to one another, did we not correct the momentary appearances of things, and overlook our present situation" (1896: III.3.1). Hume saw the effects of temporal distance on moral sensibilities as greater than those of spatial distance and of the distant future as greater than the distant past. See the discussion in Ginzburg (1994: 57).

generations far in the future than we do either to our own generation or to the generations immediately following our own. We might ask whether temporal distance in itself serves to diminish our moral obligations to others (perhaps even in cases in which what we do now will have an adverse and unavoidable impact on an as yet nonexistent future generation).

If temporal distance *does* indeed have relevance, is the relevance something other than, or in addition to, the way in which we *perceive* our obligations?

It needs to be noted, indeed, even stressed, that there is no categorical claim to be made about the relation between spatial distance and the other sorts of distance to which we have alluded. Whether and how we connect these other sorts of distance (cultural, sociological, moral, religious, etc.) with geographic distance are more than likely shaped by the social and political narratives that we construct of the "other" and that, indeed, get us to see a person (or group of persons) *as* the "other." We may find illustrations of this in the narratives that emerged (and were also deliberately advanced) after the 9/11 attack on our shores. These narratives suggested constructions of the Taliban (and others) that so distanced them from us that our use of force (including the use of drones) against them was then taken, almost without question, to have moral legitimacy.

Clearly, spatial distance is amenable to other and sometimes (either intentional or non-intentional) manipulative forms of distancing.

Distance and Obligation

As these last questions and concerns indicate, much of the current debate over the moral relevance of distance concerns the impact of various kinds of distance not only on our moral obligations but also on our perception of those obligations. Is the fact that others are spatially, sensorially, culturally, emotionally and/or epistemically distant from us relevant to (1) whether we have moral obligations to them? (2) what our moral obligations to distant others are (assuming we have such obligations)? and (3) the stringency of our moral obligations to distant others (again, assuming that we have such obligations)? Or does the distance between us as actors and others as objects of our actions (4) merely affect what we deem our obligations to be? And if there are indeed true moral differences between what we owe to those close to us and what we owe to distant others, are these differences only ones of degree? And how should these differences, whatever their character, be considered in the context of other considerations, for example, the magnitude of the needs of distant others, the causes of their needs, the effort or cost required to respond to those needs, and the degree to which, as well as rapidity with which, those needs will be alleviated or eliminated by our actions?[18]

[18] Frances Kamm has devoted considerable effort to disentangling arguments and reviewing them, usually critically. However, she *does* think that whereas distance per se is sometimes relevant to our duties to aid, it is not relevant to our duties not to harm. For a selection, see Kamm (2000, 2004). For critiques of Kamm, see Igneski (2001) and Orsi (2008).

Of course, in the case of the use of drones, we do not *find* ourselves distant from those whom our actions affect; rather, the use of drones *creates* the distance between us as agents of actions and those whom our actions affect. Does *this* fact make a moral difference?

It may be that the questions we have raised cannot be answered in the abstract (as our discussion up till now might be taken to have suggested), for whether and how distance counts may depend on how we respond to some of the contextual questions we earlier raised (such as the perceived and socially constructed presence or absence of associative relations).

Given that drone strikes, at least as we have been considering their use, are military responses to terrorism and the planning of terrorist activities, the distance necessitated by effective counterterrorism maneuvers may require us to look in novel ways at the distance between us as agents of action and others as persons acted upon. That is, the impact of distance on the moral nature of our actions, as well as on our perception of that nature, may need to be viewed within the context of *the specific employment of that distance in drone warfare*. Since the obvious benefit associated with distanced warfare of the kind enabled by drones is the avoidance of much of the cost of military combat while at the same time successfully achieving ethically defensible military goals, we have good reason for choosing drone warfare as the best military option.

But, it has been argued, although drone use may minimize (or altogether avoid) the loss of life on our side, it may do so at the cost of causing greater damage and/or death to enemy civilians.[19]

In reply, it has been claimed that drone use succeeds in minimizing damage to limb and/or life on *both* sides. Because drones are remotely controlled, their user's own citizens (and soldiers) are placed at no risk[20]; and, because of the technology associated with drones, killings are more precisely targeted than by conventional bombing so that noncombatant life is less likely to be lost. We say "less likely" because, at least until fairly recently, drone warfare *has* been dogged by complaints about the indefensible loss of noncombatant life.[21] (Some of these complaints have

[19] Several years ago, there was a vigorous debate in Israel over a decision that, to minimize the loss of Israeli soldiers' lives, greater risks were to be taken with respect to apparently noncombatant populations. That was said to be militarily and morally justified. But others argued that it was worse to increase the security of one's own military if it increased the risk to noncombatant "enemy" populations. See Kasher and Yadlin (2005a, b), Fotion (2005), Perry (2005), Haydar (2005), Kasher and Yadlin (2005c, 2006), Ramose (2008), Robinson (2008), Margalit and Walzer (2009), Kasher and Yadlin (with reply by Margalit and Walzer) (2009), Yaari (with reply by Margalit and Walzer) (2009), and Luban (2014).

[20] There is an argument, developed by Jai Galliot (2012: 355), that the asymmetrical frustration caused by drone use might lead the groups on whom they are used to adopt desperation tactics or what he calls "evoked potential": "the possibly spontaneous, dangerous and sometimes morally questionable responses likely to be provoked/evoked by radical technological asymmetry." We are not convinced that one should factor this into a *moral argument* about what to do.

[21] Recent conservative estimates from the Bureau of Investigative Journalism put the total killed in Pakistan, Yemen, and Somalia as 2945–4756, including 495–1109 civilians and 180–218 children. See note 4. Even with greater caution, however, innocents are being killed (Baker 2015; Timm 2015).

been warranted, though the failure has, for the most part, not been one of imprecise targeting but the misidentification of "targets" with the result that civilians have been killed by Hellfire missiles mistakenly directed toward them.)

Obligations to the Distant Needy

It has sometimes been suggested, as well as contested, that spatial distance has moral relevance with respect to our obligations to help the needy. Might whatever counts in favor of the view that geographic distance bears on our moral obligations of *beneficence* to others also count in favor of the view that geographic distance bears on our moral obligations *not to harm* others? Some have maintained that there is an asymmetry between the relevance of spatial distance to our positive obligations to the needy and the relevance of spatial distance with respect to our duties not to harm. Others have denied this asymmetry.

Admittedly, there are seemingly important differences between the two kinds of obligations. One difference between duties to help and the duty not to harm is that the latter is always more stringent than the former. If one has to choose between not harming Jane and helping Jill (when one cannot do both), morality bids us give priority to the moral injunction not to harm.[22]

A second difference is that our duty not to harm is a duty we have vis-à-vis *all* persons (and, according to some, vis-à-vis all living or at least living sentient creatures), whereas the duty to aid is one whose fulfillment involves discretionary choice on our part. Although (absent special moral justification) there is *no one* I may kill, I am under no strict moral obligation to help *everyone* in need. (This point is sometimes expressed by means of the Kantian distinction between perfect and imperfect duties.)[23]

A third difference, already alluded to, between duties of beneficence and duties not to harm is that with respect to the former we are (generally speaking) not responsible for the need that our beneficence is intended to alleviate (except insofar as our failure to aid may exacerbate their situation), whereas the duty not to harm is a duty not to be an *agent* of injury, damage, destruction, etc. (for which aid might then be called).[24]

---

[22] We must assume, of course, that the amount of benefit is not greatly disproportionate to the harm (If the benefit is great, say, of preventing the certain starvation of hundreds of people, that may affect the morality of choosing to inflict a slight harm on a few persons).

[23] This connects up with an ongoing and long-standing debate about the moral significance of a distinction between omissions and commissions, whether the former have any causal significance and whether (and if so under what circumstances) they should be enforceable. We leave this debate to one side; though see Kleinig (1986).

[24] Some, particularly Thomas Pogge, have questioned that division. According to Pogge, the plight of the distant needy is to some extent *caused by* those in western countries. See, e.g., Pogge (2002, 2005). The causal argument might be run in a number of different ways, but the general idea is that the desire for commodities, and cheap or profitable commodities, has created an exploitative economy that is seriously harmful to people in Third World countries and that we therefore have a strong moral responsibility to alleviate their situation. So here is an argument that despite physical distance there is a causal connection between what we do and what they suffer that overcomes any attempt to make a moral argument out of distance. There has, however, been a vigorous debate over Pogge's alleged causal link. See, e.g., Steinhoff (2012) and Patten (2005).

It is not obvious to us that the factors that are said to be relevant to our obligations of beneficence to the distant needy are also relevant to our obligations not to harm a distant enemy.

It is sometimes argued that, so far as aiding the needy is concerned, spatial distance counts simply in terms of the effort or risk that is likely to be involved when assisting those near as against those who are far away. The child found starving in my neighborhood can be aided more directly and easily than the starving child in a faraway country. But, given that we could wire-transfer money to an aid organization located where the needy, but faraway, child is, should spatial proximity make a moral difference? (This was the burden of Singer's article.) In the end, does spatial distance resolve itself into other factors?

Additionally, suppose the needy in our own very large country are geographically more distant than needy persons of a country on which we border. Do we owe more to our *fellow citizens* even if helping them involves effort and risk, than we owe geographically closer but just as needy noncitizen others? Do Arizonans owe more to needy New Yorkers than to needy Mexicans?[25] If we do, that would presume not only the relevance of the associative category "fellow citizen" but also that that particular association is one that overrides other morally important considerations.[26]

In our discussion of the moral permissibility of using drones to carry out a lethal attack, we start with the contestable premise that the killing of our intended target *is morally permissible (and perhaps even morally obligatory)*.[27] The question that remains to be answered and which this paper means to address is whether the morality of our acting on that permission (or obligation) is affected by the distance between us and our intended target. If we are morally permitted (or obligated) to target Abdul in Afghanistan (because of his terrorist-related activities), does it make any difference to that permission (or obligation) that Alan and Alice are in Nevada rather than close-by in Afghanistan?

---

[25] It would not follow that one owed everything to one and nothing to the other; if we are thinking in distributive terms, it might be a question of more or less rather than all or none.

[26] Bernard Williams offers an example of two drowning people, only one of whom a bystander is able to save, and one of whom is his wife. Williams claims that the person who ponders which person he should save, given that he can save only one, is a person who has "one thought too many" (1981: 18). Williams's position derives from the preeminent (even if not always overriding) role that our deepest personal attachments should have in our determinations about what we should do. For Williams, allowing spatially distant needs to weigh as (or even more) heavily in our moral deliberations about what we should do as the needs of those associatively closer to us threatens to alienate us from ourselves. See his remarks in Smart and Williams (1973: 116). Of course, contra-Williams, we might raise the question of whether one *should* always give priority to the projects with which one is most closely identified without regard to the nature of those projects, a question that does not impugn Williams's concern that an undifferentiated utilitarianism would invariably discount or ignore the very special importance of "our deepest personal attachments."

[27] Here we need to recognize the great diversity of situations: from protecting convoys of one's own soldiers to targeting suspected terrorists. In some cases there will be important issues associated with *targeted killings*. In other cases, there will be important issues about *due process*, at least where the targets are citizens of the targeting country. See note 45. See also McNeal (2014) and Miller (2014).

Drones and Depersonalization

One argument in favor of the view that we ought to have moral qualms about using drones for lethal as opposed to surveillance purposes is that the spatial distance between the attacking agent and the attacked subject leads to a morally reprehensible *depersonalization* of the enemy. The argument is causal in that it claims that spatial distance *brings about* moral distance (perhaps via other kinds of distance, such as epistemic and psychic distance).[28] The depersonalization brought about by the use of drones used for killing distant others is abetted, it is claimed, by the technology involved. Hence the charge that using drones for the purpose of killing distant others induces a "Playstation mentality" (Cole et al. 2010), a mentality that distances us from the seriousness of our actions and so from a true moral appreciation of them. For this reason, drone use may be said to constitute a moral hazard.[29]

The link claimed to exist between drone operation and depersonalization is sometimes differentiated into three overlapping phenomena[30]:

(a) Dehumanization
(b) Deindividuation
(c) Moral disengagement

Although these phenomena are probably best seen as conceptually and causally overlapping elements within a complex phenomenon and not as neatly differentiated, there may be some heuristic value in distinguishing them: (a) Dehumanization involves morally downgrading the objects of intended drone strikes by referring to them in ways that obscure their human qualities, deeming them "targets," or "objects" rather than persons, or else morally dismissing them by characterizing them using derogatory epithets; (b) deindividuation occurs when drone operators subsume the drone "target" within some group category that reduces the person to

---

[28] A personal example of how spatial distance "naturally" contributes to depersonalization: When the World Trade Center was attacked on 9/11, one of the two authors of this paper was about a mile away, the other about three short blocks away. Both of us observed objects falling from the topmost stories of the 100-storey northern Twin Tower. But only one of us had a vivid perception of these objects *as* human beings and so was confronted by the unbearably horrific conditions within the burning building that must have driven them to jump to what they must have known was their certain death. The psychological and emotional impact of what we saw was, on each of us, very different. Clearly, distance mattered to how we saw what we saw (not that, in our own case, one of us depersonalized the objects so much as failed to have a strong sense of them *as* persons).

[29] Although the notion of a moral hazard has its home in the business world, especially that of insurance, where it points to the potential for an insurance policy to breed carelessness, it is more generally applicable to a context in which the details of that context may affect our conduct in morally deleterious ways.

[30] We've adapted them from G.I. Wilson (2013). Wilson draws heavily on Bandura (2004) and McAlister, Bandura, and Owen (2006).

be killed merely to "one of them"[31]; and (c) moral disengagement involves the use of various social and psychological mechanisms (such as deindividuation) so that killing by means of drones is more easily justified: attention is deflected from the seriousness of drone use, or responsibility for drone use is diffused or mitigated.

Moral trivialization (through depersonalization or other means) is always a serious matter, but moral trivialization of the use of lethal drones is especially serious because the killing of other human beings is always to be undertaken for only the most pressing reasons. The right to life is of fundamental importance, and what it protects is a condition for almost every other right we have. Loss of life is something for which there is no adequate recompense. So it is important that we do not create or foster circumstances in which the value of a human life may be viewed as diminished, taken without an appropriate justification, or taken without seeing the need for justification as being of utmost importance.[32]

The question we have been looking at is whether the use of drones to kill distant others undermines, erodes, or shields us from having a proper sense of the seriousness of what we are doing. Does the fact that the manned cockpit of a drone is many thousands of miles from the site of the "action" lead to an immoral detachment from the seriousness of what is intended and done?[33]

We review two arguments to the effect that it does: one presented as a philosophical argument about the conditions under which humans "can and cannot" countenance the killing of each other and the other an argument based on the psychological effects of distance.

[31] It can also occur when drone operators come to see themselves simply as functionaries rather than as individual moral agents (mere cogs within the organization with a job to do).

[32] "Engagement in terror-related activities" needs precising. It may take a number of forms each of which raises its own questions. Abdul may be doing no more than advocating terrorism, or conspiring with others to engage in terror-related activity, assisting others who are more centrally involved, on his way to perform a terrorist act, in the process of performing a terrorist act (burying an IED on the road), and so on. Arguably, not all of these justify killing and therefore do not justify killing by means of drones.

[33] Not all detachment may be immoral. We may hope for a professional detachment by those tasked with killing others – a sense that, though the role they have is a supremely serious one, they are not only morally comfortable with it but also able to approach it with an unclouded mind. Might we compare this with a physician who can professionally work on a body that has been ravaged by disease or injury not by depersonalizing it but through the development of a needed professionalism? See the report on Col. D. Scott Brenton in Bumiller (2012): "'I see mothers with children, I see fathers with children, I see fathers with mothers, I see kids playing soccer,' Colonel Brenton said. [But] When the call comes for him to fire a missile and kill a militant – and only, Colonel Brenton said, when the women and children are not around – the hair on the back of his neck stands up, just as it did when he used to line up targets in his F-16 fighter jet. Afterward, just like the old days, he compartmentalizes: 'I feel no emotional attachment to the enemy,' he said. 'I have a duty, and I execute the duty.'"

The Significance of Face

Emmanuel Lévinas, believing that humans possess a fundamental inhibition against killing each other, argues that once the personhood of another is recognized, a recognition that is impossible to avoid when we behold the other's face,[34] we can no longer kill or at least must overcome an enormous natural resistance to doing so. If this view is correct, then the deployment of drones enables us to destroy other humans without the normal and normally intense human inhibition against doing so.

Although presented as a philosophical position, Lévinas's contention may more accurately be described as a psychological position, a recognition that, as we look at another's face and into his or her eyes, we experience that person as one of our own, a creature like ourselves, and therefore to be treated as no less.[35] Lévinas attempts to go further, however: we see ourselves as both interrogated and addressed by the face of the other, and this constitutes a moral barrier to our destroying him or her.

We find Lévinas's view interesting and suggestive. But in the end, we find it taken to justify more than is warranted. For even if we grant that we are psychologically inhibited from killing someone into whose eyes we gaze, that fact (if it is a fact) does not constitute a *moral* argument against killing that person. The connection between what is psychologically odious and what is morally prohibited has to

---

[34] Lévinas (1961). The face, for Lévinas, is not just a face but the other's "living presence" (66), which makes a moral demand of us (201, 207) and "forbids us to kill" (1985: 86). In recent times, Lévinas's views have been controversially appealed to in the French debate concerning face-concealing clothing such as the niqab. See Patton (2014).

[35] The view that Lévinas puts forth here concerning the moral significance of face may inform the work of those who, in trying to help desperately needy persons by seeking donations of funds for this purpose, try to shorten the psychic distance between us and those for whom the funds are sought by presenting their faces to us in dramatic images on TV, in vivid photographs in brochures, or in graphically and movingly detailed descriptions in solicitation letters. It is hoped that the haunted, sad look in the eyes of those presented to us will not only move us to act but also move us to feel obligated to help.

A somewhat different use of the same psychological phenomenon can be found in an early argument in the abortion debate: the "windowed womb." See Wertheimer (1971). Cf. those US states that require women seeking abortions to view a sonogram before proceeding with their abortion (Guttmacher Institute 2017).

One other matter: When we are talking about distance and drones, we are not simply talking about surveillance. If Alan and Alice are in Nevada and keeping an eye on what may turn out to be terror-related activities in Afghanistan, that need not be too problematic. There are also issues of *privacy* (seeing what people are doing on their rooftops), and we might argue in that case, as we tend to in some others, that security and privacy may sometimes have to be traded off. The fact that Abdul is believed to be engaged in terror-related activities justifies some infringements on his privacy. So it pays to keep in mind that what is at issue in the case of Predator drones is the *targeted killing* for which they are used. Abdul is not merely being surveilled but he is being surveilled with a view to killing him if it is determined that he is engaged in terror-related activities. Moreover, given the specific capacity of drones, there is a desire to kill him with minimal damage to innocent others, and so he may be surveilled for an opportune time when he is alone and vulnerable.

be argued for and not merely asserted. As applied to drone use, we should keep in mind that when we use drones to kill, the presumption is that the targeted person has been established (by independent means) as an enemy (terrorist) whose life is *justifiably* taken. The moral justification of the killing is independent of whether that killing is something we could bring ourselves to do, were we to gaze into our intended victim's eyes.

Lévinas does not claim that killing a person into whose face we look is psychologically impossible but rather that such a killing requires an overpowering of natural human inhibitions. (If this is true, then it is a psychological truth about human beings that, we might reasonably say, is also a moral good: Killing another human being *ought* not to be a psychologically easy thing to do.)

But where does this leave the *morality* of killing by means of drones?

One of the promises, if not quite the fulfillment, of drone technology is that it need not deprive drone operators from seeing others in their humanity. That is the source of Mark Coeckelbergh's claim for there being an "empathic bridge" between drone operators and those whom they track (Coeckelbergh 2013).[36] To be sure, the empathy of which Coeckelbergh writes is not one borne of personally seeing the face of the other but rather one that arises out of an appreciation of the personhood of the other through the hearing of that other's voice, through seeing the other's interactions with his or her family and associates, and sometimes through the reading of that person's written thoughts. All of these are not only accessible to the drone operator but are sometimes a critical part of the process of identifying the targeted person as the truly intended target.

The Psychological Effects of Spatial Distance

It is sometimes claimed that the use of drones reduces killing to something like a computer game. The spatial distance between Alan and Alice at their consoles in Nevada and Abdul in Afghanistan generates a sensory, epistemic, and social distance that obscures the seriousness of what is at issue (Sharkey 2012): Whatever the dangerousness of Abdul and the moral magnitude of the activity in which he is involved, these are not brought home to Alan/Alice on account of the risk to them from him, for there is no risk to them from the visually reduced tiny two-dimensional image of him on their screen. Additionally, in the most likely event that Alan and Alice are operating a "predator" drone armed with Hellfire missiles, they may be inclined to have the sense that they are hunting down nonhuman prey or possibly even delivering a divinely sanctioned punishment.

The argument that distance may reduce killing to something like an arcade game was argued at length in Lt Col. David Grossman's 1995 book, *On Killing: The*

[36] As we will suggest, the prevalence of burnout among drone operators may provide some if inconclusive empirical support for this. See note 40 and surrounding text.

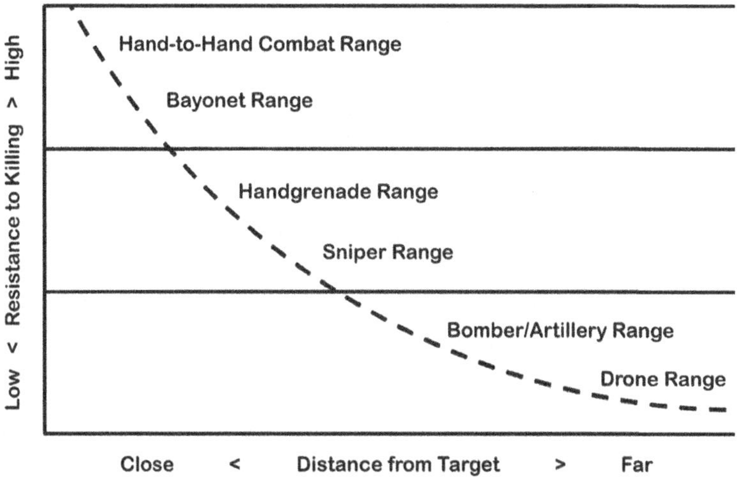

Fig. 2.1 Effect of distance on resistance to killing (Galliott 2015: 137)

Psychological Cost of Learning to Kill in War and Society (1995; rev. ed. 2009: 98).[37] Here we reproduce Jai Galliott's updated and slightly revised version of Grossman's graphic representation of his position, one intended to accommodate the introduction of weaponized drones (Fig. 2.1).

According to the chart – although as we will see it may simplistically represent our moral inhibitions – it appears that with the advent of armed drones, the resistance to killing would (or at least could) be reduced to practically zero, a matter that, understandably enough, is worrisome for many of us.[38]

To the extent that the graph accurately reflects how distance influences the springs of action, killing at greater and greater distances becomes increasingly easy, so easy at *very* great distances that such killing is evacuated of moral seriousness. Because of this, some have claimed that drone operators are reduced to skilled computer game players, needing only to strategize timing and to coordinate eye and hand movements. Of course, Alan and Alice need to be sure that it is Abdul they are targeting, and they need to be correct in believing that Abdul is what he is presumed to be, namely, a terrorist/enemy of some kind. But those issues are usually determined by others, most likely their supervisors.

Epistemic requirements, including the requirement that we have learned enough about the person we are targeting to give us a lively and accurate appreciation of the

[37] Some of Grossman's theses, esp. his thesis about the link between arcade games and violence, viz., that arcade games erode our (natural) inhibition against killing, have been hotly contested. The thesis considered in this essay is rather different, viz., that the use of drones reduces killing to an arcade game played by the drone operator.

[38] This point harks back to Stanley Milgram's experiments (1974). Although Milgram was primarily concerned about the power of authority in relation to conscience, distance significantly affected the experimental subjects' willingness to inflict pain.

moral seriousness of what we are about to do to him or her, may not always be easily satisfied. Although the technology is improving, along, we might hope, with the quality of intelligence according to which persons to be killed by attacking drones are identified and tracked, drone operations have in the past sometimes (all-too-often) resulted in botched and controversial killings.

Defenders of drone warfare claim that those who deploy the drones are well aware that the targets of their activity are human, albeit humans whom they are justifiably ordered to kill. They work against the (perhaps controversial) background view that the person or persons they are targeting cannot be captured and brought to trial but must, as imminent or ongoing threats to others, be killed as quickly as possible. They see the situation they are in as a classic "defense-of-life" situation: even if they themselves are not endangered, they are taking aggressive action on behalf of those who are. If they do not kill the person identified as the sought-after terrorist when they can, the blood of that terrorist's future victims will be on their hands. The seriousness of their task is not only not lost on them, they are acutely aware of it, and this awareness is what lies behind the considerable pains that they take to isolate, albeit not always successfully, the target terrorist or terrorists from other surrounding persons.

Their second claim, intended to counter the objection that drone use inevitably depersonalizes its victims, is that the task of determining whether someone is a terrorist, and then tracking and isolating him, often takes an extended period of time: identities must be checked and an opportune time to fire the missile sought. Those who are tracking the alleged terrorist often begin to relate to the object of their interest as a person with a life – a life of family, friends, and other associates – someone, that is, who is often engaged in, for the most part, commonplace and familiar activities. Indeed, for the period that the person is being tracked, there may be no signs of terror-related activity, and if the identity of a terrorist has already been established, it may have been established by others; the role of the drone operators may be simply to locate the terrorist and choose an opportune time to trigger the missile that is intended to kill him, say, when isolated from his family and innocent others.[39] Against this background, drone operators may come to empathize; they form Coeckelbergh's "empathic bridge" with the person as a participant in a larger and identifiable life and in many ways a life not too dissimilar from the lives that they themselves lead. Some drone operators report that this empathic identification is reinforced by the fact that after their day's work, they leave their "office" and go home to their own families.

According to a recent article in the *New York Times,* US Air Force officials reported their concern about losing drone pilots "who are worn down by the unique stresses of their work" (Drew and Philipps 2015). It also referred to a 2013 Defense Department study which found that drone pilots experienced depression, anxiety, and post-traumatic stress disorder at the same rate as pilots of manned aircraft who

[39] This diffusion of responsibility, however, may be a further source of depersonalization. If mistakes are made, whose fault is it? Anyone's? The fog of war? See the section on "Fragmenting Responsibility".

were deployed to Iraq or Afghanistan. One of the drone pilots quoted in the article, Bruce Black (who as part of a team, watched Abu Musab al-Zarqawi, founder of Al Qaeda in Iraq, for 600 h before al-Zarqawi was killed by a bomb from a manned aircraft), has this to say: "After something like that, you come home and have to make … choices about the kids' clothes or if I parked in the right place. And after making life and death decisions all day, it doesn't matter. It's hard to care."

Third, there are other aspects of the use of lethal drones that, in adding to the potential stress on the operators of these drones, make the stereotypical "Playstation" scenario, in which "the enemy" is "taken out" when he appears on the screen, a fiction that fails to capture the actual and tense scenario that is more likely to be the case in a drone operation. For example, sometimes drone operators have the responsibility of protecting convoys of their own soldiers who, in real-time battleground situations, are in need of cover as they progress from point A to point B in hostile territory. In these cases, the drone operators must keep their eyes peeled for and respond to unusual movements or happenings that may prove threatening to their own or allied troops. Such drone operators must be alert to everything from a live ambush to newly dug earth at the roadside that may conceal an improvised explosive device (IED). Spending an 8-hour shift at the controls of a monitoring lethal drone with the sort of riveted attention needed for their tasks is, understandably, both psychologically taxing and emotionally draining.[40]

Complicating the situation in the case of drone warfare (and frequently commented upon) is the fact that, unlike artillery fire from a distance or from a plane that then moves on beyond its target, drone technology not only allows but frequently requires operators to home in after they have launched an attack on their target in order to verify the attainment of their objective. They may then be confronted by a grisly scene of dismemberment and agonizing death.[41]

The picture we have drawn here draws support not only from the statements of those who themselves operate drones but also from the psycho-medical data collected from and about them. A report commissioned by the US Air Force indicated that 29% of the drone pilots who were surveyed reported suffering from burnout and high levels of fatigue, including 17% of the survey total who were judged to be clinically distressed (Stewart 2011).[42]

---

[40] See Kelly McEvers' interview (2013) with former drone operator, Brandon Bryant; see also Abé (2012).

[41] As the technology improves, the scenes will become more graphic. See, e.g., Kopstein (2013).

[42] Despite the secrecy around the US drone program, various operators and ex-operators have also spoken about their experiences, and they have for the most part confirmed the psychological and moral cost of drone piloting. See, e.g., Klaidman (2012), Power (2013), Linebaugh (2013), and Asaro (2013). As noted earlier, there is an argument to the effect that those pilots who are unmoved by the lives their work will destroy have developed capacities for professional compartmentalization that would serve them as well in other combat situations. See the remarks of Col. D. Scott Brenton in Bumiller (2012). It has led to suggestions that drone operators should be eligible for special military awards. See generally, Wikipedia authors, "Distinguished warfare medal"; see also Lubold (2014), AAP (2013), and Wood and Harbaugh (2014). Ironically, given the criticism of drone piloting, the US Air Force is struggling to find sufficient drone operators (Drew and Philipps 2015). On the matter of recognition, a compromise has since been reached.

From their personal reports, we have reason to believe that a significant source of the stress experienced by some drone operators was their realization that those they targeted were sometimes mistakenly identified and/or that they sometimes misjudged situations with the result that (among) those they killed were innocent persons, some of them children. Although we do not intend this as a criticism of drone use *as such*, and do not view these tragic happenings as a function of distance per se, we do believe that this situation highlights the critical importance of good intelligence and technology: one should have grave qualms about using killing technologies while they and the intelligence that guides them are still in development and when the high costs of failure fall mostly on the receiving side.[43]

Although we are aware of the argument that in the real world technologies have to be used "while still in development" as a way of ironing out their kinks, that argument should not carry as much weight as it is sometimes accorded.[44]

Throughout our discussion, we have underscored the fact that some sorts of distance associated with drone use may render drone operators unable to appreciate fully the moral gravity of their activity and its consequences. But we are mindful that the ability of drone operators to distance themselves psychologically from what they do may be a helpful, and perhaps even necessary, feature of their work. Given the high level of psychological stress and strain reported among drone operators, it might well be the case that some psychological distancing on their part is required to provide a measure of emotional protection without which it would be difficult (if not impossible) for them to continue doing the work that they do. Of course, were intelligence and judgment better than they have often been in the past, so that drone operators could be (legitimately) assured that risks imposed by drone use on innocent lives were minimized, the psychological toll and therefore the need of psychological distancing would be lessened.

---

[43] The problem may be intensified if some of the moral constraints on killing are increased in "short-of-war" contexts. See note 11.

[44] Heart transplant technology, which in its early uses resulted in many failures and in many deaths, might be cited in this connection. But the pioneering heart transplant surgeons, though subject to a considerable amount of public criticism when they failed, as they often did, were at least trying to help people who, given the state of medicine at the time, had no other realistic options. That is very different from drone operators who, because of flawed intelligence, blow up a wedding party rather than a convoy of terrorists or who are mistakenly led to target some poor villagers collecting scrap metal rather than Taliban burying land mines. Ironically, the psychological pressure may be intensified by a factor that we note later: the fragmentation of responsibility. If things go wrong, the drone operators may be left feeling that they have not acted as a result of their own best judgment, but rather at the behest of others, though it was *their* act that ended the innocent life (Brandt 2013).

Asymmetric Unfairness

One of the moral objections to using lethal drones is that doing so is *unfair*.[45] Rather than two antagonists (whether countries, armies, or individuals) "facing off" under conditions of rough equality, drone operators are thousands of miles away, insulated from harm and in possession of a super-lethal weapon, whereas the other is, at best, modestly armed and, moreover, eminently accessible and so exceedingly vulnerable to air attack. The relative capabilities and vulnerabilities of those who use lethal drones to attack and of those who are the targets of those attacks are completely asymmetrical. With respect to one another, they are radically unequally situated with respect to military advantage. Drone use is not analogous to the use of a rifle against an attacker or even to the use of a bomber against an army. Rather, it is the unleashing of a Goliath against a David.[46] In the contest between a terrorist and drone operators, the terrorist doesn't stand a chance.

The charge of asymmetric unfairness involves several disparate claims, only some of which are related to the issue of distance, whereas some others are only marginally about unfairness (Strawser 2010: 355–358; Galliott 2012).

1. First, there is the "shotgun to a fly" dimension. The use of a Hellfire missile to take out an individual or small group seems, at the least, to involve the use of a disproportionate means, whether or not the end is legitimate: a single bullet would do the same job. Although this is true, we do not see this kind of disproportionality between means and ends as having intrinsic moral import. Nor does the issue of distance appear to have any moral relevance here.
2. The second claim is that there is a fundamental disparity in the vulnerability of each side to harm by the other. Drone operators are completely insulated from harm, a product of being situated at a distance from the damage that they cause, whereas the other side, because of the technology possessed and adroitly used by drone operators, is visually and always geographically accessible. Does this significant difference in vulnerability have moral import in its own right?

   We do not see this to be the case. Presumably, one important strategy in warfare and counterterrorism is to kill without being killed, and if one of the parties can manage to protect or conceal him/herself in such a way as to be invulnerable (or practically so), that is, a matter of strategic superiority relative to the other, a clear disparity between them but not one that, in itself, we see as being of moral consequence.

---

[45] Sometimes "due process" arguments are advanced that are different from those we advance under this heading. One is that unless people pose an imminent threat, we should be trying to capture them and bring them to justice rather than eliminating them. The other arises if the alleged terrorist is a citizen of one's own country. See the debate over the drone killing of Anwar al-Awlaki (Mohamed 2011; Coll 2012).

[46] Though *that* story (I Sam. 17) is about David's triumph in an unequal and unfair contest. Moreover, it is instructive, because much of the story of asymmetric warfare is a story of the little guy who beats the big guy (Arreguín-Toft 2001). The issue in the present context is whether the asymmetry creates some form of unfairness.

3. The third charge, one that has become fashionable as a result of recent work by Jeff McMahan (2006; cf. Rodin 2008), is that wartime combatants are not to be viewed as moral equals.[47] If one party has a just cause and the other does not, then (given the principles of *jus in bello*) soldiers fighting for the just cause may justly kill those on the other side without regard to whether those on the other side have comparable military resources.

   Might it then be argued that if the side using drones is *not* the side with a just cause, its use of drones *exacerbates* the injustice of what is done in the name of that cause? We do not see this as obviously the case. To be sure, what is done in the name of an unjust cause is unjust, whatever the means for doing it. However, the use of drones to inflict injury does not in itself make matters worse than otherwise. If it is true, as it is usually argued, that the use of drones allows for more targeted and so more accurate killing and consequently less infliction of harm on innocent parties, then although it will be unjust for the side that pursues an unjust cause to use drones, or indeed any weapons deployed through *any* delivery system, that injustice may in fact be limited rather than increased by the use of drones as opposed to other means of attack.[48]
4. The fourth claim is that drones disturb what would or should otherwise be a level playing field. Certainly the distance that the technology allows, along with its killing capability, gives the operators of drones a decisive military advantage. The question is whether this advantage is to be regarded as an *unfair* advantage. It certainly would be were we involved in some kind of contest in which an initial level playing field is important. But it is not reasonable to hold that a level playing field *is* important or even relevant in war and in the taking of military measures to counter terrorism (Mowery 2014). In traditional theory of principled warfare, that is, warfare undertaken in response to unprovoked aggression, the taking of military measures amounts to engaging in actions required for self-defense. To be sure, this does not mean that there are no constraints on the actions one may take to secure one's defense. The means used must not be inhumane or indiscriminate so far as civilian or innocent deaths are concerned. For this reason, the use of nuclear, chemical, and biological weapons is condemned. Such weapons are notoriously difficult to direct precisely, and the suffering caused as

---

[47] It needs noting that McMahan's claim about the moral inequality of combatants at war with one another has not gone unchallenged. The doctrine of the moral equality of combatants whatever we might want to say about the countries that send them to fight is fairly well entrenched in (even if not original to) Just War theory. Even if we take as given that soldiers fighting for a country will feel patriotic toward that country and that the patriotism they feel may not be unthinking but morally self-reflective, it is (except in special circumstances) generally risky to view and therefore hold individual soldiers responsible for the decisions of their governments to go to war. We may not want to say that soldiers fighting on the wrong side of an unjust war are *justified* in killing those whom their government has declared as the enemy, but we would probably see these soldiers, at least generally speaking, as morally *excusable* for doing so. For (sometimes partial) defenses of the moral equality of combatants, see Walzer fourth edn. (2006), Zupan (2006), and Ceulemans (2007–2008). See also Steinhoff (2008) and Lang (2011).

[48] What if it is the drones that make the difference between loss and victory for the unjust participant?

a result of their use is both indiscriminate and protracted. The use of drones, at least in intent, does not run afoul of this stricture, for drones are designed to make surgically accurate strikes (which is not to say that their design always results in success). It may be argued, then, that drone use is not unfair, at least so long as it is morally legitimate to kill the target in the first place.

5. A fifth charge of unfairness is that although there is always some risk to and therefore fear for civilians who live in a war zone or in areas inhabited by terrorists, drones unwarrantedly traumatize civilian populations in those areas that they target. As drones are presently used, there are frequent reports in the local media of "individuals who speak of the psychological terror from the daily presence of drones … [with locals] constantly wondering which patterns of behavior drone controllers find suspicious" (Amoureux 2013; cf. Bhojani 2014). Civilians have reported persistent fears that they might come to the attention of a drone operator (sitting many miles away) who cannot be communicated with and whose suspicions cannot therefore be allayed. Villagers who hear the humming presence of hovering drones have reported being afraid to go to the market or even outside their homes lest they attract the unwanted attention of a Hellfire missile. The situation is almost like *Nineteen Eighty-Four*, not simply a loss of privacy but an uncontrollable, oppressive, unstoppable, menacing presence for the civilian population. Do these effects on the local citizenry caused by drone use constitute unfairness in the conduct of war and/or the countering of terrorism?

   However unfortunate the effects on the local population – especially unfortunate because those affected are clearly innocents – the problem here is not related to distance per se, though it must be granted that the spatial distance is accompanied by inaccessibility. The traumatization of civilians arises from the awful fact that all-too-often drone strikes have been misguided and, as a result, have killed innocent persons. Clearly civilians cannot take comfort and feel physically and/or psychologically safe on account of their innocence when even innocent actions may be (and have been) interpreted as suspicious acts, and there is, at least at present, no way of signaling or establishing one's innocence to an operator who is inaccessibly thousands of miles away. This has been one of the truly terrible costs of using drones before they were "ready" and without the requisite intelligence to avoid target errors.[49]

6. A sixth claim said to be connected to considerations of fairness is the way in which distantly controlled drones potentially increase what is referred to as "the theater of war." That drones are being controlled from Nevada (and other parts of the United States) might be taken to justify an expansion of the war zone from, say, Afghanistan to those parts of the United States (or elsewhere where US drone operators sit at the controls). This, it is claimed, would give legitimacy to

[49] The spike in drone use occurred when Barack Obama became the US President and was not unrelated to his concern about military deaths of US soldiers in Afghanistan and Pakistan. Drones were rushed into service ahead of important technological and intelligence safeguards and capabilities.

attacks on American (or other) soil and lead to US or other civilians/citizens being unfairly placed at greater risk.[50]

7. A seventh and final claim concerns what might be referred to as "mission creep." It is arguable that the immense distance and therefore invulnerability of drone users from counterattack make it *easier* to engage in military or warlike activities without the kind of last resort justification that such killings ought to have. Indeed, if the costs of war are borne *only* by the enemy and not by our own soldiers (or civilian citizens), decisions to *initiate* military action might come to be decisions that are increasingly easier to make, and this would be most unfortunate. The moral justification for our killing intended targets, whether by means of drones or by other, more conventional methods, depends on our (judicious) assessment that that killing will remove the lethal danger posed by those intended targets if they are left alive. That assessment should not be influenced and thereby perhaps skewed by the fact that the killing of those targets can be done safely and efficiently with no cost to ourselves. We assert this last point as true independent of whether the context of drone use is war or counterterrorism (which involves the use of force short of all-out war).

   We raise this last point mindful of those who have argued that although one enters into war only because other, less drastic options have been exhausted or are not pursuable – traditionally, a condition for *jus ad bellum* – once engaged in war, "last resort" principles may drop out of consideration, though principles of proportionality continue to operate. We believe that "last resort" principles in military actions of *any* sort are essential to the moral pursuit of our ends (assuming those ends themselves to be morally legitimate). We worry that the option of drone warfare may both incline a country to lower the barrier on going to war and, in addition, tempt a country to engage in disproportionate activities once in it.

   If, as is now largely the case, what is being waged through the use of drones is the so-called war on terror, then the situation is still murkier, and the possibilities for disproportionate and therefore unjust use of drones are amplified because, unlike other wars, the "war on terror" is not an officially declared war with an explicitly declared enemy.[51] People are included on "hit lists" as targets in the war on terror who, it is sometimes argued, ought to be dealt with in other ways.[52]

---

[50] This also reflects a concern that many have that drone warfare succeed in large measure because it is carried out against an enemy that is not capable of retaliating in like measure. Were a drone warfare conducted against an enemy with similar capabilities, would it be conducted as readily or in the same way?

[51] Even though there may be fewer constraints on *jus ad vim*, there may be greater constraints on noncombatant deaths. In addition to Ford (2013), see Walzer (2006: Preface).

[52] Capture, for example. The fact that acting on these lists is seen as a presidential prerogative based on classified evidence adds a further dimension to the concern. In his 8 years in office, US President George W. Bush authorized 44 such strikes. President Obama authorized 239 in his first 3 years. They subsequently diminished. Nevertheless, the theory of preemptive strikes, which underlay many of these decisions, was quite contentious.

> These considerations do not speak definitively against the legitimacy of drone use in dealing with the threat of terrorism, but they point to moral hazards to which we need to be especially sensitive.[53]

What, then, should we conclude about the legitimacy of the broad claim of asymmetric unfairness in the use of drones?

We do not see the asymmetry that is created by drone use as proving unfairness in the treatment of others. But we do think that asymmetric warfare of the kind that drone use involves may create serious temptations to behave in ways that are morally questionable. The invulnerability that drone use allows for those who operate the drones may weaken what should be our commitment to the obligation to use lethal military force reservedly, justly, and honorably. This latter consideration provides a link to the next objection to drone use at which we shall look.

The Charge of Cowardice or Lack of Courage

There has been complaint that drone warfare is *cowardly* or at least is associated with a lack of the sort of courage that is often considered integral to military engagement. Military engagement is generally thought to require a resolute determination not to shrink from fear or risk to self in the pursuit of a worthy objective. Because drone operators fight from "behind a screen" rather than confront their enemy face to face,[54] there is, so the complaint goes, no call for the display of military courage; on the contrary, drone warfare displays the trappings of cowardice.[55]

---

[53] This is one of the problems emanating from the fact that the CIA has been the primary US agent for drone warfare. There is thus relatively little transparency and accountability.

[54] Although this charge might seem to emanate from oppositional sources, it is also heard within military circles: drone operators lack the macho qualities of real soldiers – they have been referred to as "cowardly button-pushers" (Abé 2012).

[55] The argument is not a new one. In *Don Quixote*, a paean to "chivalry," the Knight of La Mancha inveighs against the invention of "the devilish instruments of artillery" whereby "a cowardly base hand takes away the life of the bravest gentleman" by means of a bullet "coming nobody knows how or from whence," Cervantes Saavedra (1993, vol. 2: 318). Old or new, the argument could probably be employed about other forms of long-distance or aerially directed combat. Indeed, direct physical contact with the enemy is sometimes said to morally distinguish the foot soldier from the bombardier, although, as modern technology has developed, ground-to-air missiles may place the bombardier at considerable risk as well.

The complaint that use of military drones is cowardly is put forth on the grounds that drone operators are military personnel who display no military courage. We wish to note the mistake that is made here.[56]

As noted earlier, courage is about resolutely confronting fear. Admittedly, there is no risk and no threat to military personnel who sit at consoles in Nevada tracking movements and waiting, or looking, for the opportunity to trigger Hellfire missiles. There is therefore no physical fear to confront. As a result, whether the challenges of drone use are handled well or badly by the military persons who operate the drones, the execution of their duties does not call for courage on their part. This does not mean, however, that drone operators *lack* courage. It is rather that in meeting the challenges of their position, there may be no call for its display.[57] The issue of physical courage simply does not arise.

Of course, we might wonder why a virtue traditionally associated with *one* way of engaging in military activity needs to be displayed if we find another, more effective and efficient, way of engaging in that activity.[58] Given the ways in which war was traditionally fought (mano a mano), physical courage *was* required and so came to be recognized as a military virtue. But there is no reason why we should continue to fight wars in the traditional way if, for at least (what is believed to be) a just cause, we can fight them in other ways, even if those other ways do not call for the exercise of physical courage. (Moreover, there are other virtues, patience, concentration,

---

[56] We would also draw attention to an irony involved in the charge of cowardice. The use of a technology developed largely to pursue the so-called war on terror is now complained (by some) to display the same vice as was popularly and insistently imputed to terrorists. Those who commandeered the planes that were used as weapons in the 9/11 attacks were early and frequently referred to as "cowards," and those questioning that attribution were often the objects of characterizations meant to shame or censor them (for references, see Weber (2005)). "Cowardice" became not only a widely affirmed characterization of terrorists but also a politically correct one.

The charge of cowardice, though insistently propagated by political authorities, may have been inapt as applied to the 9/11 terrorists, for they did not secure themselves behind a protective wall that shielded them from risk to their own lives but sacrificed their lives in order to destroy the lives of others. Their suicides might be said to have made manifest the courage of their convictions.

Perhaps the charge that drone operators act with cowardice is fuelled by something to which we alluded earlier: their ability to depersonalize. In depersonalizing, drone operators shield themselves from the moral enormity of what they are doing, namely, killing vulnerable human beings, often in horrible ways and in ways that keep those who do the killing not only safe but also hidden, not only separated from the moral seriousness of what they are doing (avoiding "the look") but also avoiding the sight of the bloody aftermath to which they have given rise. That this may be what feeds the complaint is suggested by the fact that it is also a common complaint about snipers (Blahnik 2003).

[57] Depending on the circumstances, some form of moral and psychological courage may be called for if drone operators are required to make their own judgments about whether a situation calls for the use of a missile.

[58] Nor does courage take only one form. We recognize the possibility of "moral and psychological courage," getting ourselves to do something that we believe is right or even morally called for when we have not the stomach for it. From interviews with drone operators, it is clear that they are sometimes called upon to exhibit *these* forms of courage.

competence, care, and a sense of responsibility, which *are* associated with operating a military drone.)

Perhaps it is felt that since military actions involving drone warfare do not require the traditional military virtues of courage, loyalty, or selflessness, they run the risk of being actions in which agents fail to recognize what some view as their "high calling" and to appreciate the human costs involved in what they are doing to others (Vallor 2013).[59]

In answer, we would like to suggest that the virtues associated with traditional military combat may be neither as deeply emblematic of military engagement as their proponents claim nor, indeed, as morally constraining as it is often maintained. We believe that all too often the glorification of war serves (perhaps ignoble) political rather than moral purposes, and if, given right and compelling reasons, we decide that we *must* wage war, then there are plenty of other virtues: virtues such as care, constraint, loyalty to country, and competence that may equally well and nobly be brought into play. Certainly the use of drones alters the moral configuration of combat, an alteration that opens discussion of what constitutes noble military action in the newly constructed and now highly technologized military arena.

Fragmenting Responsibility

A final objection to military drone use is that it encourages a fragmentation of responsibility.

The archetypal war situation is one in which two armies confront each other and fight it out. Each is enemy to the other, and, on the battlefield at least, each is conventionally justified in killing the other. There is, of course, a chain of command, a coordinating mechanism with the "higher ups" for the purpose of planning strategy and determining when and which foot soldiers are to charge or to fire. Obviously, this description is highly idealized, for fighting may also take place in jungles, in villages, and in cities, and innocents or civilian populations may to varying degrees and in varying ways find themselves in the cross fire. In many such cases, military decisions are no longer clearly structured by strategic planning and may need to be made on the spot in response to unexpected and perhaps even unimagined contingencies. Nevertheless, the basic hierarchical structure of responsibility seems to be clear enough.

The workings of drone warfare, however, are such that the locus of responsibility for the deaths that result from its use may be deeply fragmented and diffuse; there are those who gather and sift intelligence for the purpose of determining who may be a potential enemy, other persons who construct "hit lists", and still others whose job is to locate those identified on such lists. Yet others may be charged with deciding who on the lists are to be dealt with by drone attack and who (where fea-

[59] See also Wood and Harbaugh (2014: A29), who argue that "the moment we conflate proficiency and valor, we cheapen the meaning of bravery itself."

sible) are to be captured. Still others are charged with sitting at their consoles with different, albeit associated, responsibilities. Responsibility for targeting a particular person or population is thus diffused over many people, each (or each set) of whom is involved in a different operation relevant to the use of drones as a means of armed attack.

We see this diffusion as unfortunate, even if in some sense necessary, for insofar as there is diffusion of responsibility, there will inevitably be a sense of dilution of responsibility. The decision of who is to be justifiably killed, and when and where this is to take place, involves so many people at so many of the preparatory stages that deflection of responsibility should something go wrong is tempting (and even in some cases justified). On the other hand, and this is a different criticism, the fragmentation of responsibility may unfairly burden a drone operator who, as the last link in the chain of command, triggers the missile that may target the wrong person or set of persons. If one takes the (classical military) view that each soldier is morally responsible for what he himself does,[60] irrespective of his acting in the context of, and perhaps on the orders of, multiple other decision-makers, then killing the wrong person will bring his judgment into question, including his judgment that he respect the judgment of other decision-makers.

Perhaps the complexity of drone warfare (i.e., the multitudinous skills involved and the different personnel required) requires a division of labor and thus of responsibility. But this should not serve as a reason for its diffusion, deflection, or diversion. However allocations of responsibility are made, and we believe that the model for moral responsibility should not be viewed as a closed system in which there is a "fixed quantity" of responsibility to be allocated among participants so that the greater the number of participants, the less responsibility is to be borne by any one participant. Rather, each participant may be seen as significantly, albeit not equally, responsible for what comes about, even if each has made a different contribution to it. (No doubt, the hierarchical character of military responsibility tends to moderate this way of conceiving the allocation of responsibility (Osiel 1998)).

In Summary

It is our view that the use of drones presents distinctive moral risks rather than that their use constitutes a distinctive moral wrong. Spatial distance is not, we think, a morally relevant consideration *in and of itself*, but because the geographic separation between drone operators and the human objects of drone attacks requires that human targets be viewed via computer screens, the spatial distance involved in drone use imposes sensory and other limitations that do have relevance to our moral perceptions, to our judgments, and (therefore) to our actions.

[60] "Men who take up arms against one another in public war do not cease on this account to be moral beings, responsible to one another and to God" (Lieber Code, 1863, art 15).

Drone use runs a high risk of numbing our moral sensibilities to the horror of war, whether generally or for the purposes of eliminating terrorists, for two other reasons: (1) The distance between drone operators and their targets is such that drone operators remain hidden and therefore invulnerable not only to counterattack from, but even to identification by, those who are targeted for death; and (2) responsibility for identifying who are to be attacked, when they are to be attacked, and where, is all-too-frequently hard to pinpoint, with the result that moral accountability for what is done is easily diffused and therefore (perceived to be) diluted.

The challenge, as we see it, is to be able to employ the available modern technologies that allow us effectively and efficiently to carry out our justified military missions while leaving intact and even further developing the moral acuity necessary for us to both fully grasp the moral enormity of our actions and effectively sharpen the moral sensibility that we need to appreciate the full measure of that enormity. One of the dangers of technology is that it tempts us to overreliance on its possibilities. We say *over*reliance because, as we have suggested, a potentially useful technology is as likely to detract from the purposes of morally justifiable conflict as it is to advance them. So we must always keep in mind, indeed, in the forefront of our minds, that of all options that are technologically possible, only a subset of those options is worthy of pursuit by humans who care about the moral worth of their actions and of their character.

The last couple of years have suggested a greater awareness of the importance of these issues, though it remains to be seen whether future users of military drones will learn from and embrace the moral lessons imparted by misadventures of its earlier use. We hope that open discussion of the issues raised in this chapter will lead in that direction.

References

AAP. (2013). Medals for drone warriors cancelled. *New York Times*, April 15. http://www.nytimes.com/2013/04/16/us/politics/medals-for-drone-warriors-canceled.html?_r=1&

Abé., N. (2012). Dreams in infrared: The woes of an American drone operator. *Spiegel Online*. December 14. http://www.spiegel.de/international/world/pain-continues-after-war-for-american-drone-pilot-a-872726.html

Amoureux., J. (2013). Are drones ethical? *Christian Science Monitor*, April 1. http://www.csmonitor.com/Commentary/Opinion/2013/0401/Are-US-drones-ethical

Aristotle, *Rhetoric*. Multiple editions.

Arreguín-Toft, I. (2001). How the weak win wars: A theory of asymmetric conflict. *International Security, 26*, 93–128.

Asaro, P. M. (2013). The labor of surveillance and bureaucratized killing: New subjectivities of military drone operators. *Social Semiotics, 23*, 196–224.

Baker, P. (2015). Obama apologizes after drone kills American and Italian Held by Al Qaeda. *New York Times*, April 24. http://www.nytimes.com/2015/04/24/world/asia/2-qaeda-hostages-were-accidentally-killed-in-us-raid-white-house-says.html

Bandura, A. (2004). The role of selective moral disengagement in terrorism and counterterrorism. In F. M. Moghaddam & A. J. Marsella (Eds.), *Understanding terrorism: Psychosocial roots,*

consequences and interventions (pp. 121–150). Washington, DC: American Psychological Association.
Bhojani, H. H. (2014). The constant presence of U.S. drones in the sky traumatize and ruin lives on the ground. *AlterNet*, January 23. http://www.alternet.org/world/armed-drones-breed-stress-trauma-anxiety-and-death
Blahnik, T. (2003). True bravery. *Snipercountry.com*, April 11. http://www.snipercountry.com/Articles/TrueBravery.asp
Blom, J. D. (2010). *Unmanned aerial systems: A historical perspective*, Occasional Paper 37. Kansas: USACAC, Combat Studies Press. http://usacac.army.mil/cac2/cgsc/carl/download/csipubs/OP37.pdf
Boyle, A. (2012). The US and its UAVs: A cost-benefit analysis. American Security Project. http://www.americansecurityproject.org/the-us-and-its-uavs-a-cost-benefit-analysis/
Brandt, M. R. (2013). Cyborg agency and individual trauma: What Enders Game teaches us about killing in the age of drone warfare. *M/C Journal, 16*.6. http://journal.media-culture.org.au/index.php/mcjournal/article/viewArticle/718
Brunstetter, D. R. (2012). Can we wage a just drone war? *The Atlantic*, July 19. http://www.theatlantic.com/technology/archive/2012/07/can-we-wage-a-just-drone-war/260055/
Bumiller, E. (2012). A day job waiting for a kill shot a world away. *New York Times*, July 29. http://www.nytimes.com/2012/07/30/us/drone-pilots-waiting-for-a-kill-shot-7000-miles-away.html?pagewanted=all
Bureau of Investigative Journalism. Covert drone war. https://www.thebureauinvestigates.com/category/projects/drones/drones-graphs/
Cervantes, S., Miguel De. 1993. *Don Quixote*. Ware, Hertfordshire: Wordsworth Editions. 2 vols.
Ceulemans, C. (2007–2008). The moral equality of combatants. *Parameters*. Winter: 99–109. http://strategicstudiesinstitute.army.mil/pubs/parameters/Articles/07winter/ceuleman.pdf
Coeckelbergh, M. (2013). Drones, information technology, and distance: Mapping the moral epistemology of remote fighting. *Ethics and Information Technology, 15*, 87–98.
Cole, C., Dobbing, M., & Hailwood, A. (2010). *Convenient killing: Armed drones and the 'playstation' mentality*. Oxford: Fellowship of Reconciliation. http://dronewarsuk.files.wordpress.com/2010/10/conv-killing-final.pdf
Coll, Steve. Kill or capture. 2012. *The New Yorker*, August 2. http://www.newyorker.com/online/blogs/comment/2012/08/kill-or-capture.html
Diderot, D. (1749; 1966). Lettre sur les aveugles à l'usage de ceux qui voient. (Letter on the blind, for the use of those who see). Trans. Derek Coltman. In L. G. Crocker (Ed.), *Diderot's Selected Writings*. New York: Macmillan.
Drew, C., & Philipps, D. (2015). As stress drives off drone operators, air force must cut flights. *New York Times*, June 17: A1. http://www.nytimes.com/2015/06/17/us/as-stress-drives-off-drone-operators-air-force-must-cut-flights.html?_r=0
Enemark, C. (2013). Unmanned drones and the ethics of war. In F. Allhof, N. G. Evans, & A. Henschke (Eds.), *Routledge handbook of ethics and war: Just war theory in the 21st century* (pp. 327–337). Abingdon: Routledge.
Ford, S. B. (2013). *Jus ad vim* and the just use of lethal force-short-of-war. In F. Allhof, N. G. Evans, & A. Henschke (Eds.), *Routledge handbook of ethics and war: Just war theory in the 21st century* (pp. 63–75). Abingdon: Routledge.
Fotion, N. (2005). Transforming and expanding the Kasher/Yadlin theory on the ethics of fighting wars against terrorism. *Journal of Military Ethics, 4*, 33–43.
Freiberger, E. (2013). Just war theory and the ethics of drone warfare. *E-International Relations*, July 18. http://www.e-ir.info/2013/07/18/just-war-theory-and-the-ethics-of-drone-warfare/
Galliot, J. C. (2012). Closing with completeness: The asymmetric drone warfare debate. *Journal of Military Ethics, 11*, 355.
Galliott, J. C. (2012). Uninhabited aerial vehicles and the asymmetry objection: A response to Strawser. *Journal of Military Ethics, 11*, 58–66.
Galliott, J. C. (2015). *Military robots: Mapping the moral landscape*. Aldershot: Ashgate.

Ginzburg, C. (1994). Killing a Chinese Mandarin: The moral implications of distance. *Critical Inquiry, 21*, 46–60.

Grossman, D. (1995; rev. ed. 2009). *On killing: The psychological cost of learning to kill in war and society.* New York: Back Bay Books/Little, Brown & Co.

Guttmacher Institute. (2017). Requirements for ultrasound. https://www.guttmacher.org/state-policy/explore/requirements-ultrasound

Haydar, B. (2005). The ethics of fighting terror and the priority of citizens. *Journal of Military Ethics, 4*, 52–59.

Hume, D. (1896). In L. A. Selby Bigge (Ed.), *A treatise of human nature*. Oxford, Clarendon.: http://oll.libertyfund.org/?option=com_staticxt&staticfile=show.php%3Ftitle=342.

Igneski, V. (2001). Distance, determinacy, and the duty to aid: A reply to Frances Kamm. *Law and Philosophy, 20*, 605–616.

Kamm, F. (2000). Does distance matter morally to the duty to rescue? *Law and Philosophy, 19*, 655–681.

Kamm, F. (2004). The new problem of distance in morality. In D. K. Chatterjee (Ed.), *The ethics of assistance: Morality and the distant needy* (pp. 59–74). Cambridge, UK, Cambridge University Press.

Kasher, A., & Yadlin, A. (2005a). Assassination and preventive killing. *SAIS Review, 25*, 41–57.

Kasher, A., & Yadlin, A. (2005b). Military ethics of fighting terror: An Israeli perspective. *Journal of Military Ethics, 4*(1), 3–32.

Kasher, A., & Yadlin, A. (2005c). Military ethics of fighting terror: Response. *Journal of Military Ethics, 4*, 60–70.

Kasher, A., & Yadlin, A. (2006). Military ethics of fighting terror: Principles. *Philosophia, 34*, 75–84.

Kasher, A., & Yadlin, A. (2009). Israel and the rules of war: An exchange. *New York Review of Books* 56, June 11 (with reply by Avishai Margalit and Michael Walzer).

Kilcullen, D., & Exum, A. M. (2009). Death from above, outrage down below. *New York Times*, May 17. http://www.nytimes.com/2009/05/17/opinion/17exum.html?pagewanted=all

Klaidman, D. (2012). The mind of a drone pilot. *The Daily Beast*, June 8. http://www.thedaily-beast.com/articles/2012/06/08/daniel-klaidman-on-the-mind-of-a-drone-strike-operator.html

Kleinig, J. (1986). Criminal liability for failures to act. *Law and Contemporary Problems, 49*, 161–180.

Kopstein, J. (2013). DARPA's 1.8 gigapixel drone camera is a high-res fourth amendment law-suit waiting to happen *The Verge*, February 1. http://www.theverge.com/2013/2/1/3940898/darpa-gigapixel-drone-surveillance-camera-revealed

Lang, G. (2011). Excuses for the moral equality of combatants. *Analysis Reviews, 71*, 512–523.

Lévinas, E. (1961). Totality and infinity: An essay on exteriority. Trans. Alphonso Lingis. Pittsburgh: Duquesne University Press.

Lévinas, E. (1985). Ethics and infinity: Conversations with Philippe Nemo. Trans. Richard A. Cohen. Pittsburgh: Duquesne University Press.

Lieber Code. (1863). Instructions for the government of armies of the United States in the field. April 24. http://avalon.law.yale.edu/19th_century/lieber.asp

Linebaugh, H. (2013). I worked on the US drone program. The public should know what really goes on. *The Guardian*, December 29. http://www.theguardian.com/commentisfree/2013/dec/29/drones-us-military

Luban, D. (2014). Risk taking and force protection. In R. Walzer (Ed.), *Yitzhak Benbaji and Naomi Sussman* (pp. 277–301). Abingdon: Routledge.

Lubold, G. (2014). Medals for drone pilots? Hagel faces a tough choice. *The Complex/FP*, January 27. http://complex.foreignpolicy.com/posts/2014/01/27/medals_for_drone_pilots_hagel_still_cant_decide

Margalit, A., & Walzer, M. (2009). Israel: Civilians and combatants. *New York Review of Books*, 56. 8, May 14: 21–22.

McAlister, A. L., Bandura, A., & Owen, S. V. (2006). Mechanisms of moral disengagement in support of military force: Impact of Sept. 11. *Journal of Social and Clinical Psychology, 25*, 141–165. http://www.uky.edu/~eushe2/Bandura/Bandura2006JSCP.pdf.

McEvers, K. (2013). The hidden cost of the drone program. NPR, May 5. http://www.npr.org/2013/05/05/181403067/the-hidden-cost-of-the-drone-program
McMahan, J. (2006). On the moral equality of combatants. *Journal of Political Philosophy, 14*, 377–393. http://philosophy.rutgers.edu/dmdocuments/Moral_Equality_of_Combatants.pdf.
McNeal, G. S. (2014). Targeted killing and accountability. *Georgetown Law Journal, 102*, 681–794. http://papers.ssrn.com/sol3/papers.cfm?abstract_id=1819583.
Milgram, S. (1974). *Obedience to authority: An experimental view*. New York: HarperCollins.
Miller, S. (2014). The ethics of targeted killing: Osama bin Laden, drones, and counter-terrorism. *Public Affairs Quarterly, 28*, 317–340.
Mohamed, F. G. (2011). Farewell to due process: The assassination of Anwar al-Awlaki. *Huffington Post*, October 3. http://www.huffingtonpost.com/feisal-g-mohamed/anwar-al-awlaki-killed_b_989485.html#
Mowery, R. (2014). Drones vs. fair chase. http://bowhunting.net/2014/02/44814/
O'Connell, M. E. (2012). Unlawful killing with combat drones: A case study of Pakistan, 2004–2009. In S. Bronitt, M. Gani, & S. Hufnagel (Eds.), *Shooting to kill: Socio-legal perspectives on the use of lethal force* (pp. 263–291). Oxford: Hart Publishing.
O'Hara, W. (2010). Drone attacks and just war theory. *SmallWarsJournal.com*, September 14. http://smallwarsjournal.com/blog/journal/docs-temp/541-ohaire.pdf
Orsi, F. (2008). Obligations of nearness. *Journal of Value Inquiry, 42*, 1–21.
Osiel, M. J. (1998). Obeying orders: Atrocity, military discipline and the law of war. *California Law Review, 86*, 939–1129.
Patten, A. (2005). Should we stop thinking about poverty in terms of helping the poor? *Ethics and International Affairs, 19*, 19–27.
Patton, C. (2014). Defacing Levinas: Vision, veiling and the ethics of republican citizenship in France. *Social Identities*. https://doi.org/10.1080/13504630.2013.878990.
Perry, D. L. (2005). Ambiguities in the 'war on terror'. *Journal of Military Ethics, 4*, 44–51.
Pogge, T. (2002). *World poverty and human rights: Cosmopolitan responsibilities and reforms*. Cambridge: Polity Press.
Pogge, T. (2005). Severe poverty as a violation of negative duties. *Ethics and International Affairs, 19*, 55–83.
Power, M. (2013). Confessions of a drone warrior. *GQ*, October. http://www.gq.com/news-politics/big-issues/201311/drone-uav-pilot-assassination
Public Intelligence. (2012). DoD current and future U.S. drone activities map. https://publicintelligence.net/dod-us-drone-activities-map/
Ramose, M. B. (2008). Military ethics of fighting terror: A response to Kasher and Yadlin. *Philosophia, 36*, 209–212.
Raskin, M., & West, D. (2008). *Collateral damage: A U.S. strategy in war?* Washington: Institute for Policy Studies, 2008. http://www.ips-dc.org/reports/collateral_damage
Robinson, P. (2008). The ethics of the strong against the tactics of the weak: A response to Kasher and Yadlin's 'Military ethics of fighting terror'. *Philosophia, 36*, 195–202.
Rodin, D. (2008). The moral inequality of soldiers: Why jus in bello asymmetry is half right. In D. Rodin & H. Shue (Eds.), *Just and unjust warriors: The moral and legal status of soldiers* (pp. 44–68). New York: Oxford University Press.
Sharkey, N. (2012). Killing made easy: From joysticks to politics. In P. Lin, K. Abney, & G. A. Bekey (Eds.), *Robot ethics: The ethical and social implications of robotics* (pp. 111–128). Cambridge, MA: MIT Press.
Sifton, J. (2012). A brief history of drones. *The Nation*, February 7. http://www.thenation.com/article/166124/brief-history-drones
Singer, P. (1972). Famine, affluence, and morality. *Philosophy & Public Affairs, 1*, 229–243.
Singer, P. (1979). ch 8. In *Rich and poor. In Practical Ethics* (3rd ed.). Cambridge: Cambridge University Press.
Smart, J. J. C., & Williams, B. (1973). *Utilitarianism: For and against*. Cambridge: Cambridge University Press.

Smith, A. (1790). *The theory of moral sentiments.* sixth ed., MεταLibri, http://www.ibiblio.org/ml/libri/s/SmithA_MoralSentiments_p.pdf
Steinhoff, U. (2008). Jeff McMahan on the moral inequality of combatants. *Journal of Political Philosophy, 16*, 220–226.
Steinhoff, U. (2012). Why 'we' are not harming the global poor: A critique of Pogge's leap from state to individual responsibility. *Public Reason, 4*, 119–138.
Stewart, P. (2011). Overstretched U.S. drone pilots face stress risk. *Reuters*, December 19. http://www.reuters.com/article/2011/12/19/us-drone-pilots-stress-idUSTRE7BI24N20111219
Strawser, B. J. (2010). Moral predators: The duty to employ uninhabited aerial vehicles. *Journal of Military Ethics, 9*, 342–368.
Timm, T. (2015). The hostages killed by US drones are the casualties of an inhumane policy. *The Guardian,* April 24. http://www.theguardian.com/commentisfree/2015/apr/24/the-hostages-killed-by-us-drones-are-the-casualties-of-an-inhumane-policy
Unger, P. (1996). *Living high and letting die: Our illusion of innocence.* New York: Oxford University Press.
Vallor, S. (2013). The future of military virtue: Autonomous systems and the moral deskilling of the military. In K. Podins, J. Stinissen, & M. Maybaum (Eds.), *5th international conference on cyber conflict.* Tallin: NATO CCD COE Publications. http://www.ccdcoe.org/publications/2013proceedings/d2r1s10_vallor.pdf.
Walzer, M. (2006). *Just and unjust wars: A moral argument with historical illustrations* (4th ed.). New York: Basic Books.
Weber, M. (2005). Are terrorists cowards? *Public Affairs Quarterly, 19*, 331–342.
Wertheimer, R. (1971). Understanding the abortion argument. *Philosophy & Public Affairs, 1*, 67–95.
Wikipedia authors, Distinguished warfare medal. http://en.wikipedia.org/wiki/Distinguished_Warfare_Medal
Williams, B. (1981). Persons, character and morality. In *Moral luck: Philosophical papers 1973–80.* Cambridge: Cambridge University Press.
Wilson, G. I. (2013). The psychology of killer drones action against our foes; reaction affecting us. Fabius Maximus blog, August 30. http://fabiusmaximus.com/2013/08/30/drones-syria-54434/
Wong, E. (2013). Hacking U.S. secrets, China pushes for drones. *New York Times*, September 20, 2013. http://www.nytimes.com/2013/09/21/world/asia/hacking-us-secrets-china-pushes-for-drones.html
Wood, J., & Harbaugh, K. (2014). The limits of armchair warfare. *New York Times*, May 21: A29. http://www.nytimes.com/2014/05/21/opinion/the-limits-of-armchair-warfare.html
Wyler, G. (2013). Yemeni journalist gives a powerful description of what it's like when your life is at the mercy of a drone. *Business Insider,* April 25. http://www.businessinsider.com.au/drone-strike-hearing-yemeni-journalist-farea-al-muslimi-2013-4
Yaari, M. (2009). Israel: The code of combat. *New York Review of Books* 56, October 8 (with reply by Avishai Margalit and Michael Walzer).
Zupan, D. (2006). The moral (in)equality of combatants. http://isme.tamu.edu/JSCOPE06/Zupan06.html

Chapter 3
War as Play, War as Slaughter, and the Laws of War

Karsten J. Struhl

The idea that war can be play may seem strange, as play often conveys the idea of something which is not serious and also not harmful. This idea has been challenged by the Dutch historian Johan Huizinga (1955), who wrote a groundbreaking work on play and its relation to culture in 1938. This book, entitled *Homo Ludens*, makes a strong case for the more general claim that the play function in human culture is as important as the work function and human reasoning; in short, for Huizinga, our species is not only *Homo Sapiens* and *Homo Faber* (man the maker) but also *Homo Ludens* (man the player). Huizinga, in making his case, attempts to demonstrate the relation of the play motive to the development of language, to knowledge, to law, to art and poetry, to philosophy, and to war. It is this last function of play which I intend to further elaborate in this paper. My purpose is not to defend everything Huizinga says about war as play but to develop some of the implications of his analysis for thinking about modern warfare and just war theory, specifically about its implications for twentieth-century total war and the twenty-first-century war on terrorism. I shall put forward several claims – first, that the play motive of war is intimately bound up with just war theory; second, that the play function in tandem with just war theory functions not only to limit the horrors of war but also in part to obscure the slaughter that is the horrible reality of all wars; third, that, the warfare of the twentieth century developed a techno-culture which in large part vitiated the play motive and which also made it almost impossible to have a just war; and, finally, that the continued development of war technology in the twenty-first century in conjunction with the ideology of the war on terrorism has revived the play motive with a vengeance that conceals the slaughter without the need for just war theory.

I would like to thank John L. Hammond for his insightful criticisms and comments on an earlier version of this chapter.

K. J. Struhl (✉)
John Jay College of Criminal Justice (CUNY), New York, NY, USA
e-mail: kastruth@tiac.net

G. J. Andreopoulos et al. (eds.), *The Rule of Law in an Era of Change*,
Springer Series on International Justice and Human Rights,
https://doi.org/10.1007/978-3-319-89908-4_3

What is the play motive? For Huizinga, play can be very serious. When the child plays, even when she knows that it is pretend, the play is often performed with utmost seriousness. Chess is generally played with the most serious intent and absorption. What is at stake is winning, victory, showing one's superiority to the opponent, which is a pleasure independent of any prize that may be obtained. Play, for Huizinga, carves out a sphere distinct from ordinary life. It creates, as it were, its own universe with a playing field, a playing field which may be elevated to the level of the sacred. Play, for Huizinga, is limited in time and space. It has a beginning and end of the game. It has an order of its own, its own distinct set of rules which the players must not transgress. "As soon as the rules are transgressed the whole play-world collapses. The game is over" (Huizinga 1955, p. 11).

Play most often takes the agonistic form of two opposing persons or groups who contest for supremacy. The Olympic contests of ancient Greece reveal play in its contending, agonistic nature. In fact, the games were referred to as *olympiakoí agones*. Most of them were "fought out in deadly earnest" (Huizinga 1955, p. 48) and included duels sometimes fought to the death. In such agonistic play, something is at stake, which can give immense satisfaction to at least one of the participants. What is at stake is not so much the external rewards but the idea of winning esteem and honor, and this is greatly enhanced by the presence of spectators. Huizinga sees this as the outgrowth of a competitive instinct which "is not in the first place a desire for power or a will to dominate. The primary thing is the desire to excel others, to be first and to be honoured for that" (Huizinga 1955, p. 50). The prize, even if materially significant, is essentially a symbol of this achievement.

Once we understand that play often has a significant agonistic dimension, it should not be strange that play can involve the drawing of blood and even killing. The play motive can be discerned in blood sports from the Roman gladiatorial combats to contemporary boxing. It can be seen in the duel when one party wishes to avenge what he considers an outrage to his honor. While the duel has as its immediate object to draw blood, its real goal is symbolic and its formal structure is that of play. "...it is the shedding of blood and not the killing that matters....The spot where the duel is fought bears all the marks of a play-ground; the weapons have to be exactly alike as in certain games; there is a signal from the start to the finish, and the number of shots is prescribed. When blood flows, honor is vindicated and restored" (Huizinga 1955, p. 95).

What about war? At first glance, it may seem obscene to characterize war as play. Perhaps we can allow that blood sports and duels have a play element, but war seems to be qualitatively different, especially given the enormity of the slaughter. However, Huizinga offers considerable support for the claim that war, with all its carnage, has historically manifested a significant play dimension. A large part of his analysis focuses on the many ways in which war in ancient and medieval societies was regarded as a contest between equals, a contest whose goal was glory and honor. He notes the ways in which much of ancient war had stringent rules that could not be explained by material calculations. One interesting example of this, from ancient Greek history, was the war between two Euboean cities, Chalcis and

Eritrea, in the seventh century B.C.E. "A solemn compact in which the rules were laid down was deposited beforehand in the temple of Artemis. The time and place for the encounter were therein appointed. All missiles were forbidden: spears, arrows, slingshots; only the lance and the sword were allowed" (Huizinga 1955, p. 96). Huizinga also cites examples from ancient non-Western cultures. For example, during hostilities, Chinese war lords "used to exchange jugs of wine which were solemnly drunk amid reminiscences of a more peaceful past and protestations of mutual esteem" (Huizinga 1955, p. 98). In the Middle Ages, kings and princes often attempted to replace armies with single combat to settle their dispute. Preceding the battle of Crécy, there was an exchange of letters "in which the King of France offered King Edward the choice of two places and four separate days of battle, or more if desired" (Huizinga 1955, p. 99). Huizinga (1955) further notes the ideal of the noble warrior, which imagines war as "an exhilarating game of courage and honour" (p. 101) and suggests the way in which this ideal functions in stories about both the knights of the Middles Ages and the Japanese samurai. While many of these stories are myths, it would be wrong to say that they had no influence on the warriors themselves. Furthermore, the idea of war as encompassing certain warrior virtues persists in the modern era. As Huizinga (1955) puts it, the image of "war as the fountain-head of human virtues" (Huizinga, p. 103) has found its way into much of modern poetry and art. A typical example is the poet John Ruskin who praised war as a fundamental component of the aesthetic imagination. "No great art ever yet rose on earth but among a nation of soldiers….The love of contest among men are disciplined, by consent, into modes of beautiful – though it may be fatal – play" (quoted in Huizinga 1955, p. 103). Huizinga (1955) concurs with Ruskin and concludes as follows: "Epic and lyrical expression of the noblest kind, brilliant decorative art…all have sprung from this immemorial conception of war as a noble game" (p. 104).

Of course, Huizinga recognizes that the lyrical and artistic expression of war creates a myth which may often be at odds with the reality. Still, what is important for him is that this myth of war demonstrates the way in which human beings have historically understood war as a form of play and that, furthermore, the artistic expression of this myth is itself a form of play. Huizinga does, however, offer an important caveat. The play element in war can only exist insofar as the antagonists perceive each other as equals and attempt to limit violence through the use of certain rules of war. The play element is destroyed "as soon as war is waged outside the sphere of equals, against groups not recognized as human beings and thus deprived of human rights -- barbarians, devils, heathens, heretics, and 'lesser breeds without the law'" (Huizinga 1955, pp. 89–90). Furthermore, for Huizinga (1955), various kinds of war activities are excluded from the idea of war as play: "the surprise, the ambush, the raid, the punitive expedition and wholesale extermination cannot be described as agonistic forms or warfare" (p. 90). Finally, "it remained for the theory of `total war' to…extinguish the last vestige of the play element" (Huizinga 1955, p. 90). This, as we shall see, has significant implications for modern warfare and the possibility of the applicability of just war theory.

Just War Theory and the Play Motive

I now want to consider certain implications of Huizinga's analysis. I shall begin with some thoughts about the relation of the play motive in war to just war theory. Just war theory is generally said to have begun with Augustine who was, in part, attempting to reconcile Christianity's pacifist message with its allegiance to the Roman Empire. However, in its more explicit form, developed by Thomas Aquinas and other thinkers within the Catholic philosophical tradition, its stated historical function was to promote limits to war. To achieve this goal, just war theory uses two kinds of criteria. The first is whether a given war itself is justified (*jus ad bellum*) and the second is whether the way in which the war is conducted can be justified (*jus in bello*). The main criterion for *jus ad bellum* is that the war be fought for a just cause, which is usually taken to mean that it be a war of self-defense against aggression. Other criteria of *jus ad bellum* is that war must be a last resort, that it must be waged by a legitimate authority and for the right motive, and that the good to be achieved must outweigh the probable harm of going to war (the proportionality criterion). The most important criterion for *jus in bello* is that of noncombatant immunity, which is taken to mean that civilians must not be the object of direct attack and that the infrastructure necessary to support the life and health of the civilian population not be the object of direct attack (e.g., destroying the water supply of the city). *Jus in bello* also invokes a proportionality criterion, insisting that the military means used be no more than is necessary to achieve its aim and that there be an attempt to avoid harm to civilians. Finally, *jus in bello* prohibits certain means and methods of warfare, e.g., using chemical weapons, and also prohibits killing or torturing prisoners of war.

The criteria for *jus ad bellum* are the criteria of the legitimacy of embarking on war. In terms of understanding war as a form of play, we might regard these criteria as the criteria for deciding to enter the game of war in the first place. In contrast, we might say that the rules of *jus in bello* are the play rules of war. Recall that, for Huizinga, agonistic play requires that the protagonists regard each other as equal and agree to play by certain rules which put limits on what they can do to each other. In other words, once the war has begun, the game of war requires both sides to play by the same rules. If these rules are broken, then war can no longer be conceived as a noble game and winning no longer can bring the victor honor and glory. Thus, the game of war requires that each side adheres to the rule of noncombatant immunity as well as the rules which prohibit the maltreatment of prisoners. If they do not, war is no longer play but simply slaughter.

Here's the problem. War is, in fact, always slaughter on a massive scale. Whatever justification is given for it, it takes the form of organized murder and often seems quite senseless to its participants. However, as Chris Hedges (2003) has argued, war also takes on a mythic form which can be distinguished from the experiential reality. This mythic form allows human beings to tolerate what would otherwise be intolerable. In this mythic form, "we imbue events with meaning that they do not have" (Hedges 2003, p. 21). We try to make sense of the horror. The myth of war tries to give "a justification to what is often nothing more than gross human cruelty and stupidity" (Hedges 2003, p. 23). The myth of war depends upon our ability to think of war as a noble game, and this requires the play rules of just war theory. Thus, while just war theory has as its stated purpose to limit war, it tends, in fact, to perpetuate the tolerance for warfare in general. If this is correct, then just war theory keeps the game of war going by concealing behind its play rules the reality of war as senseless, murderous slaughter.

However, something happened to war in the twentieth century which made the play rules of just war theory especially problematic. In the early part of the century, there seemed to be a consensus, at least among European nations with regard to each other's citizens, that directly targeting civilian areas through bombardment was a war crime. Article 25 of The Hague Convention of October 1907 stated that "bombardment, by whatever means, of towns, villages, dwellings or buildings which are undefended, is prohibited."[1] But this consensus was soon to be eroded. Between World War I and World War II, there was a moral slide that eroded the rule of noncombatant immunity, a moral slide which made it possible to accept the direct targeting of civilians as a legitimate act of war. World War I witnessed the extensive use of naval blockades. During World II, the allies used saturation bombing on a regular basis. When in 1940 Winston Churchill made the decision to bomb Germany, the decision was to bomb military targets only (although this included communication and transportation). However, once Germany responded with an aerial Blitz that killed 40,000 civilians, the order was given to firebomb German cities. In the bombing of German cities by the British alone, at least 300,000 were killed and 780,000 wounded. During World War II, the United States dropped 200,000 tons of bombs. Overall, the total number of civilians killed through the Allied bombing raids in Europe was over half a million. The US firebombing of Tokyo and Dresden took 100,000 lives each. The "strategic" bombing in Japan resulted in perhaps a million casualties, the majority of which were civilians. And that was before the bombing of Hiroshima, where 100,000 were immediately killed and another 100,000 soon died as the result of radiation, and the bombing of Nagasaki, where 70,000 died, some immediately and some within the year. In all, the pretense of bombing only military targets was gone. The new concept was called "area bombing." Jonathan Glover (2001) offers a succinct summary of this slide: "The blockade made area bombing seem acceptable. Area bombing was reached from a gentle slide from military bombing. The bombing of German cities made acceptable the bombing of Japanese ones, which in turn allowed the slide to the atomic bomb. The slide went on from the Hiroshima bomb to Nagasaki" (p. 115).[2]

---

[1]The Hague Convention of October 1907 can be accessed at http://www.opbw.org/int_inst/sec_docs/1907HC-TEXT.pdf. Sadly, this consensus did not apply to natives in foreign lands. The British bombed the Pathans in India in 1915, revolutionaries in Egypt in 1916, Afghanistan in 1919, and Iran and Transjordan in 1920. Sven Lindqvist (2001) suggests that "bombing natives was considered quite natural. The Italians did it in Libya, the French did it in Morocco, and the British did it throughout the Middle East, in India, and East Africa, while the South Africans did it in Southwest Africa" (p. 74).

[2]See Walzer (2015, pp. 254, 265, and 260) for the general statistics on the terror bombing of the German cities and specifically of the bombing of Dresden and Tokyo. See Glover (2001, pp. 77 and 99) for the statistics on the results of the bombing of Hiroshima and Nagasaki.

This moral slide has constructed a moral culture of insensitivity in which the massive destruction of civilians and of the civilian infrastructure has become accepted. Each escalation of warfare set a precedent for a further escalation so that what was considered barbaric earlier soon became the norm. This new norm then becomes part of the military culture of war.[3] In addition, as the military technology develops, it becomes almost unthinkable not to use it. Thus, what might be called the techno-cultural system of modern warfare dictates how war in general is waged and the kinds of acts that are necessary to win.

The rest of the twentieth century continued the pattern. As a result of the US invasion of Vietnam under the pretense of "saving it from communism," it has been estimated that 415,000 civilians died in South Vietnam alone (Tirman 2011, p. 167). They died from the effects of Napalm, cluster bombs, and Agent Orange. Although it is difficult to get clear estimates of civilian deaths in North Vietnamese cities, it is clear that many more civilians died as the result of saturation bombing. During this war, the United States designated certain areas as "free-fire zones" in which anything that moved was a legitimate target. American soldiers destroyed whole villages in South Vietnam and sometimes deliberately massacred the civilian population. Overall, it is estimated that the United States dropped "7 million tons of bombs…on Vietnam, more than twice the total bombs dropped on Europe and Asia in World War II" (Zinn 1990, p. 469).[4]

The NATO war in Yugoslavia is an especially interesting example of the moral slide, as it was justified as a "humanitarian intervention" to protect Albanian civilians in Kosovo. It, however, took the form not of direct military intervention in Kosovo but of savage aerial bombardment of Belgrade and other major cities in Serbia. Schools, hospitals, water purification plants, electric generators, railways, automobile factories, bridges, and marketplaces were hit and hit with deliberate intention. Every major city and many villages were attacked not just once but many times. Bombs were dropped on the downtown centers of cities. Cluster bombs, which are explicitly designed to kill human beings, were dropped in heavily populated civilian areas. Within 20 min of the first bombing attack, there was often a second round of bombing whose function was, in part, to kill rescue workers. Hence, a war fought to protect civilians in one area used methods which not only put other civilians at risk but, in fact, directly targeted them.[5]

Consider a traffic system. It is not very easy to ride a horse through a modern city and would be next to impossible to do it on a highway. On the interstate it is necessary to maintain a certain speed in order to be in accord with the general flow of cars. Going too slow is as much of a danger as going too fast. In the same way, the Internet is a system which places demands on what kinds of programs I need and

[3] What was, for the most part, only allowable (at least in principle) against the natives of foreign lands now became acceptable against anyone, European as well as non-European.

[4] For more details on the civilian casualties as a result of the American invasion of Vietnam, see Young (1991).

[5] For these and other examples of the civilian casualties as a result of the NATO bombing of Yugoslavia, see Arkin (2000) and Amnesty International Report (2000).

how much memory I need for my computer. If I am going to use the Internet, I must periodically upgrade or replace my computer as the Internet is upgraded. And so it is with war. Here is my hypothesis. Modern war has been upgraded to the point that it is necessary to build and to employ weapons and methods of attack which make it difficult to discriminate between combatant and noncombatants. The deterioration of the ability to discriminate and the targeting of the civilian infrastructure and of civilians themselves are built into the techno-cultural system of modern war. The play rules of war have been vitiated by the techno-cultural system of modern war.[6]

Of course, the reality of all war is that civilians will be killed, but what is striking is that throughout the wars of the twentieth century, the ratio between civilian casualties and military casualties has so increased that now the former far outnumbers the latter.[7] Just war theory has attempted to allow for this with the doctrine of double effect. The doctrine of double effect, in its minimal form, claims that the killing of civilians is permissible so long as it is not the direct intent of the action and so long as it is not a means to our ends. The idea is that we distinguish between two effects of our actions – that which is intended and that which is not intended. We are not, according to the traditional doctrine of double effect, responsible for the evil unintended effects of our action. Thus, a military action may cause the death of many civilians, but so long as its goal is not specifically to kill these civilians and so long as we do not target these civilians as a means to this goal (and so long as the goal is itself morally acceptable within the rules of war), it does not violate the criteria of noncombatant immunity. There are a number of problems with this doctrine, which has resulted in a number of attempts to revise it. For example, Michael Walzer (2015) has suggested the following amendment to the traditional doctrine – that in addition to the evil effect not being intended or a means to the intended end, the agent, "aware of the evil involved...seeks to minimize it, accepting costs to himself" (p. 156). On Walzer's revision, the doctrine of double effect requires a second intention – an intention to minimize civilian casualties even if this requires a greater risk for the military agent. While this seems like a reasonable amendment to the traditional doctrine, it is not clear how it can function within the techno-cultural conditions of modern warfare. The problem is not merely that modern war causes massive civilian casualties, because the agents of war are insufficiently concerned with the loss of civilian life (although that is certainly true). The problem is that the warfare

[6] I use the phrase "techno-cultural system of modern war" to indicate that the problem is not just the upgrading of war technology but the combination of that technology with the development of the culture of the modern military and its imperatives. My hypothesis should not be construed as a form of technological determinism.

[7] A 2001 study supported by the International Committee of the Red Cross states that "civilians have – both intentionally and by accident – been moved to the center stage in the theater of war" and notes that while in World War I, there were nine soldiers killed for every civilian, in the wars today "it is estimated that ten civilians die for every soldier or fighter killed in battle" (Greenberg and Boorstin 2001, p. 19). While these specific statistics have been challenged by Epps (2013), because of the difficulty of compiling such statistics, she nevertheless concludes "that since the turn of the twentieth century, civilian deaths have outnumbered military deaths in nearly all wars" (p. 329).

of the twentieth and now twenty-first century deliberately targets civilians while hypocritically pretending that the civilians killed are simply "collateral damage." In his private diary, Harry S. Truman claimed that when he gave the order to drop the atomic bomb on Hiroshima, he instructed the Secretary of War "to use it so that military objectives and soldiers are the target and not women and children" (quoted in Glover 2001, pp. 101–102). Of course, this is a clear example of self-deception, but it highlights the problem. How, in an age when we have such weapons of mass destruction, and given our techno-culture of war, do we minimize civilian casualties? Truman's self-deception was a symptom of a larger problem. Given the techno-culture of modern war, we can no longer play by the rules of war. If we were to acknowledge this, then we would have to acknowledge that the game is over, and just war theory is obsolete. By the middle of the twentieth century, war had become the "total war" which Huizinga saw as extinguishing "the last vestige of the play element." War was no longer play. It was simply slaughter.

The War on Terrorism

This is not, however, the end of the story. What is now called "the war on terrorism" began shortly after the attack on the World Trade Center on September 11, 2001. The beginning of the war on terrorism took the form of a war against the State of Afghanistan, even though there was no evidence that the Taliban government had helped plan the attack or even that they knew about it. The main justification that the Bush Administration gave for going to war was that the Taliban "harbored" Al-Qaeda. In other words, the United States had arrogated to itself the right to attack another country not because that country had attacked it, which would, on just war theory, be a legitimate act of self-defense, but because Al-Qaeda resided on that country's soil. Thus, the war on terrorism in its first incarnation was potentially a war on any nation-state which harbored terrorists. The second incarnation of the war on terrorism was the war against Iraq. In order to convince its own citizens to support this invasion of a sovereign country, all the US government needed to do was to suggest that Iraq might have weapons of mass destruction and that it might also have some relations with Al-Qaeda. However, once the war had begun and no weapons of mass destruction were discovered, more emphasis was put on the latter rationale in spite of the fact that no specific links to Al-Qaeda were revealed. The public relations strategy was then altered to suggest that even if there were no links to Al-Qaeda at the moment, there might be some in the future. Thus, with the war in Iraq, the doctrine of the war on terrorism extended not just the spatial but also the temporal scope of war. The war on terrorism now proclaims that if a country could conceivably at some future time ally itself with a terrorist organization, the United States can declare war against them. In effect, the war on terrorism entails that the US government arrogates to itself the right to make war against whomever it chooses, wherever it chooses. It can bomb suspected terrorists in any country with little regard for civilian casualties. It can attack any country suspected of harboring terrorists. It can employ the doctrine of preventive war, as it did in Iraq. It can fly pilotless Predator drones over any country and can selectively assassinate anyone it chooses anywhere in the world simply by Presidential Decree. It can kidnap anyone it deems a suspected terrorist from any country and perhaps subject them to what the Bush administration euphemistically termed "enhanced interrogation," in other words, torture.[8]

The war on terrorism has inaugurated a new form of total war. It is a war without limits not only in that it ignores the rules of *jus in bello* but because it envisions the whole world as a battlefield. Free-fire zones are no longer restricted to certain designated areas, as they were in Vietnam. The whole world is now a potentially free-fire zone. In other words, there is no longer a specific playing field or rather the whole world is the playing field. There is no longer a foreseeable conclusion of the war, as terrorism is an ongoing problem that could continue into the indefinite future. In all, the war on terrorism has no limit in time and space. It does not even attempt to play by the rules of just war theory.[9] It does not recognize the combatants on the other side as warriors with an equal status. The war on terrorism is a war against an enemy who is to be hunted down, assassinated, and killed often with their families. It is a war of extermination. On Huizinga's analysis, this kind of total war should extinguish once and for all the play motive. Yet, I want to suggest that in an odd way, the opposite has occurred. The war on terrorism has revived the play motive in a different and more insidious form.

War as a Video Game

Here is an additional line of thought. This new form of play is made possible through the recent development of war video games, new visual technologies, and robotics. In conjunction with the ideology of the war on terrorism, these technological developments have organized war as a new form of play, one which blurs the difference between the virtual and the reality of war. In this section, I will discuss the development of war video games and their function as recruitment tools, as a form of military training, and as a narrative that functions to legitimate the war on terrorism. In the next section, I will discuss the significance of the application of the new visual technologies and of robotics to war.

As I am writing this paper, there are a number of websites on the Internet which allow you to play a variety of war video games for free, e.g., a website entitled *War*

[8]This was the official policy of the Bush administration. While the Obama administration has removed many of the "enhanced interrogation" techniques, e.g., "waterboarding," from the official manuals, the United States continues to use various forms of psychological torture as well as to outsource torture. See Kaye (2014), Roth (2014), and Cook (2010).

[9]Perhaps there was no time in history where war was really conducted according to the rule of just war theory. But there was often the attempt or at least the pretense of the attempt to play by these rules. In the war on terrorism, the attempt is no longer operative and even the pretense has very little to do with the rules of *jus ad bellum* or *jus in bello*.

Games (2015). One of the most popular war video games is entitled *America's Army* and was developed by the US army explicitly for recruitment purposes and first released in 2002 (Stahl 2006; Mead 2013). Lt. Colonel Casey Wardynski, the creator of *America's Army* and also the director of the Army's Office of Economic and Manpower Analysis, told Corey Mead (2013) that that the main target audience was 12- and 13-year-old boys. The point, he said, was "to capture the youth mind share," because by age 13, they are already beginning to decide what they want to do with their lives. "You can't wait until they're seventeen, because by then they will have decided they're going to college or to a trade school.…You have to get them before they've made those decisions" (quoted in Mead 2013, Chapter 4). The game immediately proved itself to be an effective recruitment tool. In 2005 it was determined that 40 percent of army enlistees had previously played the game (Stahl 2006).[10] According to a 2008 MIT study, "30 percent of all Americans age 16–24 had a more positive impression of the army because of the game [*America's Army*] and, even more amazingly, the game had more impact on recruits than all other forms of Army advertising combined" (quoted in Mead 2013, Chapter 4). *America's Army* has also invaded the classroom. In 2008, the Army's third Recruiting Brigade in Ohio partnered with *Project Lead the Way*, a nonprofit educational curriculum provider. Since *Project Lead the Way*'s curriculum was preapproved in every state, *America's Army* was now able to be presented as a basic learning module in public schools throughout the United States. This is one example of a more general phenomenon where military-endorsed video games enter the public educational system. What all this means is that the military now "creates curricular areas where the immersion in, say, army-branded virtual worlds may define the learning experience itself" (Mead 2013, Chapter 8).

While *America's Army* is one of the most popular war video games, it is only one of many examples of what has been developed by "the military-entertainment-complex" (Mead 2013; Shaw 2010) or, more elaborately, the "military-industrial-media-entertainment network" (Der Derain 2001). The history of this relation is complex, as the military initially "took the lead in financing, sponsoring, and inventing the technology used in video games, while game companies were the happy beneficiaries" (Mead 2013, introduction). However, while today the video game industry is the main developer of war video games, it often does so in partnership with the military. One of the main examples of this was a partnership between the Defense Department and the University of Southern California's Institute for Creative Technologies (ICT), which was initiated with a $45 million Defense Department grant. ICT "brings together video game developers, f/x artists, research scientists and Pentagon experts to create faster, cheaper, and more effective ways of preparing recruits for their jobs on the front line" (Silberman 2004). In addition,

[10] To be sure, correlation is not causation. Nonetheless, this high correlation between a video game intentionally constructed by the military for recruitment purposes and the high use of that game by those who eventually decided to enlist suggests that there is at least a fit between the way many enlistees understand war and the way in which *America's Army* (and other war video games) depicts contemporary warfare.

"such partnerships allow commercial game developers access to up-to-the-minute details of new weapons systems the public is hungry to test drive. ICT is a microcosm of much broader trends in military and game industry collaboration..." (Stahl 2006, p. 117).

Over the last two decades, the cooperation between the military and the commercial-entertainment industry has focused on the development of video games not only for recruitment but also increasingly for military training purposes. While virtual military training was used through much of the twentieth century,[11] what is new is that virtual learning in general and war video games in particular have now become perhaps the most important tools for military training. For example, the Pentagon has developed a video game entitled *Close Combat Tactical Trainer* which simulates the experience of tank warfare (Silberman 2004). The Pentagon commissioned a game entitled *Full Spectrum Warfare* to train foot soldiers, and the marines have, in cooperation with a private software company, developed a game entitled *Close Combat: First to Fight*, which was later released commercially (Stahl 2006). The ICT developed, in cooperation with Pandemic Studios, a training package called *Full Spectrum Warrior*, which was also released commercially and which won awards for the Best Original Game and Best Simulation (cited in Silberman 2004). The result of this development is nothing less than a qualitative transformation of the military, not only its technology but also its culture. Michael Macedonia (2002), who, as chief technical director of the army's simulation training programs, was instrumental in the development of ICT, makes this point emphatically. "What has changed dramatically is the emergence of a military culture that accepts computer games as a powerful tool for learning, socialization, and training" (Macedonia 2002, pp. 166–167).

There are a number of reasons for this qualitative leap in the military use of virtual technology and video games for training purposes. The first is that the new recruits of the last two decades need a different form of training. Macedonia (2002) has this to say about these new kind of recruits: "Young people coming of age in this new century have spent years immersed in video games and complex multiplayer games....Army studies show that this 'wired generation' is very different in terms of skills and attitudes than its predecessors" (p. 158). Since most teenagers are already users of video games and often specifically of war games, military training for new recruits with war video games is a natural extension of their previous experience. In other words, a generation already hooked on video games can most easily develop the skills and attitudes which the military needs through video game training.

This brings me to the second main reason that video games are given such a prominent place in military training. The wars on terrorism are asymmetric wars. In the wars on terrorism, the one major superpower and its allies now face a more decentralized set of opponents which requires more agile and mobile decentralized armed forces. These army units need to be deployed rapidly anywhere in the world,

[11] In 1929, Ed Link invented the flight simulator which was first used in amusement parks but later was further developed by the Roosevelt administration for use in World War II (see Silberman 2004).

and this requires a new set of skills for which, according to a 2003 army study entitled "Training for Future Conflicts," a "game-based approach to learning" is especially useful (Mead 2013, Chapter 3). A third reason for the military's interest in the development of video war games is that they are a highly cost-effective tool for training. As Mead (2013, Chapter 3) points out, training exercises which would be very expensive to repeat in real physical space can easily be performed 30 or 40 times in virtual space at very little additional cost. A fourth reason has to do with the way in which war has been reorganized through the development of thermal imaging and robotics. With these developments, many of the elements of the video game now prefigure the experience of actual combat. I will discuss these developments in the next section.

The overall goal of video-based training is to create a virtual game environment where soldiers are always training, where, as Michael Macedonia puts it, the military would have "soldiers, always be[ing] part of the game…real people in real places interacting with real people in virtual places that are copies of the real world" (Quoted in Mead 2013, Chapter 3). The result is that these games not only teach certain skills but blur the distinction between reality and the virtual world. In other words, the point of the training is to prepare the soldier for the experience of actual combat which (with the assist of thermal imaging and robotics) will have the feel of the video games which the soldier has already practiced and to allow the experience of combat to feel like the extension of video game training. Steve Silberman (2004) offers the following comment on this process: "Immersive scenarios, high-payoff targets, limited lethality, people simulators, networked fires. These young warriors will live, play, fight, and die in the Matrix."[12]

The development of war video games does much more than provide a tool for recruitment and for military training. I have already mentioned the way in which *America's Army* has insinuated itself into the curriculum of public schools in the United States. In so doing, it provides a narrative which functions to legitimate the war on terrorism. As Ian Graham Shaw (2010) points out, "*America's Army* is more than a recruitment tool….It is also a platform for a new type of cultural consent, providing players at home with a transitional space to participate in the 'war on terror'" (p. 797). Americans of all ages play *America's Army* and other war video games. As a result, to quote Shaw (2010) again, many American children and adults "participate collectively" in the war on terrorism "just as if they were members of the military….the divide between the real and the virtual – between civilian and military, domestic and foreign – is erased as we wage war through gaming" (p. 798). Shaw's use of the phrase "transitional space" draws on the psychoanalyst D.W. Winnicott's (2005) analysis of play as a transition between the inner world of

[12] There is an interesting relation between science fiction and the development of the war video game industry. For example, Michael Macedonia claims that *Ender's Game*, a young adult novel written by Orson Scott Card, was one of the inspirations for the military's decision to become heavily involved in the development of war video games (Mead 2013, Chapter 3). In the novel, the protagonist practices outer space war maneuvers in video games only to discover after the fact that his last "video game" (against aliens) was not a simulation at all but real combat in real space.

fantasy and the outer world of objective reality. Play, for Winnicott, is a transitional space in which these two worlds intersect, and there are no clear boundary lines between them. For Shaw (2010), "video games are transitional spaces defined by play….The political question then becomes what kind of political space is the transitioning into?" (p. 793). To answer this question, we need to look more closely at the narrative which is constructed within this transitional space.

The most popular war video games today are video games about terrorism in which the players take the role of special operatives whose task is to counter the terrorists. According to Marcus Schulzke (2013), these counterterrorist games "attempt to make the players feel that they are embodied in the game…[but] restrict players to the perspective of the characters they control" (p. 592). This perspective is almost always that of western military forces and their special operatives. There is no attempt to understand the perspective of the terrorist or their reasons for fighting. "Terrorist threats emerge from nowhere, as if there were no social or economic forces causing them to come into existence or sustaining them….terrorists simply exist and…they are enemies because they have been deemed terrorist" (Schulzke 2013, p. 595). Terrorists are portrayed not as decentralized and often competing relatively small units, as they are in reality, but as a unified force in which all units are linked. "The enemy is not reducible to a particular terrorist organization. Rather, the enemy is global terrorism itself" (Schulzke 2013, p. 598). The reified abstraction "global terrorism" makes the enemy appear all the more ominous, creating the sense that anything necessary to combat it is legitimate. Furthermore, in these games, the terrorists seem to be everywhere in the world, but there are almost no civilians present. Therefore, "players are usually free to kill all non-player characters aside from their teammates…there is no need to discriminate between those who can be attacked and those who cannot" (Schulzke 2013, p. 596). And since terrorism is such an extreme existential threat to all of western civilization, the icon "heroes" whose perspective is adopted by the player can "disobey all the rules with impunity….Any tactic, no matter how destructive, turns out to be permissible" (Schulzke 2013, p. 599).[13] In short, the laws of war, and especially the criteria of discrimination and proportionality for *jus in bello*, are effectively nullified in the narrative of the game. In the virtual reality of the war game, there are no moral limits.

The narratives of these war games have a number of other features which support the ideology of the war on terrorism. As the players of these war games find themselves going to many parts of the world and often play the role of operatives involved in covert operations, these games collectively function to legitimate the US military as a "global police force that functions secretly with small rapid deployment teams

[13] Schulzke (2013) forefronts one particular series of games entitled *Call of Duty: Modern Warfare* which is representative of this genre and which had sold (at the time that his article was written) almost 65 million copies and has about 40 million active online players. The characters in this game are Americans and British, and players have an option of destroying the civilian infrastructure in order to prevent terrorists from destroying them, including such buildings as the White House, the British Parliament, and the New York Stock Exchange. They can contradict the orders of their commanding officer and the laws of whatever country they are in. They can even launch nuclear weapons.

in a context of low-intensity warfare" (Stahl 2006, p. 118). These video games also support the idea that war is preferable to diplomacy (Stahl 2006) and that it can be waged with precision so that there are no civilian casualties (Schulzke 2013). They also convey the idea that almost anyone foreign is a threat (Schulzke 2013) and that the Islamic world is always a realm of continued violence and war (Shaw 2010).

At this point one may object – aren't these war games only games? Can the players not tell the difference between the rules of the game and the moral and legal rules that govern the conduct of actual wars? Can they not distinguish between what happens in the virtual world and what happens in reality? These questions assume that while video games may be used to recruit and train soldiers and while they may represent war in a particular way, war itself is not a game, certainly not a video game. But this assumption misses what playing these war games does to the sense of self. Whether used by children in schools, by teenagers or young adults as leisure entertainment, or by soldiers in training, one's avatar in the virtual world can only win by adopting a virtual identity constructed by these values and assumptions. When played over and over again, this virtual identity becomes internalized, and playing them involves participating in a narrative which reinforces the ideology of the war on terrorism. Even if the user is a civilian, she is a participant in the war on terrorism, thus forming a hybrid sense of identity, a "civilian-soldier" or a "citizen-soldier" (Shaw 2010; Stahl 2006). The war video game, precisely because it is both interactive and engaging, becomes the player's internal psychic reality and helps construct her sense of identity. "The video game is increasingly both medium and metaphor by which war invades our hearts and minds" (Stahl 2006, p. 127). By playing the game, the user is inducted into a war which is now "deprived of its substance – a virtual war fought behind computer screens, a war experienced by its participants as a video game, a war with no casualties" (Zizek 2002, p. 37). One does not have to be recruited into the army to be inducted into the war on terrorism. The war video game calls each player personally to take her place within this war. To borrow a term from Louis Althusser (1971), it "interpellates," or hails, the player as an active subject into the ideology of the war on terrorism. "Hey, you there," it says, play the game by the rules and strive to win, and you personally will become a warrior whose goal is to combat terrorism by whatever means are provided by the game.[14] In short, for the frequent player of video war games, the ideological narrative becomes part of one's subjective identity.

The assumption that the player can distinguish between the way war is represented in the video game and the reality of the war itself also misses the way that war in the twenty-first century has been reconfigured by this virtual reality training and, as we shall soon see, by new visual technologies and robotics. The idea that war is a video game is not a mere metaphor. It is, in fact, the way war is now being

[14] For Althusser, all ideology interpellates, or hails, individuals as subjects of the ideology, subjects both in the sense of being a subject who plays the role dictated by the ideology and as being subjected to the ideology. The individual, now called to take her place within the ideology, then practices the rituals which constitute both the ideology and her subjective identity. In the case of war video games, the rituals are the rules and practices involved in playing the game.

organized. As Janice Kennedy, a columnist for the *Ottawa Citizen*, observes, "War, they said wisely, is not a game. Except that it is, soldier, get used to it" (quoted in Stahl 2006, p. 113).

War Reorganized as an Extension of Virtual Reality

In the last section, I discussed the role of war videos in military training and suggested that part of the point of this training was to blur the relation between the virtual world and reality of war. In this section, I want to consider the way in which the development of new visual technologies and robotics reconstructs war as a video game as it reconfigures the relation between the virtual and the real.

The new visual technologies include night vision, thermal imaging, and virtual reality training. Night vision goggles make it possible for combat troops in Iraq and Afghanistan to conduct raids under the cover of darkness, invading the homes of suspected terrorists and often terrorizing the whole family. It is common for soldiers in Iraq and Afghanistan to wear these goggles several hours a night. What the soldiers see through the goggles is a screen with a green hue and the residents of the household which they invade look like figures in a video display. And as one former reconnaissance specialist has commented, "night vision enhances the soldiers' ability to see through darkness while looking past the human beings in front of them" (Vasquez 2009, p. 93). The consequences of this can be deadly. "Seeing enemy combatants as merely figures on a screen, identical to how bad guys are depicted in video games, makes it all too easy to kill them without hesitation" (Vasquez 2009, p. 91). Furthermore, the use of night vision technologies also distances civilians from the horror of war. CNN's reports of the first Gulf War was full of nighttime footage in which the war was viewed as a "techno-spectacle of precision guided bombs, made possible through visual technology" (Vasquez 2009, p. 92). Hollywood films also exploit night vision technologies to create the illusion in the audience of being there while simultaneously distancing the audience from the reality. "Watching bombs splashing on the green (night vision) or grey (infrared) screens as they pulverized bridges, bunkers, and tank berms, tele-spectators were drawn closer to the awesome violence of war while distancing themselves from the reality of human carnage happening right before their eyes" (Vazquez 2009, p. 92).

Tanks and helicopters have thermal imaging devices which construct a visual field in which objects that produce heat are seen as a gray image. The problem, of course, is that these images make no distinction between combatants and noncombatants. Videos leaked by Private Manning to Wikileaks show helicopter air strikes killing civilians. One video in particular shows a helicopter strike in 2007 in which two Reuters' journalists are killed along with other civilians. The most chilling thing about these and other videos which can be viewed on the Internet is the callous disregard for life exhibited by the dialogue between the helicopter pilot and the gunner. One video used for training by US forces shows the helicopter pilot telling the gunner to fire at the images on the screen without it being clear who they are. "Hit this one," says the pilot. "Now hit the other one." The white objects explode. No weapons are identified. The white objects are pulling an object from a tractor. Perhaps it is an explosive. Or perhaps they are farmers plowing a field. There is no way to know. What appears on the screen is that white objects explode. For the pilot and the gunner, what they are doing has no more significance than when icons and images are shot down in a video game. What happens in reality is that human beings are blown to bits. But for these soldiers, what they are doing often has the feel of play in virtual reality.[15]

Dave Grossman (2009), a former military psychologist, notes that the greater the distance in war, the easier it was for soldiers to kill. During World War II, what allowed the bomber crews of planes to kill millions of civilians was the distance which protected them from seeing the carnage they were causing. "Intellectually, they understood the horror of what they were doing. Emotionally, the distance involved permitted them to deny it....From a distance, I can deny your humanity; and from a distance, I cannot hear your screams" (Grossman 2009, pp. 101–102) The distance factor produced by these new visual technologies is not just spatial distance. What is seen through these new visual technologies is a virtual world whose distance from the real world is a psychological distance of a new kind. Keith Shurtleff (2002) observes that "as war becomes safer and easier, as soldiers are removed from the horrors of war and see the enemy not as humans but as blips on a screen, there is a very real danger of losing the deterrent that such horrors provide" (p. 103). The American military is well aware of this tendency and has been developing a new form of virtual reality training called "Close Combat Tactical Trainer" (CCTT). The soldier is fitted with a body suit and helmet which supply sophisticated digital data creating a set of images. The camera in the headgear will track the movement of the soldier's body and adjust the picture accordingly. The point of the training is to create a virtual reality in which the soldier feels like she is in real combat. The long-range goal is to create a cyber-warrior who can be equipped with "a completely opaque helmet – identical to those used in training – inside of which he would see as real images and icons the data that was being fed into the system as sensors" (Friedman and Friedman 2004, p. 362).

The military's interest in development of new visual technologies works hand in hand with its interest in the development of robotics for military purposes. Robotics, in its broad sense, is that branch of engineering which deals with the development of technology that can perform complex tasks with little or no human intervention. In the contemporary understanding of the term, the ultimate goal is to build robots that can be programmed to monitor the environment, process information, decide how to respond, and to manipulate the environment in accord with that decision. To create such robots requires the continued development and integration of such fields as electronics, computer science, and artificial intelligence (AI). Also included in the future development of robotics may be the use of nanotechnology (using electronic circuits at the molecular level).

[15] This example comes from Vasquez (2009).

The military's interest in robotics today focuses on the development and use of unmanned vehicles, of which there are four kinds – unmanned ground vehicles (UGVs), unmanned surface vehicles (USVs), which operate on the surface of the water, unmanned underwater vehicles (UUVs), and unmanned aerial vehicles (UAVs) or drones.[16] While the military's attempt to create UAVs goes back as far as World War I,[17] the possibility of robotic unmanned vehicles could not exist until the development of computer technology. According to P.W. Singer (2009b), the contemporary interest in the development of unmanned vehicles occurred in the late 1990s, as a result of "a shrinking U.S. military…and an increasing belief that public tolerance for military risk and casualties had dropped dramatically after the relatively costless victory of the Gulf War" (p. 30). However, the really significant increase in military spending for robotic unmanned vehicles occurred after the attack on the World Trade Center on September 11, 2001. In that year, the Congress gave the Pentagon the task of making one third of all aircraft with firepower UAVs by 2010 and making one third of all ground combat vehicles UGVs by 2015 (Arkin 2009b; Markoff 2010). It should not be surprising, then, that 80% of all funding for AI research comes from the military, which means that "while firms like Microsoft and Google lead and the military follows in other parts of the information technology world, the military sets the agenda in AI" (Singer 2009a, p. 78). Major companies like iRobot, which made the first mass-marketed robot vacuum cleaner, obtains one third of its revenue from the military (Singer 2009a).

The increase in the number of unmanned vehicles used by the military has been enormous since 2001. When the United States first invaded Iraq, there were no UGVs. By the end of 2004, there were 150. "By the end of 2008, there were about 12,000 robots operating on the ground in Iraq. As one retired Army officer put it, the 'Army of the Grand Robotic' is taking shape" (Singer 2009b, p. 26). The Army is investing $230 billion on a Future Combat System (FCS) program in which they hope to reorganize their units into FCS brigades and in which unmanned vehicles will eventually predominate (Singer 2009b). In 2014, General Robert Cone, commander of the Army Training and Doctrine Command, predicted that very soon one third of all brigade combat teams would be robots (Scholl 2014).

In 2008, there were twice as many UAVs operating in Afghanistan and Iraq as they were manned fighter planes (Singer 2009b). According to a 2012 Congressional Research Report by Jeremiah Gertler, a specialist in military aviation, while in 2005 drones were only 5% of military aircraft, the military in 2012 had 7494 drones, which was 31% of all military aircraft (Ackerman and Shachtman 2012). US killer drones now fly regularly over Afghanistan, Iraq, Pakistan, Yemen, Somalia, and the Philippines. The most extensive use of drones outside immediate war zones is operated secretly by the CIA and, therefore, without any clear oversight. According to

[16] Although there are now many women in the military, the military has not yet attempted to find a gender neutral term for these kinds of vehicles.

[17] According to Jeremy Stamp (2013), "The first functioning unmanned aerial vehicle was developed in 1918 as a secret project supervised by Orville Wright and Charles F. Kettering." However, the war ended before it could be used in combat.

the British-based Bureau of Investigative Journalism, between 2004 and 2012 the CIA-operated drones killed between 2600 and 3400 people in Pakistan, many of whom were civilians (cited in Benjamin 2013, p. 61).

There are a number of reasons that the military has opted to allocate a considerable part of its budget for the development and use of robotic unmanned vehicles. I have already alluded to two of these reasons – the lack of public tolerance for military risk and casualties and the sense of emergency generated in the aftermath of September 11 by the war on terrorism. P.W. Singer (2009a) has suggested the following additional reasons: they don't lose concentration after a certain number of hours; they don't need to eat or sleep; they can operate in environments which would require human beings to wear protective gear; they can withstand gravitational pressures that would knock out a human pilot; and they can process information more quickly than humans and share them easily with other robots. In addition, they have a number of psychological advantages over humans. "They don't show up at work red-eyed from a night of drinking, they don't care about their sweethearts back home when they are supposed to be on mission, and they don't get jealous when a fellow soldier gets a promotion" (Singer 2009a, p. 65). Gordon Johnson, who was one of the members of the Pentagon's Joint Forces of Command, put the military's case for preferring robots to humans succinctly. "They're not afraid. They don't forget orders. They don't care if the guy next to them has just been shot. Will they do a better job than humans? Yes" (quoted in Singer 2009a, p. 63).

However, humans are not yet out of the loop. Much of what unmanned vehicles do still requires an operator who must monitor and at least guide some aspect of the robots' behavior as well as making the decision to kill, and this requires the kinds of skills that video games teach. In fact, it tends to create the feeling in the operator of the unmanned vehicle that she is still playing a video game. For example, one of the first weaponized UGVs used in combat was a Special Weapons Observation Reconnaissance Detection System (SWORDS). It is remotely controlled by either radio or fiber optic wire. It has several cameras which can see in all directions, which can magnify the selected target, and which is equipped with night vision technology. It can carry any weapon that weighs less than 300 pounds which is locked into stable platform, along with ammunition, grenades, and rockets. It can also be equipped with hellfire missiles that can vaporize its target, and it can provide a power system for its own weapons.[18] Finally, it comes with a control unit which weighs thirty pounds and which "opens up to reveal a video screen, a handful of buttons, and two joysticks that the soldier uses to drive the SWORDS and fire its weapons" (Singer 2009a, p. 30). The operator can, in effect, operate SWORDS, as one operates an icon in a video game.

The same is true of UAVs or drones. Like UGVs, drones can also be equipped with a variety of weapons including machine guns, hellfire missiles, and even cluster bombs. They also have high-resolution cameras, heat censors, and various other

[18] Singer (2009a) gives the example of a power system called Metal Storm which is a gun that uses electricity to shoot as many as a million rounds per minute. As a result it can "deconstruct a target, by shredding it apart bullet by bullet.…The makers also note that this electric machine gun is good for 'crowd control'" (p. 83).

visual technologies.[19] Operators may use joysticks to control their UAVs and more recently may use touch screens with Google Earth satellite technology to point to a target area they wish to bomb.[20] As a result, there is an almost seamless transition between the video game training and the operation of UAVs. An air force lieutenant, who was coordinating unmanned air strikes in Iraq, says, "It's like a video game, the ability to kill. It's like…[he pauses, searching for the rights words] freaking cool" (quoted in Singer 2009a, p. 395). In this case, the operator of the UAV was in the same country as his target. However, the operator may also be sitting 8000 miles away at an air force base in Nevada[21] while her target may be in Afghanistan, Iraq, Pakistan, or Yemen. The psychological distance here may then be compounded by the spatial and physical difference of the terrain. Furthermore, the orders for targeting the victim may come from somewhere else up the line of command. What happens in reality is that a human being is killed in a foreign country. But what happens on the screen can have the feel of an image exploding in a video game. The reality is the air force base and the home and family to which the operator of the drone returns after the kill. The virtual world is the world in which the kill seems to take place, which is on the computer screen. A 2010 report on targeted killings by the United Nations Special Rapporteur on extrajudicial, summary, or arbitrary executions noted that the increasing use of drones by the United States was undermining the rules of war. "Because operators are based thousands of miles away from the battlefield, and undertake operations entirely through computer screens and remote audio-feed, there is a risk of developing a 'PlayStation' mentality to killing" (Alston 2010, p. 25).[22] Philip Alston, the author of the report, said in an interview that the United States was putting forth legal justifications that would make the rules of war "as flexible as possible" (quoted in Savage 2010).

The "PlayStation" mentality is not just a confusion of the real and the virtual. It is also a split between one's "real" self and one's "virtual" self. It tends to create what researchers have termed a "doubling" effect. "Participation via the virtual world also seems to affect not merely how people look at the target, but also how the person looks at themselves.…Otherwise nice and normal people create psychic doubles that carry out some terrible acts that their normal identity would never do" (Singer 2009a, p. 396). Thus, the distancing factor here is not only a psychological and physical distance from what the operator sees on the screen but also a distance from oneself. In short, twenty-first-century warfare is in the process of blurring not

[19] One of the main kinds of killer drones is the Predator. Benjamin (2013) notes that the "Predator's infrared camera can even identify the heat signature of a human body from 10,000 feet in the air" (p. 19).

[20] The GPS technology also allows the operator to know precisely where the drone is located and enables her to guide and communicate with the drone.

[21] Drone operators are also located in air force bases in Arizona, New Mexico, California, North Dakota, Texas, Florida, Indiana, Maryland, Missouri, New York, Ohio, and North and South Dakota.

[22] The PlayStation Network, provided by Sony Computer Entertainment, provides video game consoles as well as a number of other electronic devices, e.g., smartphones. One of the early UGVs' operating controls was modeled on the control system of PlayStation video games (see Singer 2009a, p. 68).

only the distinction between physical reality and the virtual world but also blurs the distinction between the self as virtual and the self as real.

One of the consequences of the increasing use of drones in the war on terrorism is an increasing erosion of the laws of war.[23] The technology itself presents a problem for discriminating between combatants and noncombatants. For example, it is not possible for heat sensors, which most drone systems use to identify human beings from a distance, to make this distinction. Are they human beings working in the field with farm implements or are they carrying weapons? Are they armed forces of a country allied with us or are they enemy forces? Is their activity in preparation for a terrorist action or are they praying? Furthermore, the fact that the drone operator is not at risk has as one of its consequences that the public is relatively unconcerned about whether the laws of war are violated. "With no American soldiers coming home in body bags, few US citizens will care what else is happening…turning the Afghanistan-Pakistan war into a UAV turkey shoot" (Webb et al. 2010, pp. 36–37). In addition, as drones (and other lethal unmanned vehicles) proliferate, as more nations begin to use lethal unmanned vehicles, and as even terrorist groups may soon have drones, we can expect that there will be even less attempt to discriminate between combatants and civilians.[24] Finally, the experience of drone operators in the control room (the video effect, the blurring of reality and the virtual, the doubling of one's sense of self, etc.) makes it less likely that they will adhere to the rules of war.

A Possible Objection, a Reply, and the Future of War

I now want to consider a serious challenge to the argument presented above. In replying, I hope to further clarify my position and to consider its implications for the future of war. The objection I want to consider arises from the fact that many of the operators of drones have been found to suffer from post-traumatic stress disorder (PTSD) in the same proportion or even higher proportion as do soldiers engaged in combat (Webb et al. 2010; Holmqvist 2013; Benjamin 2013). On the basis of these findings, Caroline Holmqvist (2013) argues that what the drone operator is doing cannot be so easily characterized as playing a video game, since she is viscerally impacted by the reality of what she is doing:

[23] There are many news reports of civilians killed by drone strikes. For example, a drone attack which was intended for Ayman al-Zawahiri, who was bin Laden's deputy, instead killed 18 civilians and resulted in a protest involving thousands shouting "Death to America" (cited in Singer 2009a, p. 399). However, it is difficult to get accurate statistics. According to one estimate by the Bureau of Investigative Journalism based in Great Britain, from 2004 to 2011, the number of people killed as a result of drone operations *outside of Afghanistan and Iraq* was between 2372 and 2997. In this same period, the number of civilians killed by these strikes was between 391 and 780, of which 175 were children (cited in Benjamin 2013, p. 105).

[24] Drone technology is increasingly being used by other countries. As of 2012, more than 75 countries had drones, a number of which either already had or were seeking weaponized drones. This was almost double the amount of countries having drones in 2005 (see Benjamin 2013, pp. 70–71).

> Contrary to common perception, drone warfare is 'real' for those staring at the screen and, as such, the reference to video games is often simplistic. It is the *immersive* quality of video games, their power to draw them into the virtual worlds that make them potent….The video streams from the UAV are shown to have the same immersive quality on the drone operator – they produce the same 'reality-effect.' (Holmquist 2013, pp. 541–542)

I have several answers to this objection. First, while I would agree that video games have an immersive quality, this does not change the fact that this immersive quality is an immersion in virtual reality. Second, as Holmquist notes, it is precisely this immersive quality of video games that gives them their power over the player. Without this power, people would not be drawn to playing them over and over again, and there is no reason to think that one cannot be viscerally affected by a continual immersion in the virtual. In fact, play of various kinds often viscerally affects the player. Think of the way children are immersed in play, pretending to be certain imaginary characters. Think of the way in which competitive games like chess can create stress to the players. Third, the stress that these drone operators experience may result from precisely the way that what they do in the control room *blurs* the real and the virtual. This very comingling of the two may be a source of great stress, especially as they might observe the target and his family for some time before the kill. Finally, while it is true that some drone operators experience PTSD, many others "relish the idea of engaging in combat missions while remaining at home" (Benjamin 2013, p. 95). For these operators, what they do is go to work, play a video game with lethal consequences, and then return to their family where they play other video games with less lethal consequences. I suspect that many of them enjoy the kill in a world which is simultaneously real and virtual and in which one's double can act with impunity. Recall the drone operator in Iraq who thought that the kill from afar was "freaking cool."

Nonetheless, I think the fact that many drone operators suffer PTSD suggests that the virtual and the real cannot be so easily separated. As Holmqvist (2013) correctly puts it, "the relation between 'virtual' and 'material' in drone warfare is complex and full of contradictions…the corporeal and the incorporeal and blurred in contemporary war" (pp. 551–52). Thus, while war in the twenty-first century takes the form of a video game, this does not make war a purely virtual enterprise. Rather, it is a video game in which the play in the virtual world and the activity in the real world interpenetrate, which can often create tension and, as the evidence indicates, even PTSD.

Thus, in all, war in the form of the war on terrorism is still play, but it is not the kind of play which Huizinga analyzed. War is still a game, although it is not an agonistic game between equals. It is not a game that respects the rules of war in the traditional sense. It does not respect the rules of *jus in bello* or even those of *jus ad bellum* (except perhaps to invoke these rules for the purpose of public relations). The game of war does not need a specific playing field, because the entire earth is its playing field and also because it is a game in virtual reality. But it is not just a game in virtual reality, since the virtual and the real cannot be separated. It does not need a conclusion, because, like a video game, it can be played over and over again, and also, as in a video game, the player does not die and can have multiple lives. Nonetheless, the reality can seep into the players' "real" life and even affect their physical being. War is still slaughter, but the player of this game of war does not confront her mortality. Nonetheless, she cannot completely avoid the reality of what is happening. She cannot completely avoid the slaughter for which she is responsible.

The military is beginning to realize this problem, which is one of the reasons that there is now a push to get the human being out of the loop, to make war fully robotic. The military solution to the problem of drone operator PTSD is "to replace the pilots with automated, autonomous killing machines" (Benjamin 2013). This is also their answer to a number of other problems with the human operator. For example, according to Ronald Arkin (2009a), the time available is too short for a human being who is operating an unmanned vehicle to make an informed decision about whether or not to kill. The "pressure of an increasing battlefield tempo is forcing autonomy further and further towards the point of robots making the final lethal decision" (Arkin 2009a, p. 30).[25] For these and other reasons, the military is more enthusiastic about the future development and use of completely autonomous killer robots. Gordon Johnson, who is part of the Joint Forces Command at the Pentagon, told the *New York Times* in 2005 that autonomous lethal robots will eventually be a significant part of the military's arsenal. "It's not a question of if, it's a question of when" (quoted in Sharkey 2008, p. 15). What this will mean for the future of war cannot easily be predicted, but it is unlikely that robots can be programmed to adhere to the rules war, to discriminate accurately between combatants and noncombatants, to make good ethical judgments about proportionality, or to care about the horror that they are inflicting.[26]

Will it even be war? Steve Featherstone (2007) speculates that "within our lifetime, robots will give us the ability to wage war without committing ourselves to the human cost of actually fighting a war. War will become routine, a program….Absent fear, war cannot be called war. A better name for it would be target practice" (p. 52). Will it be autonomous robots against autonomous robots, or, as I suspect, will it be autonomous robots on all sides killing both combatants and noncombatants without much attempt to discriminate? If the latter, then war will become simply slaughter. The rules of war will be thoroughly nullified. And if there are any elements of play left, it will be as a spectator sport for those who are in military command positions or who profit from war.

[25] Arkin is a proponent of having the military develop and use autonomous lethal robots. In fact, he thinks that it will soon be possible to embed an ethical conscience into the autonomous system of these robots and offers a number of reasons in favor of his claim that such robots will eventually be able to perform more ethically than do human beings. See Arkin 2009a, b, and 2010.

[26] To quote Mark Garlasco, who is a senior military analyst at Human Rights Watch, "You can't just download international law into a computer. The situations are complicated; it goes beyond black-and-white decisions" (quoted in Singer 2009a). For other arguments which challenge the ability of autonomous lethal robots to behave in accord with the rules of *jus in bello* and the international laws of war, see Singer 2009a, Chapter 20; Gubrud 2014; Sharkey 2008; and Anderson and Waxman 2012 and 2013.

Concluding Thoughts: Implications for Just War Theory and International Law

If the above observations are correct, then unless we can change the techno-culture of modern war, there can be no just wars between nation-states. Neither can the war on terrorism be a just war. This might still allow for the possibility of rescue efforts by the United Nations, or some other international agency, or an international police agency to counter terrorism, but given the way nation-states tend to control these agencies, these efforts are unlikely to be genuinely international. Is it possible that we can change the techno-culture of war in such a way that waging war is no longer unjust? Unfortunately, this is unlikely, given the historical development of war technology and the culture that has developed around it. Furthermore, given my hypothesis about the way in which the development of new visual technologies and robotics is conjoined with the war on terrorism to construct war as a video game without limits, there are no longer rules of the game that would impose moral limits on the players. At the most, there will be the pretense of the rules of war presented as the rules of engagement which, in reality, will rarely be followed and which can be changed at the whim of those in power. And if the full agenda of the military becomes a reality, if war will eventually be waged predominantly by autonomous robots, then it is likely that even this pretense will no longer exist. War will then no longer be play but simply murder on a grand scale.

What then are we to do with just war doctrine and the international laws of war? Do we simply discard this doctrine and these laws as relics of times past? I think that would be a mistake for two reasons. First, it is precisely because the international laws of war contain agreed-upon criteria to judge wars as just and unjust that we can come to the conclusion that in the modern era there can be no just wars. Second, once wars have begun, it is still useful to criticize the conduct of the players and at least attempt to hold them accountable for atrocities, and just war theory as it is embodied in international law provides a basis for doing so. However, given the reliance on robotics in contemporary warfare and its likely trajectory toward autonomous killer robots, it will become increasingly difficult to know who is responsible. Is the operator of the lethal robot responsible? Or if the robot is autonomous, is it the manufacturer or the programmer of the robot? Is it some officer in the command hierarchy? Is it the robot itself?

Given the nature of war in the twenty-first century, the solution needs to be more radical. We need to move beyond just war theory and the international laws of war. The only hope is to create an international system that would make war no longer tenable, and sadly this is an unlikely development for the near future. However, unless we do this, we will continue to construct war as a game in an increasingly virtual (and contradictory) space, and the laws of war will remain an ideological cover for the slaughter that is the reality of war. Or, if the era of the army of autonomous robots arrives and the laws of war are completely nullified, we will face a slaughter that could threaten the existence of humanity.

References

Ackerman, S., Noah S. (2012). Almost 1 in 3 U.S. warplanes is a robot. *Wired*, January 9. http://www.wired.com/2012/01/drone-report. Accessed 14 Sept 2015.

Alston, P. (2010). Report of the special rapporteur on extrajudicial, summary or arbitrary executions: study on targeted killings. *Human Rights Council*, 14th session, agenda 3, Addendum 6, 1–29. May 28. http://www2.ohchr.org/english/bodies/hrcouncil/docs/14session/A.HRC.14.24.Add6.pdf. Accessed 31 Aug 2017.

Anderson, K., & Waxman M. (2012 & 2013). Law and ethics for robot soldiers. *Policy Review* December & January: 35–49.

Althusser, L. (1971). Ideology and ideological state apparatuses. In *Lenin and philosophy and other essays*. Trans. B. Brewster. New York: Monthly Review Press.

Amnesty International Report. (2000). NATO/Federal Republic of Yugoslavia: "Collateral damage" or unlawful killings? Violations of the laws of war by NATO during Operation Allied Force. https://www.amnesty.org/download/Documents/140000/eur700182000en.pdf. Accessed 31 Aug 2017.

Arkin, R. (2010). The case for ethical autonomy in unmanned systems. *Journal of Military Ethics, 9*(4), 332–341.

Arkin, R. (2009a). Ethical robots in warfare. *IEEE Technology and Society Magazine, 28*(1), 30–33.

Arkin, R. (2009b). *Governing lethal behavior in autonomous robots*. Boca Raton, Florida: Chaptman and Hall.

Arkin, W. M. (2000). Civilian deaths in the NATO air campaign. *Human Rights Watch, 12*(1.) https://www.hrw.org/reports/2000/nato/. Accessed 31 Aug 2017.

Benjamin, M. (2013). *Drone warfare: Killing by remote control*. New York: Verso.

Cook, S. (2010). Torture never stopped under Obama. *Global Research*. http://www.globalresearch.ca/torture-never-stopped-under-obama/17204/. Accessed 31 Aug 2017.

Der Derian, J. (2001). Virtual war: Mapping the military-industrial-media-entertainment network. In *Boulder*. Colorado: Westview Press.

Epps, V. (2013). Civilian casualties in modern warfare: The death of the collateral damage rule. *Georgia Journal of International Comparative Law, 41*, 307–355. http://digitalcommons.law.uga.edu/gjicl/vol41/iss2/2/. Accessed 31 Aug 2017.

Featherstone, S. (2007). The coming robot army: Introducing America's future fighting machines. *Harper's Magazine February*, 43–52.

Friedman, G., & Friedman, M. (2004). The return of the poor, bloody infantry. In T. Ensign (Ed.), *America's military today: The challenge of militarism* (pp. 355–374). New York: New Press.

Glover, J. J. (2001). *Humanity: A moral history of the twentieth century*. New Haven, Connecticut: Yale University Press.

Greenberg, S. B., & Boorstin, R. O. (2001). People on war: Civilians in the line of fire. *Public Perspective November/December*, 18–22. https://www.icrc.org/eng/assets/files/other/article-public-perspective-2001.pdf. Accessed 31 Aug 2017.

Grossman, L. C. D. (2009). *On killing: The psychological cost of learning to kill in war and society (revised ed.)*. New York: Back Bay Books/Little, Brown and Company.

Gubrud, M. (2014). Stopping killer robots. *Bulletin of Atomic Scientists, 70*(1), 32–42.

The Hague Convention of October 1907. http://www.opbw.org/int_inst/sec_docs/1907HC-TEXT.pdf. Accessed 31 August 2017.

Hedges, C. (2003). *War is a force that gives us meaning*. New York: Anchor Books.

Holmqvist, C. (2013). Undoing war: War ontologies and the materiality of drone warfare. *Millennium: Journal of International Studies, 41*(3), 535–552.

Huizinga, J. (1955). *Homo ludens: A study of the play element in culture*. Boston: Beacon Books.

Kaye, J. (2014). Contrary to Obama's promises, the US military still permits torture. *The Guardian*, January 25. http://www.theguardian.com/commentisfree/2014/jan/25/obama-administration-military-torture-army-field-manual/. Accessed 11 Sept 2015.

Lindqvist, S. (2001). *A history of bombing*. Trans. L.H. Rugg. New York: The New Press.
Macedonia, M. (2002). Games, simulation, and the military education dilemma. *Internet and the University: 2001 Forum*, 157–167. https://net.educause.edu/ir/library/pdf/ffpiu018.pdf. Accessed 31 Aug 2017.
Markoff, J. (2010). War machines: Recruiting robots for combat. *New York Times*, (November 28).
Mead, C. (2013). *War play: Video games and the future of conflict [Kindle version]*. New York: Houghton Mifflin Harcourt.
Roth, Z. (2014). On torture, Obama's hands aren't entirely clean. *MSNBC*, January 10. http://www.msnbc.com/msnbc/obama-torture-hands-arent-entirely-clean/. Accessed 15 Sept 2015.
Savage, C. (2010). U.N. report highly critical of American drone attacks, warning of use by others. *The New York Times*, June 3.
Scholl, C. (2014). U.S. army to replace human soldiers with "humanoid robots." *Global Research*, March 3. http://www.globalresearch.ca/us-army-to-replace-human-soldiers-with-humanoid-robots/5371657. Accessed 15 Sept 2015.
Schulzke, M. (2013). The virtual war on terror: Counterterrorism narratives in video games. *New Political Science, 35*(4), 586–603.
Sharkey, N. (2008). Casandra or false prophets of doom: AI robots and war. *IEEE Intelligent Systems, 23*(4), 14–17.
Shaw, I. G. (2010). Playing war. *Social and Cultural Geography, 11*(3), 789–803.
Shurtleff, D. K. (2002). The effects of technology on our humanity. *Parameters, 35*(4), 100–112.
Silberman, S. (2004). The war room. *Wired*, September 1. http://archive.wired.com/wired/archive/12.09/warroom.html. Accessed 31 Aug 2017.
Singer, P. W. (2009a). *Wired for war: The robotics revolution and conflicts in the 21st century*. New York: Penguin.
Singer, P. W. (2009b). Military robots and the laws of war. *The New Atlantis Winter*, 25–45.
Stahl, R. (2006). Have you played the war on terror? *Critical Studies in Media Communication, 23*(2), 112–130.
Stamp, J. (2013). World War I: 100 years later – Unmanned drones have been around since World War I. *Smithsonian.com*, February 12. http://www.smithsonianmag.com/arts-culture/unmanned-drones-have-been-around-since-world-war-i-16055939/. Accessed 10 Sept 2015.
Vasquez, J. N. (2009). Seeing green: Visual technology, virtual reality, and the experience of war. In A. Waterston (Ed.), *An anthropology of war: Views from the frontline* (pp. 87–105). New York: Berghahn Books.
Tirman, J. (2011). *The death of others: The fate of civilians in America's wars*. New York: Oxford University Press.
Walzer, M. (2015). *Just and unjust wars: A moral argument with historical illustrations* (fifth ed.). New York: Basic Books.
War Games. http://www.wargamesnew.com/. Accessed 9 September 2015.
Webb, D., Wirbel, L., & Sulzman, B. (2010). From space, no one can watch you die. *Peace Review: A Journal of Social Justice, 22*(1), 31–39.
Winnicott, D. W. (2005). *Playing and reality*. London: Routledge.
Young, M. (1991). *The Vietnam wars 1945–1990*. New York: HarperCollins.
Zinn, H. (1990). *A people's history of the United States*. New York: HarperCollins.
Zizek, S. (2002). *Welcome to the desert of the real: Five essays on September 11 and related dates*. New York: Verso.

Chapter 4
The Quest for Accountability: The Resolution 1373 Process at the United Nations Security Council

George J. Andreopoulos

The variety of measures adopted by the United Nations Security Council (UNSC) in response to the terrorist attacks of September 11 have generated a plethora of questions concerning its role within the normative architecture of the UN Charter. In particular, questions have been raised concerning the "legislative" role of the UNSC and the legitimacy of UNSC's initiatives in the area of counter-terrorism. Closely related to such a role is the critical issue of the relevance of human rights in this endeavor and the extent to which the UNSC is subject to international legal rules. More specifically, does the UNSC have human rights obligations? If yes, what are these, how has the UNSC sought to address them in the context of counter-terrorism, and how can it be held accountable in situations of non-adherence? It is important to clarify here that the question refers to obligations that apply to the UNSC, as a separate and distinct (though related) issue from the corresponding obligations of member states.[1]

Counter-terrorism is an issue area which has registered a noticeable backsliding of human rights in at least two ways: (1) the 9/11 attacks have provided an opportunity to member states to become more open about repressive policies and practices

[1] The main point here is that states may, and occasionally do, violate their human rights obligations while implementing mandatory UNSCR resolutions. The question arises as to the responsibility incurred by the UNSC when states commit violations in observance of its resolutions. In addition, as one analyst has noted, challenges to UNSCR resolutions have been directed at states that have ratified human rights treaties; Vera Gowlland-Debbas, "The Security Council as Enforcer of Human Rights," in Fassbender (2011).

An earlier and shorter version of this chapter will appear in Alison Brysk and Michael Stohl (eds.) *Contracting Human Rights. Crisis, Accountability, and Opportunity.* Edward Elgar, 2018.

G. J. Andreopoulos (✉)
Department of Political Science, John Jay College of Criminal Justice and Ph.D./MA Program in Political Science, The Graduate Center, City University of New York, New York, NY, USA
e-mail: chrights@jjay.cuny.edu

G. J. Andreopoulos et al. (eds.), *The Rule of Law in an Era of Change*,
Springer Series on International Justice and Human Rights,
https://doi.org/10.1007/978-3-319-89908-4_4

that, in previous years, were engaged in but would not openly admit to doing so. In this sense, there is a considerable continuity between the pre- and post-911 eras; and (2) the collective processes of international law have been engaged in a way that have legitimized many of these practices under the legislative activism of the UNSC and the 1373 process. The reach of this activism and its implications for human rights are examined in this chapter in an attempt to critically discuss the key parameters of the accountability gap and its implications for the international rule of law (ROL).[2] It is a story of the dynamic interplay between normative erosion and normative resistance that has tested the strengths and limitations of the international legal process.

This chapter begins by situating the examination within the normative architecture of the UN Charter and the complex interplay between the legal regimes that shape two of the organization's main purposes: the maintenance of international peace and security and human rights. It then proceeds with the UNSC's shift into legislative activism on the immediate aftermath of 9/11. This legislative activism and the resulting practices have raised issues of legality and legitimacy, especially in the context of the 1373 reporting process and the 1267 sanctions regime.[3] By employing content analysis and process tracing, it examines member states' country reports submitted under the 1373 process and explores the factors that have constrained the "humanization" of the UNSC's counterterrorist discourse.[4] In this context, it analyzes and assesses some of the key legislative and administration of justice practices of member states. While some progress has been achieved since the initial stages of the "global campaign against terrorism," serious accountability challenges persist, and the chapter concludes by identifying some of these challenges and offers suggestions on how to address them.

The UN Charter: Purposes and Principles

A review of the legislative history of the Charter reveals that, from the organization's very inception, the maintenance of international peace and security was envisaged as hierarchically superior to all the other purposes, including the promotion and encouragement of respect for human rights and fundamental freedoms.[5] What linked human rights to the hierarchically superior purpose of peace maintenance were situations in which human rights violations were occurring in such a scale that,

[2] On the concept of accountability and its role in limiting abuses of power in international affairs, see Grant and Keohane (2005).

[3] While some references will be made to the 1267 sanctions regime, the focus here is on the 1373 process.

[4] By humanization, I refer to the process of rendering the discourse more receptive to human rights norms and standards.

[5] As the ICJ noted in the *Certain Expenses* case, "The primary place ascribed to international peace and security is natural, since the fulfillment of the other purposes will be dependent upon the attainment of that basic condition"; ICJ Reports (1962).

upon UNSC determination under Chap. VII, would constitute either a threat to the peace or breach thereof. While the post-Cold War era has witnessed a normative explosion in this issue area with a plethora of resolutions identifying situations of human rights and humanitarian law violations as constituting threats to international peace and security,[6] it is instructive to remember that important precedents were set during the Cold War era, a period in which human rights were considered a second-order issue for the UNSC.[7]

The intersections between peace maintenance and human rights in the context of terrorism are extensive. On the one hand, terrorist acts constitute violations of fundamental human rights (in particular, physical integrity rights); on the other hand, counter-terrorism measures, especially on the aftermath of 9/11, have exhibited serious disregard for certain fundamental human rights protections (among others, privacy, due process rights, and freedom of movement). In addition, the UNSC has repeatedly identified terrorist acts as constituting threats to international peace and security and, in the process, has invoked its powers under Chap. VII of the UN Charter. These intersections have generated a series of questions relating to the nature of UNSC's human rights obligations in its adoption of such measures when acting under Chap. VII.[8]

Due to space limitations, this question will be examined in the context of the UN Charter, though such an examination by no means exhausts this complex issue.[9] There are a variety of positions on this issue ranging from the view that the UNSC is only bound by the law of the Charter and nothing else (I would call this the thin legalist position) to the view that the UNSC is bound by human rights law (I would call this the thick legalist one); in between these two are situated arguments that the UNSC is bound by jus cogens norms only and that the UNSC should be presumed to act in accordance with international law, unless it explicitly authorizes actions that are in violation of international legal norms.[10]

---

[6] In this context, typical resolutions include 688 (1991-Iraq), 770 (1992-Bosnia and Herzegovina), 794 (1992-Somalia), 929 (1994-Rwanda), 1199 (1998-Kosovo), and 1264 (1999-East Timor).

[7] For example, in the UNSC meetings preceding the adoption of UNSCR 232 imposing mandatory economic sanctions and embargo on arms and ammunition against the government of Southern Rhodesia, many state representatives made direct references to the link between the continuing existence of an "illegal racist regime" and continuing threats to international peace and security; among others, see the statement by Mr. El-Farra, the delegate from Jordan: "...the answer to such rebellion is condemnation and suppression. It amounts to invasion against the right of the majority. The answer to such invasion and aggression is Chap. 7;..." United Nations Security Council Official Records (1966). UNSCR 232 determined that the situation in Southern Rhodesia constituted a threat to international peace and security and reaffirmed "the inalienable rights of the people of Southern Rhodesia to freedom and independence in accordance with the Declaration on the Granting of Independence to Colonial Countries and Peoples..."; December 16, 1966.

[8] In recent years, increasing attention has focused on the question of the human rights obligations of organs and specialized agencies of the UN system. For recent treatments of this issue in the context international financial institutions, see Clair Apodaca, "Expanding Responsibilities: the consequences of World Bank and IMF policies on child welfare," in Apodaca (2017); and Salomon.

[9] For a useful attempt to synthesize the different threads of this debate, see Bennoune.

[10] Ibid, pp. 2–14.

There are several provisions of the UN Charter that affect the relations between peace maintenance and human rights: Article 24 which stipulates that the UNSC bears "primary responsibility for the maintenance of international peace and security" and that, in discharging its duties, the UNSC "shall act in accordance with the Purposes and Principles of the United Nations"[11]; Article 25 which states that member states "agree to accept and carry out the decisions of the Security Council in accordance with the present Charter"; Article 39 which provides that the UNSC "shall determine the existence of any threat to the peace, breach of the peace, or act of aggression and shall make recommendations, or decide what measures shall be taken .... to maintain or restore international peace and security"; and Article 103 which notes that "In the event of a conflict between the obligations" of member states "under the present Charter and their obligations under any other international agreement, their obligations under the present Charter shall prevail."[12]

No matter which approach to treaty interpretation one subscribes to, there can be little argument with the proposition that, from an international legal perspective, the UNSC's capacity to make determinations as to what constitutes a threat to international peace and security and to decide on the corresponding measures is subject to very few limitations. The only express limitation is that such action should be in accordance with the purposes and principles of the organization, which include human rights. This, however, does not take us very far because the Charter offers no guidance as to how a commitment to the promotion and encouragement of respect for human rights is supposed to guide/constrain the UNSC when it acts under Chap. VII. Here, the thin legalist position would advance the argument that the Charter's approach to peace maintenance is political, not legal; in this context, human rights and humanitarian law norms should be viewed as guidelines at best that do not "establish precise limits for enforcement actions."[13]

This position, however, provides an incomplete picture of UNSC's role. It does not take into consideration the extensive case law of this organ which is clearly central to any interpretation of its legal obligations.[14] UNSC practice, both before and after 9/11, points to the linkages between respect for human rights and peace maintenance, even if these linkages often appear ad hoc, something to be expected from the political organ par excellence of the UN system. Moreover, the UNSC's foray into the area of international justice – primarily manifested in the establishment of ICTY and ICTR – not only reinforces the said linkages but also raises a troubling question for thin legalism proponents: how can the UNSC demand accountability for human rights violations, while remaining impervious to human rights obligations in its own conduct?

---

[11] This of course takes us back to Articles 1 and 2 on the purposes and principles of the organization.

[12] Needless to say, this is not an exclusive list, but it includes the main provisions relevant to the argument that follows. One could add here Articles 55(c) and 56 of the Charter.

[13] Bennoune, supra note 9, p. 8.

[14] This argument is consistent with the ordinary meaning contextual approach to treaty interpretation.

It is through this lens that the debate surrounding the interpretation of Article 103 should be viewed. While states' obligations under the Charter are supposed to trump obligations under any other international agreement, such obligations cannot entail the wilful violation of human rights; Articles 24 and 25 in conjunction with the UNSC's own evolving case law render such a reading difficult to sustain. In addition, Article 103 refers to situations in which Charter provisions are in conflict with obligations "under any other international agreement"; this does not cover conflict with rules of customary international law, a status that, arguably, many provisions of human rights and humanitarial law treaties have attained.[15] The abovementioned interpretation, leaning toward thick legalism, is conditioned by two interrelated questions: (1) what will happen in situations in which the UNSC undertakes extraordinary measures and authorizes actions to maintain international peace and security that violate human rights? And (2) under these circumstances, can it derogate from whatever constraints it may be subjected to under Article 24, akin to what states do when they declare states of emergency and seek to reestablish "order?" The Charter is silent on this issue, and there is no precedent for such a course of action. Having said that, it is difficult to argue that if states are entitled to derogate from certain human rights obligations in times of public emergency, the UNSC cannot.[16] However, this leads us to the question of what exactly the UNSC is derogating from which takes us back to the original question of what human rights norms are binding upon the UNSC.

In light of the above, it is quite obvious that the issue is not whether human rights norms are binding upon the UNSC but which ones. Probably, the most plausible argument here is that the UNSC is bound *at least* by those human rights norms that have reached the status of jus cogens norms. Leaving aside for the moment the question of which norms are included in such a list,[17] this view both acknowledges and demarcates the contours of the accountability gap. In a nutshell, the accountability gap emerges because the human rights obligations of the UNSC are underspecified, and this issue has emerged in the context of a situation that constitutes a threat to international peace and security, a situation that enables states to either declare or perpetuate ongoing states of emergency with all the abuses/excesses associated with such a course of action.

[15] See, for example, Henckaerts and Doswald-Beck (2005). While the methodology of this study has been criticized on several fronts, it does constitute a key point of reference for all subsequent discussions on the content and reach of customary IHL rules; see Bellinger and Haynes (2007); and the author's response in Henckaerts (2007).

[16] For a similar view, see Akande (2009). I do disagree with Akande though on the idea that Art. 103 only becomes relevant when the question arises as to whether ultra vires UNSC resolutions create any obligations for UN members.

[17] The "usual suspects" would include the prohibition of genocide, of slavery and slave trade, of torture, of racial discrimination, and the promotion of the right of self-determination, among others. It is important to emphasize *at least* here because an argument can be made that other fundamental norms should be included, for example, due to process norms. While it is true that these are derogable under the ICCPR, such derogability needs to be qualified by the fact that their violation can impact non-derogable norms, as noted in the Human Rights Committee's General Comment 29. On this, see discussion in the section on member states' legislation and administration of justice practices.

The UNSC in Action

Turning from the IL to the IR lenses now, the first thing to note is that there are several ways of looking at the UNSC and its role in counterterrorist activities. One way is to use the conceptual lens of realism/neorealism. In this context, the UNSC is viewed as the organ whose actions are shaped by the interests and agendas of the most powerful members of the international community. Such a reading would be consistent with the image of the UNSC as an organ that embodies par excellence the power asymmetries in the international system (permanent vs. nonpermanent members with the former having veto power). Viewed through this lens, an argument can be made that whatever measures are adopted under the collective processes of international law would be consistent with, for example, the strategic priorities of the most powerful member states. Any appeals to norms and rules would be purely epiphenomenal; their main purpose would be to justify the adoption and implementation of measures relating to the said priorities.

Another way of looking at the UNSC is through the lens of liberal institutionalism. In this context, norms and rules can have an impact on state behavior, primarily because they can alter incentives for all entities involved (not only states but organizations, interest groups, etc.) and can sustain the prospects for long-term beneficial cooperation.[18] According to this framework, the policies adopted under the said collective processes would reflect both state interests and a desire to enhance the prospects of long-term cooperation by, for example, linking the issue of terrorism with other issues of concern to the states involved, so as to more effectively address the challenges posed by transnational terrorism. In seeking to justify the UN's involvement in this issue, the former Executive Director of the United Nations Counter-Terrorism Committee Executive Directorate (CTED) noted that the necessary responses "go well beyond conventional policing and intelligence work."[19] In addition to strengthening legislation and boosting border security, there has been "a need to identify new strategies that sometime involve a much wider range of agencies and even non-governmental players in the community to address some of the technical challenges involved, as well as the social and cultural dimensions of the phenomenon."[20] In this context, norms and rules become relevant when they can facilitate such linkages.

Last, but not least, one can draw on normative-based lenses to try to explain the UNSC role. At the risk of some overgeneralization,[21] a more normative approach

[18] See remarks by Keohane (1997). Keohane discusses both realism/neorealism and institutionalism under what he calls the "instrumentalist optic."

[19] See Mike Smith, *The role of the United Nations in Counter-Terrorism*, Keynote address at the *Policing Across Borders* Workshop, John Jay College of Criminal Justice, City University of New York, 13 December 2007 (on file with the author).

[20] Ibid.

[21] It is important to stress this point because several approaches can be included under this rubric; some of them are purely normative; others combine elements of normative and rationalist approaches. I would include here the solidarist variant of the international society school. It is beyond the scope of this chapter to address this issue.

would see UNSC involvement in counter-terrorism as part and parcel of the UNSC' s expanding post-Cold War agenda and its increasing sensitivity to non-military threats to human welfare.[22] This would also be consistent with the obligation of the UNSC, as an organ of the United Nations, "to act in accordance with the purposes and principles" of the organization.[23] These purposes and principles frame, as well as are reflective of, a shared and evolving understanding of international legitimacy.

No single lens can fully explain UNSC action since the adoption of UNSC Resolution 1368. However, as the discussion below hopes to demonstrate, the realist/neorealist lens is more relevant during the earlier phase of the development of the UN's counterterrorist agenda, while normative considerations (I would include some variants of institutionalism here) become more pronounced later on. It is not until January 2003, with the adoption of UNSC Resolution 1456, that states are called upon to respect human rights while countering terrorism.

Before addressing specific UNSC activities, it is important to note that an examination of UNSC counterterrorist initiatives constitutes a useful antidote to certain simplistic assertions about the progressive marginalization/impotence of the UNSC. Such assertions are primarily drawn from the bypassing of the UNSC in the decision to use force against Iraq. However, the "war on terror" has sustained the viability of a contrasting image, that of an engaged UNSC, in line with its activist image of the early post-Cold War period. In this case, human rights/humanitarian concerns and activism have taken, at least initially, a back seat to counterterrorist activism.[24]

UNSC "Legislative" Measures and the Question of Legitimacy

The UNSC had adopted resolutions on terrorism before 9/11[25]; however, it is with the adoption of Security Council Resolution (hereinafter UNSCR) 1373, and later on with UNSCR 1540, that the question of the legitimacy of UNSC's legislative role became an issue. The key argument here, advanced by several analysts, is that, beginning with UNSCR 1373, the UNSC, with the United States at the forefront,

---

[22] I have addressed aspects of the UNSC's expanding agenda in "The Challenges and Perils of Normative Overstretch," in Cronin and Hurd (2008). Here there is a convergence between certain liberal institutionalist, international society, and constructivist arguments, since international organizations, such as the UN, are seen as contributing factors in promoting state cooperation to address these new challenges and these challenges reflect changes in the normative environment concerning the appropriateness of addressing them.

[23] See earlier discussion.

[24] For more on this, see note 19.

[25] United Nations Security Council Resolution 731 of 21 January 1992 and United Nations Security Council Resolution 748 of March 31, 1992 (Libya); United Nations Security Council Resolution 1189, S/RES/1189, 13 August 1998 (on the Embassy bombings) and United Nations Security Council Resolution 1267, S/RES/1267, 15 October 1999 (on Afghanistan).

embarked on a legislative agenda.[26] While previous resolutions had included some temporal or geographic limitations (or both) or had included references to the conditions that had to be met before terminating the obligations imposed by them, UNSCR 1373 imposed binding orders on all states without any time limits and conditions attached.[27] The driving force behind the adoption of this resolution was the United States; UNSCR 1373 appeared unconstrained by treaty and customary law obligations and rekindled the debate about the resurgence of Hegemonic International Law (HIL).[28] Even analysts, who have avoided the designation of legislative action, have acknowledged the "far-reaching" nature of these initiatives.[29]

This UNSC foray into the issue area of counter-terrorism raises three interrelated questions: (1) can the UNSC engage in such "legislative" action? (2) If it can, should it do so? And (3) if such actions raise questions of legitimacy, what are the means through which determinations as to legitimate UNSC action should be made?

As noted earlier, the legislative history of the UN Charter, as well as subsequent practice, has demonstrated that, once the UNSC decides to take action under Chap. VII, there are very few restrictions on its powers. The main goal of the drafters was to ensure "rapid and effective action to maintain international peace and security."[30] This view was reaffirmed by the Appeals Chamber of the ICTY when it noted the UNSC's "wide margin of discretion" in choosing a particular course of action, once a determination has been made that the said course of action was in response to a threat to, or breach of the peace, or an act of aggression.[31] More specifically, in the context of combating terrorism, it is important to remember that both UNSC Resolutions 1368 and 1373 were adopted unanimously and without any expressions of concern registered in the UNSC or in the United Nations General Assembly (UNGA).[32]

Having said that, as one analyst has noted, the fact that the UNSC has the legal authority to engage in such practices, it does not mean that it should.[33] There are several reasons for not engaging in such practices that include the institutional

---

[26] Szasz (2002).

[27] See Alvarez (2003).

[28] Ibid, p. 875. This was not the only development that rekindled the debate, but it was a key contributing factor. For a discussion of the key characteristics of Hegemonic International Law and the way that dominant states interact with international law, see Vagts (2001) and Krisch (2005), esp. pp. 396–399. See also the brief note in the appendix.

[29] For more on this, see Johnstone (2008), "The Security Council as Legislature," in Cronin and Hurd, supra note 22, pp. 81–84.

[30] Simma et al. (2002).

[31] Prosecutor v. Dusko Tadic a/k/a "DULE," *Decision on the Defense Motion for Interlocutory Appeal on Jurisdiction*, para. 31.

[32] It is worth noting that the UNSC meeting in which UNSCR 1373 was adopted lasted only 5 min. There was no discussion; United Nations Security Council 4385th meeting. Friday, 28 September 2001, S/PV.4385, https://documents-dds-ny.un.org/doc/UNDOC/PRO/N01/557/31/PDF/N0155731.pdf?OpenElement. In the case of UNSCR 1368, the meeting lasted 45 min with statements made only by UNSC members.

[33] Johnstone, supra note 29, p. 82.

balance between the UNSC and the UNGA, the circumvention of the treaty-making process which is the main mechanism by which states express their willingness to be bound by an international legal rule, and the concern about the nonrepresentative nature of the UNSC.[34] The latter issue will reinforce hegemonic tendencies within the international system, an outcome consistent with a realist/neorealist reading of such developments (human rights as second-order issues in the context of UNSCR 1373).[35]

The validity of these reservations notwithstanding, to argue against the assumption of greater decision-making powers on the part of the UNSC constitutes a tricky path for those concerned with the advancement of human rights. After all, one of the key goals of many human rights advocates during the early post-Cold War period was to ensure that the UNSC would transcend its traditional understanding of security threats and render itself more receptive to nonmilitary challenges that could undermine human welfare and the maintenance of international peace and security. Given the centrality of the UNSC within the organization, its embodiment of power differentials, as well as the concomitant and ongoing danger of cooptation of normative pursuits, the critical issue here was to enhance the legitimacy of the said assumption.

Legitimacy is a key attribute of authority, which is a form of power distinguished from coercive forms of power. As several analysts have noted, legitimacy is the basis for establishing claims of authority.[36] Claims of authority are premised on the existence of a "legitimate social purpose"; "it is this social purpose (as opposed to purely private gain) that facilitates recognition and legitimacy by the members of a community."[37] While authority entails legitimacy, the reverse is not true. An entity is considered authoritative if the rules and decisions that it issues are complied with due to the fact that they originate from it.[38] Thus, and in the context of our study, a UNSC action would be considered *legitimate* by member states if it is in accordance with the purposes and principles of the organization and *authoritative* if it is complied with by them due to the fact that it is issued by a hierarchically superior but rule-abiding Council. While the degree to which the UNSC possesses legitimacy is a matter of dispute, even less of a consensus surrounds its exertion of political authority.[39]

---

[34] These reasons are discussed in Johnstone, pp. 82–84.

[35] This reading is reflective of an understanding of hegemony based on material resources, as opposed to an understanding resting on shared norms that bind states as members of an international society. In the latter context, hegemony is anchored on legitimacy; see Clark (2011), and Haas (1999).

[36] For more on this, see Hall and Bierstecker (2002), and Cronin and Hurd, note 22.

[37] Cronin and Hurd, *Introduction,* note 22, p. 6.

[38] Allen Buchanan, "Political Legitimacy and Democracy," cited in Lowe et al. (2008).

[39] See also remarks in ibid, p. 31.

What are the mechanisms that will assist in the determination of the legitimacy of UNSC actions? Two such key mechanisms are *precedent* and *consensus*.[40] The value of precedent, an important concept in legal argumentation, has been increasingly used as a key indicator of the acceptability of a particular course of action by the community of states. The UNSC has repeatedly drawn from previous decisions to justify current or intended courses of action; precedent legitimizes such courses of action by demonstrating consistency (like cases treated alike; deviations have to be explained) and coherence in reasoning.[41]

Consensus relates to the existing normative frameworks that shape discussions during a particular period and which "provide both a grammar and set of principles upon which the Council can draw" either in the determination of policies or in the justification of those already chosen. These include the aforementioned purposes and principles of the Organization, those of the broader international community, as well as emerging norms.[42]

The United Nations' immediate response to the terrorist attacks of 9/11 was indicative of the challenges confronting pro-legitimacy efforts. Very early on, and with the certainty of a US response in mind, there was a lot of discussion concerning the role of the United Nations in the global anti-terrorist campaign. UN officials used arguments relating to both precedent and consensus to justify engagement in the unfolding campaign. References to precedent included the previous UNSC resolutions dealing with terrorism, which reaffirmed the link between the suppression of terrorism and the maintenance of international peace and security; references to consensus included the adoption of the 12 (at that time) international conventions which were developed under the auspices of the United Nations and its specialized agencies and the International Atomic Energy Agency (IAEA). These conventions constituted key elements of the normative framework that demarcated the necessary and appropriate policies and practices in addressing the various terrorist threats.[43]

These references were shaped, however, by a very selective understanding of the nature of the said commitments.[44] It is worth highlighting two examples of conduct that exhibited such an understanding of legal commitments relevant to our study, in

---

[40] The list is not exhaustive. One study on UNSC authority included *deliberation* and *delegation* to the list; Cronin and Hurd, *Assessing the Council's* authority in Cronin and Hurd, supra note 22, pp. 202–206. Part of the following discussion on precedent and consensus draws from that study to which the author was one of the contributors.

[41] UNSC action to protect civilian populations and to establish accountability mechanisms, the International Criminal Tribunals for the Former Yugoslavia (ICTY) and Rwanda (ICTR), are examples of this.

[42] Cronin and Hurd, note 22, p. 206.

[43] For the texts of the international conventions dealing with terrorism issues, see http://www.un.org/en/sc/ctc/laws.html

[44] Here is where arguments about Hegemonic International Law (HIL) become relevant. However, as the discussion below will show, there is no evidence that this approach generated any sustained argumentation, let alone any incentives to induce compliance among other states. The delinking of human rights considerations from counter-terrorism fell on very sympathetic ears, at least during the initial phase of the "war on terror."

particular, examples that are reflective of the human rights deficit characteristic of responses during the early phase of UNSC's engagement in the global campaign against terrorism: (1) the a la carte treatment of a key legal instrument and (2) the arbitrary confinement of human rights concerns to the human rights organs of the United Nations.

The first example refers to the treatment of the International Convention for the Suppression of the Financing of Terrorism (ICSFT) in UNSCR 1373, a treaty which receives special attention in the resolution.[45] The UNSC asked member states to sign and ratify the Convention (in its entirety), while, at the same time, demonstrating a distinct selectivity in the provisions that it considered pertinent to the task at hand. More specifically, UNSCR 1373 included the Convention's enforcement provisions that suited the counterterrorist agenda and omitted key constraining provisions such as those relating to the rights of persons accused of terrorism-related offenses and to the requisites of international human rights law.[46] The United States was the driving force behind the resolution, which was adopted by a unanimous vote.[47]

The second example refers to the Counter-Terrorism Committee's (CTC) persistent refusal, from the very beginning, to address the human rights implications of its policies.

The tone was set early on with Sir Jeremy Greenstock's statement that the mandate of the CTC did not include the monitoring of the human rights performance of member states.[48] During a UNSC meeting, he stated that "Monitoring performance against other international conventions, including human rights law, is outside the scope of the Counter-Terrorism Committee's mandate." He then went on to note "But we will remain aware of the interaction with human rights concerns, and we will keep ourselves briefed as appropriate."[49] This minimalist approach (simply remaining aware of such concerns), while framed as an issue of jurisdiction (the task of other organs in the UN system), clearly went against the UNSC's recent engagement in human rights issues. *Such a compartmentalization reflected a highly particularistic reading of the relevance of human rights in addressing the terrorist challenge: it privileged the human rights abuses of terrorism, while sidelining the scrutiny of counter-terrorism's emerging human rights deficit.*

---

[45] In one of the resolution's paragraphs in which a call is issued for all states to "become parties as soon as possible to the relevant international conventions and protocols relating to terrorism," the ICSFT is singled out for special reference.

[46] See Alvarez, supra note 27. In fact, the only reference to human rights in SCR 1373 relates to the granting of refugee status. It asks states to take into consideration, before granting refugee status, "international standards of human rights," (among other things), so as to ensure "that the asylum seeker has not planned, facilitated, or participated in the commission of terrorist acts," para 3(f).

[47] United Nations Security Council, 4385th meeting Friday, 28 September 2001, S/PV.4385.

[48] Sir Jeremy Greenstock, United Nations Security Council 445 3rd meeting, 18 January 2002, S/PV.4453, p. 5. See also Human Rights Watch, *Hear No Evil, See No Evil: The U.N. Security Council's Approach to Human Rights Violations in the Global Counter-Terrorist Effort*, Human Rights Watch Briefing Paper, August 10, 2004, p. 6.

[49] Ibid.

Thus, very early on, the stage was set for organizational responses and measures that reinforced this direction and accentuated the tensions between the UNSC and the human rights organs in the Organization.

Addressing Member States' Counterterrorist Policies and Practices

The CTC, which was established on the basis of UNSC Resolution 1373, monitors the implementation of Resolution 1373 by all states; the resolution "requested countries to implement a number of measures intended to enhance their legal and institutional ability to counter terrorist activities at home, in their regions and around the world."[50] All states were expected to report to the Committee on measures taken or planned to implement Resolution 1373.[51] This task provided an opening to many member states to use the 1373 process in order to validate legislative initiatives and related practices that violated fundamental tenets, as well as basic procedural guarantees, of human rights law and criminal law. The submission of actual or proposed legislation by member states to the CTC, as well as certain practices in the administration of justice, was reflective of the challenges posed by the lack of human rights-sensitive control mechanisms in the early phases of the 1373 process.

Concerning legislation, a key principle in the adoption of legislation is its compliance with the principle of legality. This principle, which requires precision in legislation and prohibits the adoption of ex post facto laws (Article 15 of the International Covenant on Civil and Political Rights – ICCPR), is a non-derogable right in international human rights law, as per Article 4(2) of the ICCPR.

There are at least two factors which have facilitated member states' abuse of the said process. First, and as mentioned earlier, the CTC consistently refused over a certain period of time to address in any serious manner the human rights implications of the campaign against terrorism. The second flowed from the first: as a result of this approach, there was a manifest lack of interest on the part of the CTC to scrutinize member states' records on human rights.

These observations are validated as a result of an ongoing research conducted on two key databases: (1) the list of reports submitted by member states to the CTC during the period 2001–2006 and (2) the list of reports submitted by member states

---

[50] https://www.un.org/sc/ctc/about-us The discussion that follows on the requirements of the resolution draws in part on Andreopoulos (2011). For the full text of UNSCR 1373, see http://www.un.org/en/ga/search/view_doc.asp?symbol=S/RES/1373(2001).

[51] There is wide variation in the reports submitted by states. By the end of 2006, which is when the CTC decided not to make public anymore the reports submitted by states, all (at that time) 192 member states had submitted reports, for a total of 706 reports (if one adds the Cook Islands, the total number of reports is 709). The reports vary widely in number (e.g., Chad submitted only one report during this period, while Argentina six), in length and in quality; for the texts of these reports, see https://www.un.org/sc/ctc/resources/assessments. In addition to member states, two regional organizations, OSCE and EU, and one UN mission (UNMIK) submitted reports.

to the Human Rights Committee (HRC), which is the monitoring organ of the International Covenant on Civil and Political Rights (ICCPR). The HRC has the most extensive record of monitoring member states' human rights performance among treaty-based monitoring organs. The end year is 2006 because after that year, the CTC switched into another system of monitoring states' compliance, the preliminary implementation assessments (PIAs), a matrix-type system which ostensibly facilitated a more dialogic approach between the CTC and member states. From September 2001 to 2006 period, 56 reports were submitted to the HRC, while the CTC received 709 reports.[52] The reports were analyzed on the basis of how they addressed: (1) the definition of terrorism in their criminal law code/statutes, (2) the legal provisions about detention, and (3) the jurisdictional reach of special tribunals.

The country reports submitted to the CTC and the HRC were subjected to content analysis. Since fewer reports were submitted to the HRC than to the CTC during this period, the reports submitted to the HRC were used as the basis to identify the corresponding country reports to the CTC. While the communications/responses of the CTC to the country reports (contra to the responses of the HRC to the country reports) are not publicly available,[53] follow-up reports to the CTC were examined to see if there were any significant variations, on the abovementioned issue areas, from one report to the next. For example, if a country had adopted a questionable (from a human rights-based perspective) definition of terrorism, a definition criticized by the HRC, were issues pertaining to that definition addressed in the follow-up report to the CTC? Likewise, if a country had instituted special mechanisms/proceedings for the adjudication of terrorism-related cases, was the use of such mechanisms/preceedings addressed in the follow-up report(s) to the CTC?[54] If not, we inferred that either the CTC did not raise any critical remarks about such a definition in its response to the initial country report or that the reporting state's response reflected such an understanding (i.e., absence of a critical perspective).[55] Preliminary results

---

[52] Ibid. The HRC received 55 country reports and 1 report from UNMIK.

[53] Subsequent country reports (after the initial one) submitted to the CTC often include certain questions asked by the CTC before providing responses. In other instances, answers are provided without being preceded by some of the questions asked by the CTC. However, there is no access to the communications prepared by the CTC and addressed to the member states to which the countries' follow-up reports are responding.

[54] To bring one example, in addressing the issue of special counter-terrorist measures applicable in criminal proceedings, Egypt's fourth report to the CTC indicated that "cases relating to offences of this type are then tried by High of State Security Courts (emergency courts)," United Nations Security Council. Letter dated 20 April 2004 from the Permanent Representative of Egypt to the United Nations addressed to the Chairman of the Counter-Terrorism Committee, S/2004/343, 23 April 2004. There is no reference to this issue in the two follow-up reports (2005 and 2006) submitted by Egypt to the CTC.

[55] From the reports examined so far (35 reports to the HRC and 144 reports to the CTC), we have found only one case, Paraguay, in which the reporting state indicated resistance to the implementation of the recommendations due to their adverse human rights implications, S/2004/375, 10 May 2004. This communication reinforces our argument about CTC's insensitivity to human rights issues. We have not yet examined individual petitions submitted to the HRC during this period. This will be done during the next phase of our project.

show that there is wide variation in the responses between the HRC and the CTC to these issues in country reports. *These results seem to confirm (so far) our basic hypothesis that the HRC review process would subject human rights-related issues to close scrutiny, while the CTC review process would exhibit near absence of such scrutiny.*[56] This pattern persisted even after the adoption of UNSC 1456, which was the first post-9/11 resolution that called upon states to ensure that measures undertaken to combat terrorism were "in accordance with international law, in particular international human rights, refugee, and humanitarian law."[57]

For example, Egypt's definition of terrorism contained in Act no. 97 of 1992 included, among other things, "any use of force or violence or any threat or intimidation to which the perpetrator resorts in order to....prevent or impede the public authorities in the performance of their work; or thwart the application of the Constitution or of laws or regulations." In fact, when the HRC examined Egypt's periodic report in November 2002, it expressed alarm at "the very broad and general definition of terrorism given in Act No. 97..."[58] No such concern was apparently raised by the CTC when it reviewed Egypt's initial report, submitted in December 2001, which contained the very same definition.[59]

What are some of the key issues that appeared in subsequent reports submitted by Egypt to the CTC? Among these issues were the need for greater clarity on the decisions of the central bank regarding the freezing of funds, more information on border controls to prevent terrorist mobility, progress reports on the ratification and domestic implementation of international counterterrorist conventions, improved

[56] The only occasions in which human rights issues were raised in this process were in reports that were submitted at the very end of this period, after the adoption of UNSCR 1624 (2005). Before the CTC switched to PIAs, some questions about the implementation of UNSCR 1624 were included in the CTC's interaction with member states under the 1373 process. The key question here, following on the wording of UNSCR 1624, was "what is country X doing to ensure that any measures taken to implement paragraphs 1, 2 and 3 of Resolution 1624 (2005) comply with all its obligations under international law in particular international human rights law, refugee law and humanitarian law?" Judging from the reports reviewed so far, responses vary widely. For example, Egypt, in its sixth and final report, gave a very general and vacuous answer to the effect that the country had ratified all relevant agreements and "all levels and types of courts are obligated to apply and implement them"; the Republic of Korea, in its fifth and final report, provided a very laconic answer: "we do not have much to elaborate on this topic"; El Salvador, in its sixth and final report, did not address any Resolution 1624-related issues; and last, but not least, Uzbekistan, in its fifth and final report, responded to this question by focusing, almost exclusively, on attacking UNHCR.

[57] United Nations Security Council Resolution 1456, S/RES/1456 (2003), 20 January 2003. It is instructive to note here that, during the meeting that led to the adoption of UNSC 1456, only 3 out of the 17 speakers addressed the importance of human rights in counter-terrorism: the UN Secretary-General, the Minister for Foreign Affairs of Germany, and the Minister for Foreign Affairs of Mexico. No one from the P-5 made any reference to human rights, and Sir Jeremy Greenstock, then chair of the CTC, was likewise silent on this issue; United Nations Security Council, 4688th meeting, S/PV.4688, 20 January 2003.

[58] *Hear No Evil, See No Evil,* note 48, p. 8.

[59] United Nations Security Council (2001); and ibid, pp. 8–9.

screening at border points, and the adoption of measures to counter extremism.[60] There is hardly any discussion of the impact of existing legislation, in particular of emergency laws, and of the variety of adopted measures on the human rights situation in the country.[61]

Likewise, there is no evidence that the CTC registered any objections or concerns over Algeria's definition of terrorism included in Article 1 of Decree No. 93-03; the Decree defines a terrorist act as "any offence targeting State security, territorial integrity or the stability or normal functioning of institutions through any action seeking to," among other things, "Disrupt traffic or freedom of movement on roads and obstruct public areas with gatherings; Damage national or republican symbols and profane graves;" and "Harm the environment, means of communication or means of transport."[62] In fact, all subsequent reports to the CTC, save one, did not address at all definitional issues of terrorist acts. Instead, they addressed issues ranging from the financing of terrorist activities and the obligations of lawyers and notaries "to report suspicious transactions" to the freezing of assets of nonresidents held in Algerian banks and the legal and administrative arrangements for the registration of charitable organizations.[63] In the only subsequent report in which the definition of terrorist act is addressed, the phrasing is near identical to the one included in the initial report, thus raising serious questions about the legislation's potential for abuse, given some of its very broadly phrased and vague provisions.[64]

As expected, the HRC had a different reaction. In its concluding observations on Algeria's third periodic report,[65] the HRC noted that "While it understands the security requirements associated with the fight against terrorism," it "expresses concern at the lack of details on the particularly broad definition of terrorist and subversive acts given in the Criminal Code…"[66] The Committee emphasized that:

> The State party should ensure that counter-terrorism measures are consistent with the Covenant. In addition, the definition of terrorist and subversive acts should not lead to constructions whereby the terrorist acts can be invoked to deny the legitimate expression of rights established in the Covenant.[67]

[60] See subsequent reports by Egypt:

S/2002/601	S/2003/277	S/2004/343	S/2005/288	S/2006/351;

https://www.un.org/sc/ctc/resources/assessments

[61] Ibid; and Prue.

[62] *Report submitted by Algeria to the* Security Council Committee *established pursuant to resolution 1373 (2001),* S/2001/1280, 27 December 2001.

[63] See subsequent reports submitted by Algeria: S/2002/972 and S/2003/723; note 51.

[64] S/2004/324; note 51.

[65] *Examination of Reports Submitted by States Parties under Article 40 of the Covenant. Third Periodic Report. People's Democratic Republic of Algeria,* CCPR/C/DZA/3, 7 November 2006.

[66] *Consideration of Reports submitted by States Parties under Article 40 of the Covenant. Concluding Observations of the Human Rights Committee. Algeria,* CCPR/C/DZA/CO/3, 12 December 2007.

[67] Ibid.

Turning to another region, the CTC expressed no misgivings about the pending legislation related to terrorism, when it reviewed the initial report submitted by the Philippines.[68] This attitude was in sharp contrast to the reaction of the HRC when it reviewed the country's consolidated second and third periodic reports. In its concluding observations, the HRC noted, inter alia, that "While the Committee is mindful of the security requirements associated with efforts to combat terrorism, it is concerned by the exceedingly broad scope of the proposed legislation, as acknowledged by the delegation. The draft legislation includes a broad and vague definition of acts of terrorism which could have a negative impact on the rights guaranteed by the Covenant."[69] And it concluded: "The State party should ensure that legislation adopted and measures taken to combat terrorism are consistent with the provisions of the Covenant."[70]

The most recent (2016) global survey on the implementation of UNSCR 1373, prepared by the CTC, confirms that problems in this area persist.[71] In particular, the survey noted that:

> One core issue that remains a major matter of concern, more than 14 years after the adoption of Security Council resolution 1373 (2001), is the question of the legal definition of terrorist acts…The Counter-Terrorism Committee Executive Directorate is aware of situations in several States, in various regions, in which terrorism charges or administrative designations have been framed in vague terms, allowing for their misuse against legitimate conduct, such as the expression of political dissent or human rights advocacy…[72]

Failure to address this issue can have adverse normative as well as policy implications. Imprecise/vague legislation not only undermines key norms and may lead to abusive conduct; "clearly defined and mutually-consistent offenses" can render extradition requests less contentious, thus facilitating effective international cooperation in counter-terrorism.[73]

Concerning the administration of justice, an equally troubling picture emerges.

While bringing those suspected of terrorist-related offenses to justice is a fundamental objective of UNSCR 1373, this goal has to be addressed within a framework that reflects adherence to internationally recognized rules and standards. Some of the critical issues involved here include provisions for investigative detention,

---

[68] *Philippine Action and Initiatives Against Domestic and International Terrorism,* 27 December 2001, S/2001/1290.

[69] *United Nations. International Covenant on Civil and Political Rights. Concluding Observations of the Human Rights Committee: Philippines: Philippines.* 01/12/2003. CCPR/CO/79/PHL.

[70] Ibid.

[71] *Global survey of the implementation by Member States of Security Council resolution 1373 (2001),* S2016/49, 20 January 2016; https://www.un.org/sc/ctc/wp-content/uploads/2016/10/Global-Implementation-Survey-1373_EN.pdf

[72] Ibid.

[73] See Flynn. The key principle in this context is dual criminality according to which a person may only be extradited if her/his actions constitute offenses under the criminal law of both the requesting and the requested state.

access to counsel, the use of military or other special tribunals for terrorism-related cases, and the existence of "independent judicial oversight at all stages of terrorist investigations and prosecutions."[74] A related issue is whether the country in question has declared a state of emergency. In such a case, it is important to ensure that (1) non-derogable rights are respected, (2) that adopted measures derogating from human rights obligations adhere to the principles of necessity and proportionality and are nondiscriminatory, and (3) that derogations from certain rights do not undermine adherence to non-derogable rights.

The last point is particularly important since the record of states of exception has shown that non-compliance with derogable rights (e.g., minimum fair trial guarantees as per Article 14 of the ICCPR) often leads to violations of non-derogable rights (e.g., right to life). The relation between derogable and non-derogable rights was highlighted in General Comment 29 issued by the HRC:

> It is inherent in the protection of rights explicitly recognized as non-derogable in article 4, paragraph 2, that they must be secured by procedural guarantees, including often, judicial guarantees. The provisions of the Covenant relating to procedural safeguards may never be made subject to measures that would circumvent the protection of non-derogable rights ... Thus, for example, as article 6 of the Covenant is non-derogable in its entirety, any trial leading to the imposition of the death penalty during a state of emergency must conform to the provisions of the Covenant, including all the requirements of articles 14 and 15.[75]

In this context, the CTC did not express any concern about Colombia's draft legislative act No. 10 of 2002 which sought to amend key provisions dealing with the administration of justice. On the contrary, the HRC registered its serious concern with the said act while reviewing the country's fifth periodic report.

> The State party should take into consideration the fact that some of the provisions of this draft act would be in clear contradiction with provisions of the Covenant, in particular articles 2, 4 and 14. If it were to be adopted, such fundamental remedies as amparo proceedings could be jeopardized.[76]

Likewise, the CTC did not raise issues relating to the administration of justice when reviewing Tajikistan's third periodic report submitted under the 1373 process. In particular, the conditions of detention and trial procedures for members of groups which had "engaged in particularly serious State crimes"[77] did not seem to

---

[74] Ibid.

[75] International Covenant on Civil and Political Rights. General Comment No. 29. States of Emergency (Article 4); http://www.unhchr.ch/tbs/doc.nsf/898586b1dc7b4043c1256a450044f331/71eba4be3974b4f7c1256ae200517361/$FILE/G0144470.pdf

[76] Consideration of reports submitted by states parties under Article 40 of the Covenant. Concluding observations of the Human Rights Committee. Colombia; http://tbinternet.ohchr.org/_layouts/treatybodyexternal/Download.aspx?symbolno=CCPR%2fCO%2f80%2fCOL&Lang=en

[77] Report of the Republic of Tajikistan submitted to the United Nations Counter-Terrorism

register with the Committee. On the other hand, a few months later, the HRC, when reviewing Tajikistan's initial report, expressed serious concern, among other things, "at the lack of independence of the judiciary" and the extensive jurisdiction of military courts.[78]

There is little doubt that state misconduct during the "global campaign against terrorism" has reinforced the centrality of torture and other forms of ill treatment in any consideration of the serious challenges confronting the administration of justice.

As one analyst has pointed out, "torture, in addition to being universally prohibited, undermines the goal of bringing terrorists to justice by tainting evidence and hindering effective international cooperation by virtue of the principle of non-refoulement."[79]

In the previous global survey (2011), the administration of justice was highlighted as another problematic area:

> An issue that has recently drawn attention is the application of states of emergency or other states of exception in some States, purportedly on the basis of the terrorism threat. For States that are parties to the International Covenant on Civil and Political Rights … the application of emergency measures is subject to strict requirements and may in no case infringe on non-derogable rights, such as those set out in article 4 of the Covenant.[80]

A similar concern was echoed in the 2016 survey which noted that "compliance with international standards of due process and fair treatment also remains a matter of concern…".[81]

While member states clearly bore responsibility for these developments, it would be a mistake to underplay the UNSC's contribution to the problem and concomitant responsibility. To be sure, many of these legislative acts and administration of justice practices antedated 9/11. After all, then Egyptian President Hosni Mubarak famously declared that US policy measures adopted after 9/11 proved "that we were right from the very beginning in using all means, including military tribunals, to combat terrorism."[82] However, by compartmentalizing jurisdictional issues (human rights as concerns of other UN organs), the UNSC enabled the legitimization of

---

Committee pursuant to paragraph 6 of Resolution 1373 (2001); https://documents-dds-ny.un.org/doc/UNDOC/GEN/N04/669/99/PDF/N0466999.pdf?OpenElement

According to the report, these crimes included terrorism and sabotage.

[78] CONSIDERATION OF REPORTS SUBMITTED BY STATES PARTIES UNDER ARTICLE 40 OF THE COVENANT. Concluding observations of the Human Rights Committee. TAJIKISTAN; http://tbinternet.ohchr.org/_layouts/treatybodyexternal/Download.aspx?symbolno=E%2f2007%2f22%2c%20paras.%20441-519&Lang=en

[79] Flynn, note 73.

[80] *Global survey of the implementation of Security Council resolution 1373 (*2001*) by Member States. Compiled by the Counter-Terrorism Committee 2011;* http://www.un.org/en/sc/ctc/docs/2011-globalsurvey1373.pdf

[81] *Global survey of the implementation by Member States of Security Council resolution 1373 (2001),* note 71.

[82] Author's emphasis; quoted in Huq (2006), p. 32.

questionable state practices through the 1373 process. By denuding, during its early phase, the 1373 process from any human rights-related scrutiny,[83] the UNSC failed to uphold its human rights obligations even within the most restrictive understanding of what such obligations would entail.

The overwhelming narrative of a "global war on terror" demanding security-oriented responses notwithstanding the first signs of resistance appeared as soon as some of its excesses became known. The early phase of an imposed compartmentalization between the security and the human rights organs of the Organization was progressively superceded by an acknowledgment of its unsustainability. To be sure, there was nothing new in the assertion that states' compliance with human rights norms and standards was and remains problematic; rather, the change was manifested in the UNSC's willingness to engage with human rights issues.

What began to turn the tide toward a more human rights-sensitive counterterrorist approach?

It was a combination of endogenous (to the UN system) and exogenous factors.

Early signs of resistance emerged from within the United Nations system, as well as from prominent human rights organizations. These were primarily manifested in the form of repeated requests by human rights officials and experts in the Organization for quality control mechanisms and greater collaboration between the CTC and various human rights organs. These efforts were reinforced by critical NGO reports highlighting aspects of the said human rights deficit and calling for adherence to international human rights norms and standards.

More specifically, the Office of the High Commissioner for Human Rights (OHCHR) submitted, very early on, a note to the Chair of the CTC which referred to a set of principles that "can guide an analysis of counter-terrorism measures from a human rights perspective."[84] The note reaffirmed the importance of the principles of legality, non-derogability, necessity and proportionality, non-discrimination, due process, and non-refoulement and included an illustrative list of questions that could assist the CTC in its consideration of states reports submitted pursuant to UNSCR 1373.[85]

Moreover, at a HRC meeting held with the Legal Expert of the CTC, HRC members expressed concern over the post-9/11 focus in states' legislation "on counter-terrorist measures while ignoring human rights."[86] Some committee members pointed to instances of legislation, "which empowered the executive to accept as truth the designation made by foreign countries of organizations as terrorist organizations, without examining that designation on its merits,"[87] while one mem-

[83] Although our research of all the state reports has yet to be completed, there is nothing that has been found so far that would challenge this admittedly preliminary finding.

[84] Office of the High Commissioner for Human Rights, *Note to the Chair of the Counter-Terrorism Committee: A Human Rights Perspective on Counter-Terrorist Measures,* http://www.un.org/en/sc/ctc/docs/rights/2002_09_23_ctcchair_note.pdf

[85] Ibid.

[86] Human Rights Committee Briefed on Work of Counter-Terrorism Committee. Press Release HR/CT/630, 27/03/2003.

[87] Ibid.

ber warned "that some policies, supposedly aimed at combating terrorism, were simply policies of repression."[88]

With more evidence becoming available about a pattern of abusive practices, Human Rights Watch (HRW) published in 2004 a widely discussed report on the UNSC approach to human rights violations.[89] In that report, HRW concluded, on the basis of publicly available information, that the CTC "had focused largely on steps that governments have taken on paper…not what they are actually doing in practice," for example, "when governments describe new draft anti-terror or security laws containing provisions that rights-trained experts would readily recognize as inviting abuse, the CTC says nothing," and that the CTC is likewise silent "when governments make demonstrably inaccurate statements about actions that implicate fundamental human rights."[90] To address the growing human rights deficit, HRW called upon the UNSC to appoint "at least one human rights expert" on the CTED and to "require that governments include in their reports to the CTC an accounting of the human rights implications of their counter-terrorism measures."[91]

In a similar vein, in a briefing to the UN Commission on Human Rights, HRW urged the adoption of a resolution on the protection of human rights in countering terrorism that would, among other things, request the Commission's procedures and the UN treaty bodies to monitor the counter-terrorism measures adopted by states and recommend that the Secretary-General appoint a Special Representative on Human Rights and Counter-Terrorism.[92]

Another NGO report that generated considerable discussion was *Assessing the New Normal*, issued by the Lawyers Committee for Human Rights (now Human Rights *First*).[93] While the report did not directly address the role of the United Nations in this effort, it documented the adoption of aggressive new counter-terrorism laws by a growing number of governments in the aftermath of 9/11, laws "that undermine established norms of due process."[94] The report argued that many governments (first and foremost that of the United States) had seized upon an opportunity offered by the event of 9/11 to normalize changes that may have initially appeared as "aberrant parts of a short-term emergency response."[95]

The density of interactions between the CTC and the human rights organs and mechanisms of the Organization, and the critical scrutiny to which aggressive counterterrorist laws and practices were subjected by these bodies and civil society actors, paved the way for two human rights-related appointments at the UN: a Human Rights Officer in CTC's CTED and a Special Rapporteur on the promotion

---

[88] Ibid.

[89] *Hear No Evil, See No Evil*; supra note 48.

[90] Ibid, p. 3.

[91] Ibid, p. 4.

[92] Human Rights Watch, *Human Rights and Counter Terrorism*. Briefing to the 59th Session of the UN Commission on Human Rights; http://www.hrw.org/legacy/un/chr59/counterterrorism.htm

[93] Lawyers Committee for Human Rights (2003).

[94] Ibid, p. 75.

[95] Ibid, p. i.

and protection of human rights and fundamental freedoms while countering terrorism by the then Commission on Human Rights.[96]

It is instructive to note here the active role played early on by the Special Rapporteur (SR), a role clearly enabled by the nature of the institutional context (Commission on Human Rights as opposed to CTED). In a statement before the CTC early in his tenure, the SR included a short presentation of "current trends in states' counter-terrorism measures as to their conformity with human rights."[97] One of the identified trends referred to the CTC's near nonexistent interest "in the definition of terrorism at the national level."[98] He went on to warn the Committee that "if the human rights conformity of terrorism definitions is not reviewed, then the CTC may end up encouraging the full scope of measures designed to implement resolution 1373 in respect of something that has nothing to do with terrorism."[99]

Concluding Remarks

Some analysts have been perplexed at UNSC's slow response to the necessity of taking human rights seriously.[100] Is this a puzzle? From a perspective that subscribes to the notion that the collective processes of international law and the corresponding normative framework matter, this can indeed be a puzzle. From a realist/hegemonic law perspective though, in which the UNSC is perceived as a vehicle for the interests of its most powerful member(s), this is clearly not a puzzle.[101] It is not a puzzle for two main reasons: (1) the stake that the major powers in the UNSC, led by the United States, had in shaping a prompt and robust response to the 9/11 attacks and (2) the eagerness with which many member states seized at the opportunity provided by the 1373 process to "launder" questionable, to say the least, legislative initiatives and enforcement practices through the said process. However, there are other arguments, consistent with the rationalist optic, as to why, from the very beginning, the UNSC should and could have been more human rights sensitive in its responses to the terrorist challenge. Taking human rights norms seriously would have rendered cooperation (in extradition) among states easier and thus would have contributed to one of the key goals of the counter-terrorism effort. Such arguments

[96] Both appointments were made in 2005.

[97] Statement by Mr. Martin Scheinin, Special Rapporteur on the Protection and Promotion of Human Rights and Fundamental Freedoms while Countering Terrorism. Counter-Terrorism Committee, 24 October 2005 (on file with the author). It is not clear from his statement how many reports he reviewed in order to identify these trends.

[98] Ibid.

[99] Ibid.

[100] See, for example, Nigel Rodley's separate individual opinion (concurring) in the Sayadi and Vinck case, United Nations (2008).

[101] It is important to reemphasize that though there is a lot of blame that could be laid on the hegemon's doorstep; there were many willing accomplices among member states, as their reports to the CTC indicate.

would also be consistent with a social institutional reading of hegemony emphasizing the importance of legitimacy.

To be sure, the 1373 process is only part of the problem. A lot of ink has been shed on the 1267 Sanctions Committee and its listing and de-listing practices that have raised serious concerns about the lack of adequate due process standards in its operations.[102] Arguably, the overarching notion that underscores the initial responses of these two key subsidiary organs was that human rights issues were the responsibility of other organs in the UN system, not that of the UNSC. Such a notion could not be expressed in terms of an alleged second-order status for human rights within the security discourse despite the fact that the conduct of these bodies was consistent with such reading. Instead, the initial reluctance to take human rights seriously had to be framed as an issue of jurisdiction (an indication in itself that some importance should be attached to human rights).

For those who subscribe to the notion that the collective processes of international law matter, the nonconformity to human rights norms undermines the organization's legitimacy and the prospects for accountability. There are two other factors that antedate the 1373 process and have reinforced its impact on norm erosion and accountability: the first relates to the status of the UNSC within the UN and the second to states of emergency. The former points to long-standing issues of institutional design and the second to the "price" that the human rights regime had to pay in order to ensure state adoption of the major human rights treaties.

More specifically, the first points to two main problems: the underspecified human rights obligations of the UNSC and the corresponding lack of mechanisms and procedures to address human rights issues. This lack of mechanisms and procedures has, as one analyst noted, adversely impacted the protection of targeted individuals under the sanctions regime.[103] As the preliminary examination of state reports under the 1373 process has demonstrated, the problem is not confined to the sanctions regime; it has affected the interaction of the CTC with member states, not only with targeted individuals. While the situation has improved since the adoption of a more dialogic approach with the implementation of PIAs, problems in some of the key issue areas persist, as confirmed in the most recent global survey (2016).[104]

The second issue relates to the concept of emergency which first appeared, more than 60 years ago, in a regional and subsequently in a global human rights instrument.[105] As has been well documented, this concept has provided governments with wide latitude to engage in often widespread and/or systematic abuses against their

[102] See Post (2012).

[103] Salvatore Zappala, "Reviewing Security Council Measures in the Light of International Human Rights Principles," in Fassbender, note 1, esp. pp. 185–186.

[104] See note 71. In 2013, PIAs were replaced by the Detailed Implementation Survey (DIS) and the Overview of Implementation Assessment (OIA).

[105] The European Convention on Human Rights and Fundamental Freedoms (1950) and the ICCPR (1966).

own citizens.[106] Attempts to subject determinations, as to the existence of a public emergency and of the derogations made under it, to some type of stricter judicial scrutiny have proven to be a rather elusive quest.[107] The concept of emergency "has turned out to be the Achilles' heel of the human rights doctrinal corpus."[108]

This brings us to the last point. Turning the effort to combat terrorism into an ongoing global war without geographic or temporal limitations has privileged the securitization of counter-terrorism measures at the expense of human rights and has contributed to the ongoing process of normalizing emergency situations.[109]

In an effort to enhance a more human rights-sensitive approach to the UNSC's assessment work and contribute to greater adherence to the "purposes and principles of the United Nations," four modest recommendations are advanced:

1. That the UNSC should authorize the CTC and CTED to conduct human rights impact assessments on all draft resolutions dealing with counter-terrorism.[110]
2. That the UNSC should submit a request to all member states to conduct such assessments on their proposed counter-terrorism legislation and related administrative measures. The review of such assessments should be included in countries' DIS/OIAs compiled by the CTED. Such a process would provide additional entry points for the human rights organs of the UN system to have an input in the assessment of draft UNSC resolutions and for national human rights institutions and NGOs to do the same in their respective countries.
3. That the CTC and CTED should follow up on the country visits and assessments in order to track contributions, if any, of their assessments and key recommendations to the human rights situation in the countries concerned. Such a follow-up would enable CTC and CTED to get a better sense of what works and what does not work, of the main challenges that have to be addressed in this key issue area and render feasible a more systematic and informed analysis of the impact of the whole process.[111]
4. That the UNSC should mandate that all CTED country visits for assessment purposes include, as part of the CTED delegation, one of its human rights officers. It is quite troubling that 13 years since CTED's creation and 12 years since

[106] United Nations Economic and Social Council, *Question of the Human Rights of Persons Subjected to Any Form of Detention or Imprisonment. Study of the implications for human rights of recent developments concerning situations know as states of siege or emergency.* Special Rapporteur:

Mrs. N. Questiaux; E/CN.4/Sub.2/1982/15, 27 July 1982; and United Nations, Economic and Social Council, *The Administration of Justice and the Human Rights of Detainees. Question of Human Rights and States of Emergency.* Final Report of the Special Rapporteur, Mr. Leandro Despouy; E/CN.4/Sub.2/1997/19/Add. 1, 9 June 1996.

[107] Gross and Ni Aolain (2001); and Sheeran (2013).

[108] Rajagopal (2003).

[109] See *Assessing the New Normal,* note 93.

[110] See also Bennoune, note 9.

[111] This suggestion echoes a broader proposal that has been made for follow-up visits to assess the overall implementation of the recommendations agreed by the CTC and the visited member states; see Millar (2017).

the appointment of the first (Senior) Human Rights Officer, a human rights officer has been included in fewer than one-third of such country visits.[112]

While there is no magic bullet here, these initiatives could build on the momentum generated by the work of the UN's human rights bodies (such as OHCHR and HRC), the advocacy of key human rights NGOs, the applications filed by affected individuals and entities before regional courts (such as the ECFI/General Court, the ECJ, and the ECtHR), pertinent issues raised and debated in normatively oriented intergovernmental fora (CoE),[113] and legal challenges before domestic courts. All these factors have raised the "legitimacy stakes" and in the process have increased the pressure on the UNSC to adjust its relevant policies and procedures by reinforcing the abovementioned *consensus*, as well as advancing a different interpretation of the applicable *precedent*.

These developments, though modest, have registered an impact at the discursive level.[114] It is nowadays routine to see UNSC resolutions and statements reaffirming states' obligations under international human rights law, international humanitarian law, and refugee law, when countering terrorism; the global surveys of the implementation of Resolution 1373 confirm this trend. Changes at the discursive level constitute the first step toward the creation of additional pathways to human rights scrutiny and accountability, using platforms generated by the interactions among entities inside and outside the UN system. In an issue area exposed to the perpetual risk of human rights backsliding,[115] the synergy among various entry points to accountability could potentially constitute a sustainable form of resistance to further erosion.

Appendix

A Brief Note on Hegemonic International Law (HIL)

The ability to shape rules by a hegemonic power through the collective processes of international law can take one of two forms: (1) through sheer command or (2) through a process which entails social/communal acceptance of the hegemonic

---

[112] Since 2005, there have been 133 CTED country visits covering about 95 states. A human rights officer has participated in about 40 of these visits (these numbers cover the period until November 2017).

[113] Parliamentary Assembly Council of Europe (2008). *United Nations Security Council and European Union blacklists*; available at http://assembly.coe.int/nw/xml/XRef/Xref-XML2HTML-en.asp?fileid=17618&lang=en

[114] At this stage, it is difficult to validate empirically progress beyond the discursive level. This problem can be partially addressed by the abovemetioned systematic follow-up on the country visits and assessments.

[115] Especially if there is another 9/11 type of attack.

power's "leadership" role.[116] Taking into consideration that general (state) practice is the source of customary law formation, it is primarily the degree of social acceptance of the hegemon's unilateral behavior that will determine its rule-affirming or rule creating potential. More specifically, what at juncture X may appear as an act of imposing the hegemon's will, at juncture Y may emerge as an act of leadership, anchored within a certain social context of legitimacy.

There are other occasions though in which the act in question will not gain the necessary social acceptance to be considered rule-affirming, or rule-creating. In such situations, the act in question will be highly contested, due to its "dictated" nature, and remain in a sort of a legal limbo. Certain actors will consider it as potentially paving the way for the creation of a new rule, therefore as an act which, while it delegitimizes an existing rule, also contains the seeds of normative reconstitution, while others will consider it as clearly unlawful.[117] There are many factors contributing to command and social acceptance-oriented forms, as well as to the transition from one form to the other, factors that are shaped by a combination, in varying degrees, of material and normative considerations. A key factor in the transition from one form to another is the nature of the supporting arguments. For example, does the hegemon offer a public, specific and grounded in existing norms and rules explanation for its action/failure to act, or does the hegemon opt for vacuous statements about acts that are not publicly acknowledged and lack grounding in such norms and rules?[118] These forms are represented in the diagram that follows:

[116] For related discussion, see Vagts and Alvarez, notes 27 and 28; Clark, note 35; and Ian Hurd, *After Anarchy: Legitimacy and Power in the United Nations Security Council,* Princeton University Press, 2007.

[117] A good example of such an act was the US decision to unilaterally use force against Iraq in March 2003. Although the United States led a "coalition of the willing," this act is properly designated as unilateral since the UNSC refused to authorize such military action. From a rule-based perspective, the critical question is whether the United States is and will, in the foreseeable future, remain a lawbreaker as a result of the preventive use of force or whether the designation "lawbreaker" is temporary and future developments may determine that the United States is on its way of creating a new customary rule on the permissible uses of force. Some analysts have treated this incident as an attempt by the United States to redefine the doctrine of preemption; see the discussion in Ian Hurd, "Breaking and Making Norms: American Revisionism and Crises of Legitimacy," *International Politics,* vol. 44 (2007), esp. pp. 198–203. I do not share this interpretation. Whatever the legal effect of US action in 2003, I view it as an attempt to redefine the rule governing the permissible uses of force for the purposes of self-defense, not the doctrine of preemption, by adding prevention to preemption. It is beyond the scope of this paper to elaborate further on this issue.

[118] For a discussion along similar lines, see Hurd, ibid, pp. 200–201.

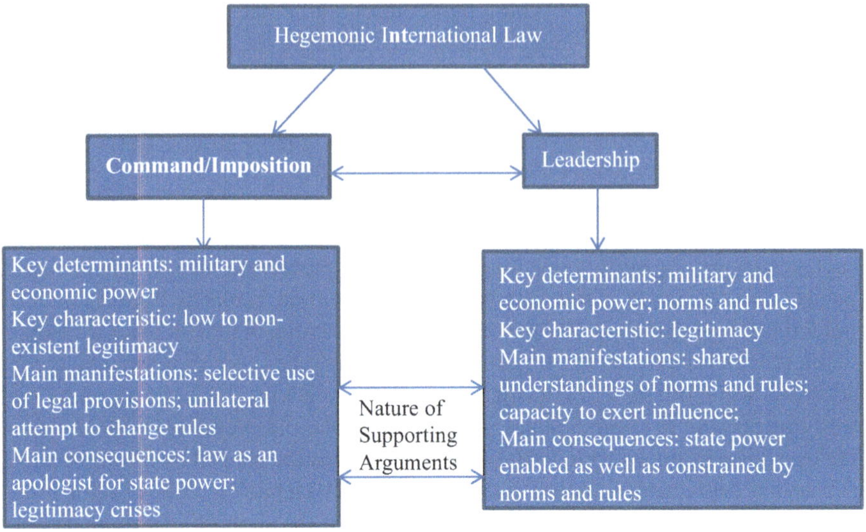

Any detailed examination of the evolution of UNSC's counter-terrorism policies and practices would probably need to be examined through the lens of an ad hoc coalitional hegemonic law model, in which these policies and practices advanced by the superpower are shared/adopted by a shifting coalition of states; the coalition at any point in time is constructed on the basis of participating states' interests and shared understandings of the issues at stake in a particular area. Such a model would combine elements of leadership and command but would not account for a particular challenge posed by the evidence unearthed so far by looking at the 1373 process: while the form and content of the review process was partially the result of the arguments offered by the "hegemon" combined with exchanges among member states in an effort to shape the parameters of the response, it was also the result of the states' self-serving and very active use of the said process to legitimize often questionable (to say the least) domestic legislative and administration of justice practices.

References

Akande, D. *The security council and human rights: What is the role of Art. 103 of the Charter? EJIL: Talk!* Posted on 30 Mar 2009.

Alvarez, J. (2003). Hegemonic international law revisited. *American Journal of International Law, 97*(4), 873–888.

Andreopoulos, G. (2008). The challenges and perils of normative overstretch. In B. Cronin & I. Hurd (Eds.), *The UN Security Council and the politics of international authority* (pp. 105–128). New York: Routledge.

Andreopoulos, G. (2011). United Nations counterterrorist strategies and human rights. In G. Andreopoulos, R. Barberet, & J. P. Levine (Eds.), *International criminal justice: Critical perspectives and new challenges* (pp. 153–168). New York: Springer.

Apodaca, C. (2017). Expanding responsibilities: The consequences of World Bank and IMF policies on child welfare. In A. Brysk & M. Stohl (Eds.), *Expanding human rights: 21st century norms and governance* (pp. 215–235). Cheltenham, Northampton: Edward Elgar.

Bellinger, J. B., III, & Haynes, W. J., II. (2007). A US government response to the International Committee of the Red Cross study Customary International Humanitarian Law. *International Review of the Red Cross, 89*(866), 443–471.

Bennoune, K. The Interplay of Legal Regimes Governing International Peace and Security and the Protection of Persons Under International Law (on file with the author).

Clark, I. (2011). *Hegemony in international society*. Oxford: Oxford University Press.

Cronin, B., & Hurd, I. (Eds.). (2008). *The UN security council and the politics of international authority* (pp. 105–128). New York: Routledge.

European Court of Human Rights / Council of Europe. (1950). *European Convention on Human Rights and Fundamental Freedoms*.

Fassbender, B. (Ed.). (2011). *Securing human rights? Achievements and challenges of the UN Security Council*. Oxford: Oxford University Press.

Flynn, E. *Pushing the limits: Human Rights at the United Nations Counter-Terrorism Committee* (unpublished paper, on file with the author).

Global survey of the implementation of Security Council resolution 1373 (2001) by Member States. Compiled by the Counter-Terrorism Committee 2011; http://www.un.org/en/sc/ctc/docs/2011-globalsurvey1373.pdf

Grant, R. W., & Keohane, R. O. (2005). Accountability and abuses of power in world politics. *American Political Science Review, 99*(1), 29–43.

Gross, O., & Ni Aolain, F. (2001). From discretion to scrutiny: Revisiting the application of the margin of appreciation doctrine in the context of article 15 of the European convention on human rights. *Human Rights Quarterly, 23*(3), 625–649.

Haas, R. N. (1999). *What to do with American primacy. Foreign Affairs, 78*(5), 37–50.

Hall, R. B., & Bierstecker, T. J. (Eds.). (2002). *The emergence of private authority in global governance*. New York: Cambridge University Press.

Henckaerts, J. M., & Doswald-Beck, L. (2005). *Customary international humanitarian law. Volume I: Rules*. New York: Cambridge University Press.

Henckaerts, J.-M. (2007). Customary international humanitarian law: A response to US comments. *International Review of the Red Cross, 89*(866), 473–488.

Human Rights Watch. Hear No Evil, See No Evil*: The U.N. security council's approach to human rights violations in the global counter-terrorist effort*. Human Rights Watch Briefing Paper, 10 Aug 2004.

Hurd, I. (2007a). *After Anarchy: Legitimacy and power in the United Nations Security Council*. Princeton: Princeton University Press.

Hurd, I. (2007b). Breaking and making norms: American revisionism and crises of legitimacy. *International Politics, 44*(2-3), 194–213.

Huq, A. Z. (2006). Extraordinary rendition and the wages of hypocrisy. *World Policy Journal, 23*(1), 25–35.

International Court of Justice (ICJ) (1962). *Certain expenses*.

International Covenant on Civil and Political Rights. General Comment No 29. States of Emergency (Article 4); http://www.unhchr.ch/tbs/doc.nsf/898586b1dc7b4043c1256a450044f331/71eba4be3974b4f7c1256ae200517361/$FILE/G0144470.pdf

International Criminal Tribunal for the Former Yugoslavia. Prosecutor v. Dusko Tadic a/k/a "DULE." *Decision on the Defense Motion for Interlocutory Appeal on Jurisdiction.*

Johnstone, I. (2008). The security council as legislature. In B. Cronin & I. Hurd (Eds.), *The UN security council and the politics of international authority* (pp. 80–104). New York: Routledge.

Keohane, R. O. (1997). International relations and international law: Two optics. *Harvard International Law Journal, 38*(2), 487–502.

Krisch, N. (2005). International law in times of hegemony: Unequal power and the shaping of the international legal order. *European Journal of International Law, 16*(3), 369–408.

Lawyers Committee for Human Rights (2003). *Assessing the new normal. Liberty and Security for the Post- September 11 United States.*
Lowe, V., Roberts, A., Welsh, J., & Zaum, D. (Eds.). (2008). *The United Nations Security Council and War. The evolution and practice since 1945.* Oxford: Oxford University Press.
Millar, A. *Mission critical or mission creep? Issues to consider for the future of the UN Counter-Terrorism Committee and Its Executive Directorate.* Global Center on Cooperative Security, October 2017.
Parliamentary Assembly Council of Europe. Resolution 1597 (2008). United Nations Security Council and European Union blacklists. Text adopted by the Assembly on 23 January 2008. Available at http://assembly.coe.int/nw/xml/XRef/Xref-XML2H TML-en.asp?fileid517618&lang5en
Post, K. (2012). Fair Process and the Security Council: A case for the office of the ombudsperson. In S. De Frias, A. Maria, K. Samuel, & N. White (Eds.), *Counter-Terrorism. International law and practice* (pp. 409–423). New York: Oxford University Press.
Prue, S. "Assessment of the Impact of UN Treaty Bodies in post 1373 Counterterrorist Strategy through the Counter-Terrorism Committee and Human Rights Treaty Bodies." The Center for International Human Rights, John Jay College of Criminal Justice, 2013 (on file with the author).
Rajagopal, B. (2003). *International law from below. Development, social movements and third world resistance.* New York: Cambridge University Press.
Salomon, M. E. *Of Austerity, Human Rights and International Institutions.* LSE Law, Society and Economy Working Papers 2/2015; www.lse.ac.uk/humanRights/documents/2015/salomonW-psAusterity.pdf
Sheeran, S. P. (2013). Reconceptualizing states of emergency under international human rights law: Theory, legal doctrine and politics. *Michigan Journal of International Law, 34*(3), 491–557.
Simma, B., Khan, D.-G., Nolte, G., Paulus, A., & Wessendorf, N. (2002). *The charter of the United Nations: A commentary.* Oxford: Oxford University Press.
Szasz, P. (2002). The security council starts legislating. *American Journal of International Law, 96*(4), 901–905.
United Nations Economic and Social Council. *Question of the human rights of persons subjected to any form of detention or imprisonment. Study of the implications for human rights of recent developments concerning situations know as states of siege or emergency.* Special Rapporteur: Mrs. N. Questiaux; E/ CN.4/Sub.2/1982/15, 27 July 1982.
United Nations Economic and Social Council. *The administration of justice and the human rights of detainees. Question of human rights and states of emergency.* Final report of the special rapporteur, Mr. Leandro Despouy; E/ CN.4/Sub.2/1997/19/Add.1, 9 June 1996.
United Nations (1966). *International covenant on civil and political rights.*
United Nations. International Covenant on Civil and Political Rights. Consideration of reports submitted by states parties under article 40 of the covenant. Concluding observations of the Human Rights Committee. THE PHILIPPINES, CCPR/CO/79/PHL, 1 Dec 2003.
United Nations. International Covenant on Civil and Political Rights. Consideration of reports submitted by states parties under article 40 of the Covenant. Concluding observations of the Human Rights Committee. Colombia; CCPR/ CO/80/COL, 26 May 2004.
United Nations. International Covenant on Civil and Political Rights. Consideration of Reports Submitted by States Parties Under Article 40 of the Covenant. Concluding observations of the Human Rights Committee. Tajikistan; CCPR/ CO/84/TJK, 18 July 2005.
United Nations International covenant on civil and political rights. Examination of Reports Submitted by States Parties under Article 40 of the Covenant. Third Periodic Report. People's Democratic Republic of Algeria, CCPR/C/DZA/3, 7 Nov 2006.
United Nations International covenant on civil and political rights. Consideration of Reports submitted by States Parties under Article 40 of the Covenant. Concluding Observations of the Human Rights Committee. Algeria, CCPR/C/ DZA/CO/3,12 Dec 2007.
United Nations. International covenant on civil and political rights. *Communication No. 1472/2006 Nabil Sayadi and Patricia Vinck v. Belgium*, CCPR/C/94/D/1472/2006, 29 Dec 2008.

United Nations Security Council. Letter dated December 27, 2001 from the Chairman of the Security Council Committee established pursuant to resolution 1373 (2001) concerning counter-terrorism addressed to the President of the Security Council Philippine Action and Initiatives Against Domestic and International Terrorism, December 27, 2001, S/2001/1290.

United Nations Security Council. Resolution 731, 21 Jan 1992 (Libya).

United Nations Security Council. Resolution 748, 31 Mar, 1992 (Libya).

United Nations Security Council. Resolution 1189, S/RES/1189, 13 Aug 1998 (on the Embassy Bombings).

United Nations Security Council. Resolution 1267, S/RES/1267, 15 Oct 1999 (Afghanistan).

United Nations Security Council. Reports by Member States Pursuant to Security Council Resolution 1373, 2001; https://www.un.org/sc/ctc/resources/assessments

United Nations Security Council., Report submitted by Egypt to the Security Council Committee established pursuant to resolution 1373 (2001), S/2001/1237, 2001b. https://documents-dds-ny.un.org/doc/UNDOC/GEN/N01/714/85/PDFN0171485.pdf?OpenElement

United Nations Security Council., Report submitted by Algeria to the Security Council Committee established pursuant to resolution 1373 (2001), S/2001/1280, https://documents-dds-ny.un.org/doc/UNDOC/GEN/N02/205/90/IMGN0220590.pdf?OpenElement

United Nations Security Council. Letter dated 27 December 2001 from the Chairman of the Security Council Committee established pursuant to resolution 1373 (2001) concerning counter-terrorism addressed to the President of the Security Council Philippine Action and Initiatives Against Domestic and International Terrorism, 27 Dec 2001, S/2001/1290.

United Nations Security Council., Letter dated 20 April 2004 from the Chairman of the Security Council Committee established pursuant to resolution 1373 (2001a) concerning counter-terrorism addressed to the President of the Security Council, S/2004/324, 23 Apr 2004, https://documents-dds-ny.un.org/doc/UNDOC/GENN04/329/60/PDF/N0432960.pdf?OpenElement

United Nations Security Council. Report of the Republic of Tajikistan Submitted to the United Nations Counter-Terrorism Committee Pursuant to Paragraph 6 of Resolution 1373 (2001b); S/2004/992, 22 Dec 2004.B36B14B17B2B4B10

United Nations Security Council Official Records, 1340th Meeting, S/PV 1340, 16 Dec 1966.

United Nations Security Council. 4453rd meeting, 18 Jan 2002, S/PV.4453.

United Nations Security Council Counter-Terrorism Committee Executive Directorate (CTED). Global survey of the implementation of Security Council resolution 1373 (2001) by Member States. Compiled by the Counter-Terrorism Committee 2011.; https://www.un.org/sc/ctc/wp-content/uploads/2016/01/2011-globalsurvey1373.pdf

United Nations Security Council Counter-Terrorism Committee Executive Directorate (CTED). Global survey of the implementation of security council resolution 1373 (2001) by member states, 20 Jan 2016.; https://www.un.org/sc/ctc/news/document/global-survey-of-the-implementation-of-security-council-resolution-1373-2001-by-member-states-2016

Vagts, D. F. (2001). Hegemonic international law. *American Journal of International Law, 95*(4), 843–848.

Chapter 5
Victims of Terrorism Associations After September 11th and March 11th: Claims, Demands, and Responses

Rosemary L. Barberet and Cristina Flesher Fominaya

Introduction and Background

This research seeks to describe and explain the claims, needs, activities, and goals of 9/11 victims via the New York tri-state area-based terrorist victims' movement that arose as a result of the attacks on the World Trade Center in 2001 in New York City, compared to those that arose after March 11, 2004 in Madrid, Spain. This project continues past comparative research on the memorialization of 9/11 and 3/11 (the Madrid bombings in 2004) (Flesher and Barberet 2011). The purpose of this research is to examine the needs, demands, claims, and activities of these victims' associations.

While most victimologists, as evidenced in victimology texts, recognize the importance of victims' associations in the victim's rights movement,[1] few have bothered to chronicle the work of victims of terrorism associations as contributors to the victim's rights movement. We surmise that this is due to two factors: first, the bias toward domestic, everyday crime in most victimological research, and, second, the notion that terrorist victimization – at least in the United States – is more of a

[1] For example, victimology textbooks in the United States commonly give importance to such groups as the Mothers Against Drunk Driving (MADD); the Clery Center for Security On Campus (formerly Security On Campus, Inc.); the National Center for Missing and Exploited Children; the Parents of Murdered Children (POMC), etc.

Support for this project was provided by PSC-CUNY Award #64276-00 42, jointly funded by the Professional Staff Congress and the City University of New York. The research assistance of Diana Rodriguez-Spahia is gratefully acknowledged.

R. L. Barberet (✉)
John Jay College of Criminal Justice, City University of New York, New York, NY, USA
e-mail: rbarberet@jjay.cuny.edu

C. Flesher Fominaya
University of Aberdeen, Aberdeen, UK

G. J. Andreopoulos et al. (eds.), *The Rule of Law in an Era of Change*, Springer Series on International Justice and Human Rights,
https://doi.org/10.1007/978-3-319-89908-4_5

disaster event than a crime, and thus transitory or "one-off," in nature. Yet we know that around the globe, terrorist victimization and its aftermath are an ongoing phenomenon. In Spain, Basque extremist terrorism has spanned five decades, spawning the creation of victims' association; in Argentina, families of victims of state terror in Argentina's dirty war formed to create the Madres de la Plaza de Mayo, a movement that continues to this day and that has internationalized. The particular nature of terrorist victimization, the needs of victims and survivors, and the types of responses that can be provided by civil society make very good reasons to study victims of terrorism associations along with other crime victims' associations.

In international spheres, victims of terrorism are generally understood to be deserving of support and compensation as part of the framework of the rule of law, as are victims in general. The report of the Secretary-General on the rule of law and transitional justice in conflict and post-conflict societies (UN Security Council 2004) mentions victims as well as their advocates (civil society organizations) repeatedly. In the summary to the document, victims are included as part of the process of achieving the rule of law: "Justice, peace and democracy are not mutually exclusive objectives, but rather mutually reinforcing imperatives... Approaches focusing only on one or another institution, or ignoring civil society or victims, will not be effective." In the context of support for reform, the considerations of victims are once again seen as paramount: "Civil society organizations, national legal associations, human rights groups and advocates for victims and the vulnerable must all be given a voice in these processes" … "Victims and the organizations that advocate on their behalf deserve the greatest attention from the international community" (p. 7). In the context of transitional justice, the report mentions other mechanisms that should be in place to "overcome the inherent limitations of criminal justice processes – to do the things that courts do not do or do not do well – in particular to help satisfy the natural need of victims' relatives to trace their loved ones and clarify their fate; to ensure that victims and their relatives are able to obtain redress for the harm they have suffered; to meet the need for a full, comprehensive historical record of what happened …" (p. 15). As such, we can clearly say that victims and their advocates are an inherent part of the "thick" definition or description of the rule of law. Attention to victims and their advocates obliges reformers to take into consideration not only rules and procedures but larger issues of justice and human rights, in national context and in the specific contexts generated by various kinds of conflict. Most importantly, there is an acknowledgement in the 2004 report that courts and formal mechanisms are not fully satisfactory for victims' needs and that other, less formal (but no less important) mechanisms are needed to fully respond to victims.

The United Nations first recognized the rights of victims of domestic crimes in a General Assembly Resolution of 1985, the Declaration of Basic Principles of Justice for Victims of Crime and Abuse of Power. General Assembly Resolution 60/147 of 2005, on Basic Principles and Guidelines on the Right to a Remedy and Reparation for Victims of Gross Violations of International Human Rights Law and Serious Violations of International Humanitarian Law, in Sections V–X, outlines the definition of and treatment to be afforded to victims, including access to justice, reparation (including restitution, compensation, rehabilitation, satisfaction, guarantees of non-repetition), and access to information. These guidelines apply to victims of international crimes. Within the United Nations Global Counter-Terrorism Strategy, victims of terrorism are guaranteed certain considerations as per UN General Assembly Resolution 60/288 of 2006.

In September of 2008, the Secretary-General convened the first symposium on supporting victims of terrorism, including victims, experts, member states, civil society organizations, and the media. The ensuing report (United Nations, 2009) noted in its conclusions the need for more networking among victims; strengthening legal instruments; establishing easily accessible health services in the short, medium, and long term for victims; creating an international rapid response team for victim support; providing financial support to victims; and creating a global awareness campaign. Under international law, it is the responsibility of the state to ensure that victims of terrorism receive services and reparation. However, as in most state responses to social problems, there are gaps in service. An indicator that the state fails at responding to victims of terrorism, despite good intentions, is the creation of terrorism victims' associations that have arisen to either deliver these services or to advocate for the creation, increase, or change in these services, as well as to advocate for the interests of victims in general in the political sphere. The creation of these groups, as well as their claims and demands, is evidence that legal remedies and their implementation are problematic in satisfying the needs of victims of terrorism. Many terrorism victims' associations have arisen within civil society to either deliver these services or to advocate for the creation, increase, or change in these services, as well as to advocate for the interests of victims in general in the political sphere. In 2012, UNODC published *The Criminal Justice Response to Support Victims of Acts of Terrorism*, which acknowledges the role of civil society in providing services and advocating for the rights of victims of terrorism. The United Nations Victims of Terrorism Support Portal lists 22 civil society organizations, but this is an underestimate of those actually working in this field nationally and globally.

In the United States, terrorist victims' associations were virtually nonexistent until the Oklahoma City bombings in 1995 and the September 11, 2002, terrorist attacks in New York, Pennsylvania, and Virginia. The United States has a long history of recognition of victims' rights and development of victim assistance, but relatively little history of victimization by terrorism on native soil. In the United States, terrorist victims' associations were virtually nonexistent until the Oklahoma City bombings in 1995 and the September 11, 2001, terrorist attacks in New York, Pennsylvania, and Virginia. However, in the United States, a strong victims' movement consisting of more than 2000 associations has formed since the 1970s. Thus, in the United States, it is very common for families of crime victims, or survivors of crime victimization, to organize and form associations. Indeed, the achievements of these organizations are notable and have been documented. For example, much of the current awareness and response in the United States to sex offender victimization, to missing and abducted children, to campus crime victims, to the victims of drunk driving, has been initiated by organizations formed by family members or survivors.

As foreign perpetrated terrorist attacks such as those of September 11, 2001 (New York), March 11, 2004 (Madrid), and July7, 2005 (London), became part of the political landscape, unfortunately replicated by many more such incidents currently, terrorist victims' associations (TVAs) are created to attempt to address the immediate and ongoing needs of their victims and families. They also make claims around anti-terrorist legislation and policy, commemoration, and judicial responses to the perpetrators. These associations not only press for the satisfaction of their needs as victims but increasingly seek to intercede as political actors in the public arena. Even in cases where they do not wish to take on an active political role, they are often drawn into political (often partisan) disputes. Thus, such associations are becoming increasingly of interest to policymakers as responsive governments need to develop instruments to anticipate and meet victims' demands but also because of their potential political impact (Hoffman and Kasupski 2007).

In the United States, federal funding was allocated after September 11th to a number of groups, but nearly all of these were pre-existing groups (Office of Victims of Crime 2003). Very few, if any, groups were formed after September 11th by victims. These groups took longer to form, and most were created by private or corporate funds. They have largely found funding outside the federal agencies. These groups now serve the more long-term needs of victims. They vary greatly in their mission, aims, and activities. Some have ceased to operate. Where still active, these groups now serve the more long-term needs of September 11th family members of victims, survivors, and first responders and, in some cases, have taken on new, broader activities.

The United States and Spain provide an empirically rich basis on which to evaluate the importance of national cultural and institutional specificity in relation to the formulation and satisfaction of victims' needs, generally formulated in universal terms in international law. Spain and the United States are located at opposite ends of the spectrum with regard to historical experiences with terrorism and the nature and history of their victims' rights movements. The United States is a liberal state, and Spain is a social welfare state with very different institutional frameworks for the assistance to victims of terrorism, yet as two developed Western democracies that were both victimized through their transportation systems by attackers tied to Al-Qaeda, the cases are sufficiently similar to provide for a meaningful comparison. Although there are differences in magnitude, the Madrid train bombing attacks were the deadliest against civilians on European soil since the 1988 Lockerbie airplane bombing.

Spain has only fairly recently made advances in the recognition of rights and assistance to victims (Aguirrezábal Quijera 2005) but has a long history with terrorism, particularly, but not exclusively Basque separatist terrorism. Spain has a long tradition of terrorist victims' associations, dating back 30 years and largely as a consequence of Basque nationalist violence. In 2000, an umbrella organization charged with representing all victims of terrorism and their associations was created as a public/private enterprise, the Fundación de Víctimas del Terrorismo, in an effort to align interests and guarantee nonpartisan attention to terrorist victim concerns. The March 11th bombings in Madrid spurred the creation of newer terrorist victims' associations responding solely to the aftermath of those bombings and generated friction as these victims sought their own recognition and assistance. But Spain's legislative commitment to the needs of victims of terrorism, no matter who the perpetrator, is in sharp contrast to the ad hoc measures adopted in the United States and resulted in a new integrated legal framework proposal passed in 2011.

Very few scholars have analyzed the work of these associations in either country, although some of the organizations have chosen to write their own account of their work. Marian Fontana wrote her own story, including the creation of the 9/11 Widows' and Victims' Families Association (Fontana 2005). The September 11th Families for Peaceful Tomorrows has their own account (Potorti and Tomorrows 2003). The most lengthy work examining these associations is RAND Association's *The Victims of Terrorism: An Assessment of Their Influence and Growing Role in Policy, Legislation, and the Private Sector* (Hoffman and Kasupski 2007), a report that arose controversy among the groups interviewed and had to be edited for a second release.[2] This report provides a detailed account of a number of 9/11 victims of terrorism associations, how they were formed and by who and what they do, and their achievements. The report is particularly concerned with how the associations mobilize politically to achieve national policy change. Other scholars have provided descriptive accounts of victims of terrorism associations within larger works (Strozier 2011) or mention the associations' specific input on aspects of the aftermath (Mollenkopf 2005).

This analysis examines the creation of 9/11-related victims of terrorism associations in the United States and the ways in which they mobilize and respond to the needs of victims and shape the public recognition of victims' plight. An analysis of web page-based documents maintained by victims of terrorism associations features an analysis of the claims, demands, activities, and goals of nongovernmental organizations formed by victims to help victims and promote social solidarity, in effort to identify civil society "best practice" in responding to the needs and victims of terrorism via national and international policymaking.

How may we expect victims of terrorism associations to be different from other crime victims' associations? First, we can generally expect victims of terrorism, and the associations they form, to be thrown into the political limelight, even if they do not seek it, because of the nature of terrorism itself as a politicized event. While many associations of victims of non-terrorist crime are politically active, their thrust is often more policy than politics. The thrust to be active politically is more

[2] After the first release of the paper, RAND "learned of concerns from some readers about the authors' way of describing distinctions among various groups. Some viewed the authors' placement of such groups into a tier system as a ranking of the groups' general influence and importance. This had not been the authors' intent. To address this ambiguity in classification, RAND undertook a second editing of the document. The tier description has been replaced by a categorization of groups—an approximation based on the groups' own stated agendas and activities—into national policy reform, state and local policy reform, and victim and family support groups... RAND also amended the dates on which various groups were formed and the types of membership categories of certain groups and their membership numbers. Other descriptions and terminology were also been modified for clarity" (Hoffman and Kasupski 2007, p. ix).

immediate on victims of terrorism. Second, there are a number of ways that 9/11 victims' associations in New York City can be expected to be different from other victims of terrorism associations. These are largely related to the particular characteristics of the perpetration of the terrorist event. The mass scale of the event generated a large number of victims, family members of victims, survivors and affected parties, and thus great media attention. The target for the attack in New York City, a workplace and an international financial hub, affected a mass of largely affiliated people in a densely populated urban area, with wide-ranging but high levels of social, political, and financial capital, as well as a contentious area upon which to rebuild and memorialize (Aronson, 2016). The nature of the attack generated a prolonged, dangerous cleanup and a huge problem of missing remains. The fact that this mass event occurred in the United States, with no special legislation in place for the compensation and treatment of large numbers of victims of terrorism, meant that responses from the State in this area were open to innovation. (Other countries such as Spain have national legislation in place and nationalized healthcare.) Thus, there was fertile ground for groups to form around a number of unique circumstances of the aftermath that the authorities were ill-equipped to handle or mediate: solidarity and social support, the deceased remains, memorialization/rebuilding, emergency and long-term compensation, mental and physical health problems, and truth-seeking. Consistent with the literature on social movement organizations (Staggenborg 1988), we should see, over time, the professionalization and deradicalization of method (Table 5.1).

The research questions were as follows:

1. How has the association evolved over time in terms of its central message and mission?
2. What are the claims and demands of the association, and how do they evolve over time?
3. What are the activities engaged in by the association, and how do they change over time?
4. Given the very diverse array of associations for victims of terrorism, what are the commonalities in civil society's response to victims of terrorism?

Method, Data, and Analytical Strategy

The data for this project come from the web pages (included cached archive web pages, especially for those organizations that are no longer active) from the 9/11 victims of terrorism associations in the tri-state area. These included 13 organizations created to provide aid to victims of terrorism and their families. In order to examine these trajectories from 2002 to 2013, cached files were obtained for each organization, for each year with the exception of one organization, the Coalition of 9/11 Families, which does not appear to have had its own website but rather a newsletter displayed on other associations' websites. Cached websites are saved by

Table 5.1 Sample of associations and years of website presence, United States

Associations	Year association was founded	URL(s)	Years of website presence covered
September 11th Widows and Victims' Families –> September 11th Families Association	2001	http://www.911wvfa.org http://911families.org	2002–2013
September's Mission	2001	http://www.septembersmission.org/	2002–2013
Skyscraper Safety Campaign	2001	http://www.skyscrapersafety.org	2002–2013
Families of September 11	2001	http://familiesofseptember11.org (suspended activity in 2012, creating the For Action Initiative, http://www.foractioninitiative.org	2002–2012
Peaceful Tomorrows	2002	www.peacefultomorrows.org	2002–2013
FSC to the 911 Commission Report	2001	http://911independentcommission.org (suspended activity in 2005)	2003–2005
Voices of September 11th	2001	www.voicesofsept11.org www.voicesofseptember11.org	2003–2013
Tuesday's Children	2001	www.tuesdayschildren.org	2003–2013
9/11 Families for a Secure America	2003	www.911fsa.org	2004–2011
WTC Survivors	2003	http://www.survivorsnet.org	2004–2013
FealGood Foundation	2005	http://www.fealgoodfoundation.com	2007–2013
WTC United Family Group -> September 11th Education Trust	2001	http://sept11educationtrust.org	2008–2013

several websites, such as Google, and provide a snapshot of particular URLs at given points in time. Results come from a content analysis of homepage banners, mission statements, and the coding of activities and claims/demands undertaken, from the start of website presence of the association to the present.

The Wayback Machine is the website used for web page retrieval. It provides a platform for searches of any URL and allows for viewing the website being searched exactly as it appeared on the date selected. The researcher then converted the websites into Portable Document Format (PDF). This data retrieval method provides the additional advantage to the researcher of analyzing the aesthetics of the website which can often say more than what is written plainly. As an example, a picture can evoke intense emotions as can slogans and logos and placement of links and quotes. In order to obtain cached files for each organization under study, the Wayback Machine Archive cached file search engine was used. URLs for each organization were searched, and depending on availability, each section of a website was converted to a PDF file. For the purposes of consistency, files were obtained on January 1 of each year or as closely as possible to the beginning.

Table 5.2 Sample of associations and years of website presence, Spain

Associations	Year association was founded	URL(s)	Years of website presence covered
FVT Foundation for the victims of terrorism	2001	http://www.fundacionvt.org/	2004 to present
AVT Association for the victims of terrorism	1981	http://avt.org/	2004 to present
A11MAT (Association for the Victims of 11-M)	2004	http://www.asociacion11m.org	2004 to present
Association for assistance to March 11 Victims	2004	http://ayuda11m.org	2004 to present

After cached websites were converted into PDFs using the Web2PDF application on Google Chrome, files were labeled and saved into appropriate categories by website, by year, and then by section of website such as home page or mission statement.

Analysis involved a content analysis of documents by type, theme, chronology, and frequency. This research provides a preliminary descriptive and longitudinal analysis of the mission, claims, demands, and activities of 9/11 terrorist victims' associations in the New York City tri-state area. The associations in the United States are compared to those active as a response to the 3/11 attacks in Madrid (see Table 5.2): Asociación Victimas del Terrorismo, Fundación Víctimas del Terrorismo, Asociación de Ayuda A las Victimas del 11-M, and Asociación de Afectados por el 11-M.

Results

Missions and Images

We examined the home page banners of the associations as well as the mission statements at founding and most recently (at present or at update). These mission statements generally show a modification of the association's original mission: a broadening of goals (e.g., Voices of September 11th), including outreach to other groups affected by tragedy, nationally and globally, the adoption of new goals (generally education and training, such as with Families of September 11th and the WTC United Family Group), a reconceptualization of goals (e.g., September 11th Families for Peaceful Tomorrows), an updating of goals (e.g., Tuesday's Children), new goals (e.g., FealGood Foundation), and the noting of achievement of past goals (e.g., Skyscraper Safety Campaign). Appendix 5.1 shows the mission statements at founding and at present (as of the writing of this chapter).

The home page banners are useful to examine because they project the image of the organization to the (global) Internet audience. One can observe generally that home page banners become sleeker and more sophisticated in their detail over time. This can be a result of technology, stable funding that allowed the hiring of more experienced web designers, but is also a general sign of professionalization of the associations.

The twin towers are present in nearly all of the home page banners, either directly in photo images or graphic form or indirectly through the use of tower-like columns in the lettering of the home page banner, such as is the case for the "i" in Voices of September 11th and for September's Mission, for which the towers are the "11" in an image of September 11, 2001. They form the background of the Skyscraper Safety Campaign, whereas the foreground is a rendering of a cityscape with other skyscrapers. The twin towers are notably absent for the Peaceful Tomorrows, whose founders are family members of 9/11 victims but whose aims are broader, and even unrelated to the symbolism of the towers. The twin towers are also not present in the logo/home page banner of Tuesday's Children, an association formed to guide those children who lost a parent on 9/11 through to adulthood.

Patriotic images (US flag, Statue of Liberty) and colors (red, white, and blue) are present on most of the home page banners that also feature the twin towers. On the home page of 9/11 Families for a Secure America, the twin towers are two US flags. The exception is the WTC Survivors' Network which has blue or purple twin towers. Besides the twin towers, the other images are those that include contemplative or happy faces (generally white); signs of solidarity and helping (the larger hand holding a smaller one, for Tuesday's Children, hands laid on top of one another for September 11th Widows and Victims' Families Association); signs of optimism (the sunrise on Peaceful Tomorrows), vigilance, and solace demonstrated by candles (Families of September 11th and September 11th Widows and Victims' Families Association); and the scales of justice (Family Steering Committee of the 9/11 Commission).

Some of the home page banners also feature a slogan or quote. The home page banner of WTC Survivors' Network features the phrase "We will never forget" in 2005, but this does not appear in later years. In 2012, the FealGood Foundation's home page banner added the words *No Responder Left Behind*. In 2003, Voices of September 11th first featured the descriptive phrase "An Advocacy Group Providing Resources and Support." In 2004, this appeared as "An Advocacy Group Providing Resources and Support to all those impacted by September 11th." In 2001, the phrase read "Providing Information, Resources and Support to the 9/11 Community," and currently, the phrase is "Healing Families and Communities After Tragedy." Families of September 11th featured their mission on their home page banner. In 2002, this was "to promote the interests of families of victims of the September 11th attacks and support public policies that improve the prevention of and response to terrorism." In 2005, the home page banner reflects a new mission statement: "To raise awareness about the effects of terrorism and public trauma and to champion domestic and international policies that prevent, protect against and response to terrorist acts." The Family Steering Committee to the 9/11 Commission includes a quote from Voltaire: "To the living we owe respect, to the dead we owe only the truth." The home page banner for September 11th Families for Peaceful Tomorrows includes a quote from Martin Luther King, Jr.: "Wars are poor chisels for carving out peaceful tomorrows." In 2005 (only) the September 11th Families' Association home page banner included the words "Working Today for a Better Tomorrow."

"Here today, here tomorrow" is the slogan that is featured on the Tuesday's Children's website in 2003 – but not at present. The Skyscraper Safety Campaign features the precision: "A project of parents and families of firefighters and WTC victims." Below as an example, we show the progression in home page banners of Voices of September 11th.

Voices of September 11th: 2003–2017

2003

2005

2006

2007

2008

2011

2014

2017

Activities

As is the case with most associations formed by victims or victims' families, associations form for social support as well as to engage in activities that are not responded to well, or at all, by the authorities. The groups that formed engaged in a variety of activities, including social support and solidarity (virtual and physical gatherings), information provision, input on memorialization, emergency funding, mental health needs, brokerage of services, services to specific populations, and political lobbying and advocacy for truth-seeking and accountability. The preservation of the twin towers footprints, the establishment of the memorial at Ground Zero, and the provision of input to the 9/11 Museum were key activities as well.

Notably, Voices of September 11th initiated a Living Memorial Project, whereby families could construct living memorials of their lost relatives. These digital archives are now in the 9/11 Museum. It is also common for the groups that form to want to engage in some kind of activity geared toward non-repetition or prevention of terrorism. In the case of September 11th Families for Peaceful Tomorrows, this means anti-war activism and solidarity journeys to other countries where people are in conflict or have experienced tragedies. Tuesday's Children has also organized similar peacebuilding missions for young people.

As the number of victims in such incidents grows, and the victims are stratified in some way (by age, occupation, role in the incident), associations will form that either specialize to cater to a subgroup (e.g., children, first responders, recovery workers, survivors, e.g., Tuesday's Children, FealGood Foundation, WTC Survivors) or somehow be inclusive and try to cater to all groups (Families of September 11th, Voices of September 11th). If the groups have competing interests, and if the environment in the aftermath is adverse to the claims and demands, then any process going forward is likely to be contentious, unless groups can form coalitions with agreed goals.

Association "Careers"

Although most of the groups examined here formed in 2001, some formed later. In the case of the Family Steering Committee to the 9/11 Commission Report, this is easily understood. In the case of the FealGood Foundation, this was due to a growing awareness of the health effects on recovery workers and the need for advocacy in this regard. The same is true for the WTC Survivors' Network – a group of people who only became conscious of their collective needs after a period of time. Not all the associations formed have lasted. Some have merged with others, and some have transformed (WTC United Family Group has become the September 11th Education Trust; Families of September 11th suspended activity in 2012, creating the For Action Initiative). The Coalition of 9/11 Families Association was formed in 2002, consisting of the 9/11 Widows and Victims' Families Association, Give Your Voice, September's Mission, Skyscraper Safety Campaign, St. Clare's WTC Outreach Committee, Voices of September 11th, and the WTC United Family Group. The Coalition's goal was to share information and provide representation of our families' voices in the development of the World Trade Center Memorial.

The contrast in activities between the associations in Spain and the United States is outlined in Table 5.3 below. The Spanish associations, in contrast, show greater permanence. Their activities mirror some of the activities of the associations in the United States, such as social solidarity and support, information provision, truth-seeking and accountability, and political activism. But in other ways, their activities are different. Direct service provision is complemented with providing assistance in accessing state services, such as the complex bureaucracy of nationalized healthcare. Commemoration in the Spanish case was so politically controversial that asso-

Table 5.3 Activities of terrorist victims' associations, United States and Spain

United States – New York	Spain – Madrid
Association "careers" – founding, dissolution, merges, and coalitions	Permanence
Activities:	*Activities*:
Social solidarity and support – virtual and physical Information provision Brokerage of services and direct service provision Input on memorialization Services to specific populations (e.g., families, survivors, children, recovery workers) Political lobbying, advocacy, and outreach Truth-seeking and accountability Political activism and international solidarity	Social solidarity and support Information provision Assistance in accessing state services and direct service provision Autonomous memorialization Services to specific populations (e.g., non-Spaniards) Truth-seeking and accountability Third-party prosecution in the trials Political activism Participation in European Federations and other types of international solidarity Watchdog of the State

ciations often mounted their own memorial services. Spanish associations also participated in third-party prosecution (*acusación popular*) in the trials of the perpetrators.[3]

Conclusion: Professionalization and Transferable Skills

There is a tendency for groups that do last over time to become progressively more professionalized. Skills learned in the process of the formation of terrorist victims' associations ("organizational learning") are transferable and can constitute good building blocks for the morphing of associations to those that embrace different or broader populations. These include not only nonprofit management and political advocacy skills but also "models" or "paradigms" for intervention. If, as Hoffman and Kasupski (2007) note, the 9/11 victims' associations learned about how to form from the experience of the Lockerbie Pan Am 101 flight victims, these victims' associations may very well have developed skills to prevent or respond to future mass tragedies and help the formation of successive groups. In the context of 9/11, they provide a diverse sample of examples of what CSOs can do that the State cannot do or chooses not to do.

[3] The Spanish Constitution and Spanish criminal procedural law permit both private prosecution (acusación particular) and popular prosecution (acusación popular) as supplementary to the role of the prosecutor. Popular prosecution is unique to the Spanish legal system and allows even citizens who have not been directly affected by a crime to exercise prosecution, in the name of the defense of legality. See Castillejo Manzanares (Castillejo and Raquel 2009) for a discussion of the restrictions increasingly placed on popular prosecution.

The Spanish 2011 comprehensive law on assistance to victims of terrorism specifically legitimates victims' associations, noting their usefulness and right to governmental subsidy, dependent on how many of their members are victims and the nature of their assistance. They have thus become conditionally but formally incorporated into the state apparatus of response to victims of terrorism. Associations in Spain are heavily dependent on state subsidy and thus seek to be declared "an association of public utility."

We have seen in this analysis an emphasis on the various activities, missions, and increased professionalization and specialization of civil society organizations created to assist and advocate for the victims of terrorism. These associations complement the efforts of the state to provide justice to victims, often offering more personalized attention since the organizations are founded by relatives of the deceased or injured and survivors of the attacks who are thus more able to empathize with others in similar situations. But these organizations, while complementing state activities, also undertake more oppositional roles, by engaging in truth-seeking, monitoring, and accountability tasks and, in the case of those organizations in Spain, by acting as a watchdog of the state. They are thus clearly emblematic of our thick description of the rule of law, providing meaning and justice to victims and survivors that goes beyond the procedures and regulations of formal justice systems.

References

Aguirrezábal Quijera, I. (2005). The United Nations' responsibility towards victims of terrorist acts. Working Paper No. 16. Madrid: FRIDE (Fundación para las relaciones internacionales y el diálogo exterior).

Aronson, J. D. (2016). *Who owns the dead? The science and politics of death at Ground Zero*. Cambridge, MA: Harvard University Press.

Castillejo, M., & Raquel, C. (2009). Hacia un nuevo proceso penal (investigación y juicio de acusación). *Estudios Penales y Criminológicos, 29*, 207–269.

Flesher, C., & Barberet, R. (2011). Defining the victims of terrorism: Competing frames around victim compensation and commemoration post 9/11 New York City and 3/11, Madrid. Chapter in Athina Karatzogianni (Ed.) Violence and war in culture and the media. London: Routledge.

Fontana, M. (2005). *A widow's walk*. New York: Simon and Schuster.

Hoffman, B., & Kasupski, A.-B. (2007). *The victims of terrorism: An assessment of their influence and growing role in policy, legislation, and the private sector (occasional paper)*. Santa Monica, CA: Rand Corporation. https://www.rand.org/pubs/occasional_papers/OP180-1.html.

Mollenkopf, J. (Ed.). (2005). *Contentious city: The politics of recovery in New York City*. New York: Russell Sage Foundation.

Office for Victims of Crime. (2003). Meeting the needs of the victims of the September 11th terrorist attacks: Department of Defense Appropriations Act of 2002. Report to Congress, April. http://www.ovc.gov/publications/infores/911victimsreptocongress03/meetingneedssept11.pdf

Potorti, D., & Tomorrows, P. (2003). *September 11th families for peaceful tomorrows: Turning our grief into action for peace*. New York: RDV Books.

Staggenborg, S. (1988). The consequences of professionalization and formalization in the pro-choice movement. *American Sociological Review, 53*, 585–606.

Strozier, C. B. (2011). *Until the fires stopped burning: 9/11 and New York City in the words and experiences of survivors and witnesses*. New York: Columbia University Press.
United Nations. (2009). *Supporting victims of terrorism*. New York: United Nations, Executive Office of the Secretary-General.
UN Security Council. (2004). The rule of law and transitional justice in conflict and post-conflict societies: Report of the Secretary-General, S/2004/616. Available at: https://www.un.org/ruleoflaw/blog/document/the-rule-of-law-and-transitional-justice-in-conflict-and-post-conflict-societies-report-of-the-secretary-general/
UNODC. (2012). *The criminal justice response to support victims of acts of terrorism*. Vienna: UNODC. Available at: http://www.unodc.org/documents/terrorism/Publications/Support_to_victims_of_terrorism/revised_edition_21_May_2012_12-53652_Ebook.pdf.

Appendix 5.1: Mission of Associations at Founding and at Present

Association	Founding year	Mission at founding	Mission at present or at last update
September 11th Widows and Victims' Families -> September 11th Families Association	2001	"Created by the families and for the families: Our most important goal is to insure the dignified recovery of your loved ones. For those families who have not yet joined us: We are dedicated to providing accurate information directly from our members working at Ground Zero Family hardships are addressed. Liaisons with the Mayor's Office, Fire Commissioner and Fire" "The September 11th Families Association supports victims of terrorism through communication, representation and peer support. Our mission is to unite the September 11th community, present evolving issues, and share resources for long-term recovery"	The September 11th Families' Association supports victims of terrorism through communication, representation and peer support. Our mission is to unite the September 11th community, present evolving issues, and share resources for long-term recovery

(continued)

Appendix 5.1 (continued)

Association	Founding year	Mission at founding	Mission at present or at last update
September's Mission	2001	The goal of September's Mission is threefold: First – The first part of the mission is to keep the memories of the people who died on September 11 alive by creating a forum where families of the victims can connect. The forum will be both online and in person. We invite family members, especially children, to email us their stories, poems and pictures for posting on the September's Mission Web site. We will also organize events where family members can come together and share their stories with one another. Second – The second part of the mission is to support the development of a memorial park on the site of the former World Trade Center and at the Pentagon. We envision these areas to be peaceful places to reflect, remember and honor those whose lives were lost at the World Trade Center, the Pentagon and on the American Airlines and United flights. We are also commissioning an author to write a memorial book to honor the lives of the victims. Please contact September's Mission if you are an author and are interested in helping us with this project. Third – The third part of the mission is help children who lost their loved ones on September 11. We support the development of an area of the memorial that would be especially geared to this often-ignored group. We believe it is important for these children to have a place to understand and accept what happened to their mothers and fathers	September's Mission is to support the development of a memorial park on the former World Trade Center site that ties into the overall redevelopment of Lower Manhattan, and to ensure its future sustainability through public/private partnerships. September's Mission is committed to working with the families, Manhattan residents, businesses and public officials to ensure that the future of the World Trade Center site not only honors the lives that were lost on September 11, but serves all New Yorkers for generations to come. Once the scope of the World Trade Center memorial is more clearly defined, September's Mission aims to work with public entities as the private arm to fund memorial development efforts as well as on-going operations and educational endeavors. September's Mission is also dedicated to helping families who lost loved ones on 9/11. By hosting and supporting events throughout the year for families and children, we strengthen personal connections and create a positive, nurturing forum that contributes to healing

(continued)

Appendix 5.1 (continued)

Association	Founding year	Mission at founding	Mission at present or at last update
Skyscraper Safety Campaign	2001	The goals of the Skyscraper Safety Campaign are: 1. To have a Federal Comprehensive Investigation, with subpoena power, into the collapse of the WTC, including design, construction, evacuation procedures and firefighting techniques. 2. To encourage better compliance with building and fire codes in NYC and nationwide, thereby safeguarding Firefighters, as well as persons who must live and work in skyscrapers. 3. To educate "codes groups" to allow the Fire Service to have more input into writing Building Codes. We call for at least 50% of all codes groups to be composed of representatives of the Fire Service and the academic field of Fire Science Engineering. (Existing groups are composed of builders, developers, financiers and bureaucrats who know little about Fire and Life Safety.) 4. To ensure that all future WTC development by the Port Authority of New York & New Jersey be characterized by quality, safety, security and New York City codes compliance	The goals of the Skyscraper Safety Campaign are: To have a Federal Comprehensive Investigation, with subpoena power, into the collapse of the WTC, including design, construction, evacuation procedures and firefighting techniques. To encourage better compliance with building and fire codes in NYC and nationwide, thereby safeguarding Firefighters, as well as persons who must live and work in skyscrapers. To educate "codes groups" to allow the Fire Service to have more input into writing Building Codes. We call for at least 50% of all codes groups to be composed of representatives of the Fire Service and the academic field of Fire Science Engineering. (Existing groups are composed of builders, developers, financiers and bureaucrats who know little about Fire and Life Safety.) To ensure that all future WTC development by the Port Authority of New York & New Jersey be characterized by quality, safety, security and New York City codes compliance. We are gratified to report that our first goal has been accomplished. The Investigation of the Collapse of the WTC has commenced. The first meeting of the National Institute of Standards and Technology (NIST) Investigation of the Collapse of the WTC was held in NYC on June 24, 2002. For ongoing information about the WTC Investigation, visit wtc.nist.gov. Much work remains to be done. It is imperative that all members of the public support the principles of the Skyscraper Safety Campaign. Our second goal is being realized as we applaud the work of NYC Mayor Mike Bloomberg and the NYC Buildings Department Commissioner Patricia Lancaster, in focusing on ensuring the safety and security of buildings in NYC. We continue to work on accomplishing all the goals of The Skyscraper Safety Campaign

(continued)

Appendix 5.1 (continued)

Association	Founding year	Mission at founding	Mission at present or at last update
Families of September 11th	2001	http://familiesofseptember11.org To promote the interests of families of victims of the September 11th attacks and support policies that improve the prevention of and response to terrorism	"To raise awareness about the effects of terrorism and public trauma and to champion domestic and international policies that prevent, protect against and response to terrorist acts." (suspended activity in 2012, creating the For Action Initiative, http://www.foractioninitiative.org) To raise awareness about the effects of public trauma and terrorism on people, societies, and the world, and to educate teachers and our youth about the history of terrorism, international relations, global security, and domestic and international policies. To inspire young people to take action—as individuals and as part of their community—and support efforts that someday might prevent future acts of global terrorism
Peaceful Tomorrows	2002	Our Mission: Peaceful Tomorrows is an advocacy organization founded by family members of September Eleventh victims. Its mission is to seek effective nonviolent responses to terrorism, and identify a commonality with all people similarly affected by violence throughout the world. By conscientiously exploring peaceful options in our search for justice, we choose to spare additional innocent families the suffering that we have already experienced—as well as to break the endless cycle of violence and retaliation engendered by war. Our goals: To make possible a safe, open dialogue on alternatives to war. To provide support and fellowship to others seeking peaceful and just responses to terrorism. To educate and raise the consciousness of the public on issues surrounding war and peace. To guard against erosion of civil liberties and other freedoms at home as a consequence of war. To promote U.S. foreign policy which places a priority on principles of democracy and human rights. To encourage a multilateral use of sensible and appropriate To encourage a multilateral use of sensible and appropriate means to bring those responsible for the September eleventh attacks to justice in an international criminal court. To recognize our fellowship with other innocent people touched by violence and war, regardless of nationality. To join with like-minded groups in furthering the causes of peace and justice	Peaceful Tomorrows is an organization founded by family members of those killed on September 11th who have united to turn our grief into action for peace. By developing and advocating nonviolent options and actions in the pursuit of justice, we hope to break the cycles of violence engendered by war and terrorism. Acknowledging our common experience with all people affected by violence throughout the world, we work to create a safer and more peaceful world for everyone. Our goals: 1. To promote dialogue on alternatives to war, while educating and raising the consciousness of the public on issues of war, peace, and the underlying causes of terrorism. 2. To support and offer fellowship to others seeking nonviolent responses to all forms of terrorism, both individual and institutional. 3. To call attention to threats to civil liberties, human rights, and other freedoms in the U.S. as a consequence of war. 4. To acknowledge our fellowship with all people affected by violence and war, recognizing that the resulting deaths are overwhelmingly civilian. 5. To encourage a multilateral, collaborative effort to bring those responsible for the September 11, 2001 attacks to justice in accordance with the principles of international law. 6. To promote U.S. foreign policy that places a priority on internationally-recognized principles of human rights, democracy and self-rule. 7. To demand ongoing investigations into the events leading up to the September 11, 2001 attacks that took the lives of our loved ones, including exhaustive examinations of U.S. foreign policies and national security failures

(continued)

Appendix 5.1 (continued)

Association	Founding year	Mission at founding	Mission at present or at last update
FSC to the 9/11 Commission Report	2001	After demanding that the Independent Commission be established, the Family Steering Committee's goal is to monitor the progress of the Commission to ensure that it assiduously follows its mandate for a broad, in depth investigation. Another important objective of the FSC is to keep the 9/11 families and the public informed about the Commission's work	(suspended activity in 2005)
Voices of September 11th	2001	Voices of September 11th is an advocacy group providing resources and support to victims' families, survivors and all those impacted by the terrorist attack on September 11th. Services include support groups, outreach, bereavement groups, lectures, workshops and special events	VOICES helps families heal after tragedy, a vital mission that began after 9/11. Today, the organization continues to address the long-term needs of those impacted by 9/11, while helping communities prepare for, respond to, and recover from other acts of mass violence and disasters
Tuesday's Children	2001	Tuesday's Children, a 'by the families – for the families' nonprofit organization founded by the brothers, colleagues and friends of World Trade Center victims, has made an eighteen year commitment to each of the thousands of children who lost a parent on Tuesday, September 11th, 2001. Our children and their families, having lost a guiding light in their lives, must not be left to walk their path alone. Tuesday's Children's programs – based on family and community interaction – create the ongoing structure and support necessary to insure a happy and healthy future	Tuesday's Children was founded to promote long-term healing in all those directly impacted by the events of September 11, 2001. Our mission today is to keep the promise to those children and families while serving and supporting communities affected by acts of terror worldwide
9/11 Families for a Secure America	2001	"What we will do: We will expose those officials who were responsible for the policies that allowed 9/11 to occur. We will work toward their removal from office and prevent their re-election. We will recommend immigration reform and will assist in election efforts of those public officials who support stringent immigration policies and the strict enforcement of these laws"	We are the families and victims of the September 11th, 2001 terror attacks and other violent crimes committed by illegal aliens. We are a group of naturalized and native born citizens of America, working together to prevent future terrorist attacks and to secure the Nation for the next generations

(continued)

Appendix 5.1 (continued)

Association	Founding year	Mission at founding	Mission at present or at last update
WTC Survivors	2003	The World Trade Center Survivors' Network is a community of interest brought together by common experience. The need for the Survivors' Network grows out of the terrorist attacks of September 11, 2001 on the World Trade Center in New York City and the high probability that large numbers of survivors of the attacks – those placed at immediate risk of injury or death during the attacks – have had their lives significantly disrupted and altered by their experiences. As a result, survivors continue to face stress, disorientation, and significant levels of grief, guilt and helplessness as they reconstruct their lives in the aftermath of the attacks. The Survivors' Network seeks to provide a forum for personal contact between survivors as a means to empower them to both deal with the circumstances of the aftermath of the attacks and to find renewed purpose in that aftermath. The Network can also function as a place for people to go and get survivors' perspectives and as a conduit for the common thoughts of survivors	In the aftermath of the attacks on the World Trade Center, many survivors felt isolated and alone. Displaced from workplaces, homes and schools, mourning the loss of friends, co-workers and loved ones, they needed to put their lives back together and move forward. In this atmosphere, a small group of World Trade Center survivors found each other online. They soon realized that, while their individual experiences were vastly different, by sharing knowledge and resources they were able to help themselves and each other. That small, initial group led to the formation of the World Trade Center Survivors' Network (WTCSN), a non-profit, non-political group currently located in lower Manhattan. Staffed entirely by volunteers, most of whom are themselves survivors, the World Trade Center Survivors' Network employs a wide range of initiatives and activities to serve survivors, including: Representing survivors' interests regarding redevelopment of the World Trade Center site including the memorial and museum Participating in conferences on terrorism and its aftermath Speaking about survivor's experiences at schools, houses of worship and community meetings forging alliances with survivors of other terrorist attacks both within and outside the US providing survivors with a forum where they can connect with each other

(continued)

Appendix 5.1 (continued)

Association	Founding year	Mission at founding	Mission at present or at last update
FealGood Foundation	2005	The primary mission of the FealGood Foundation, a non-profit organization, is to spread awareness and educate the public about the catastrophic health effects on 9/11 first responders, as well as to provide assistance to relieve these great heroes of the financial burdens placed on them over the last five years. A secondary goal of our Foundation is to create a network of advocacy on 9/11 healthcare issues. We not only advocate for Ground Zero workers, but show others how they can advocate for themselves and help others through grassroots activism	The primary mission of the FealGood Foundation ("FGF") is to assist First Responders, and/or any individual, who may have been injured, physically or mentally, as a direct result of their rescue, recovery and clean up efforts at the World Trade Center Site following the terrorist attacks of September 11, 2001. The secondary mission of the FGF is to assist all emergency personnel, including but not limited to, construction workers, police officers, firefighters, nurses, volunteers, sanitation workers and transportation workers, within the United States who have been injured, or face serious injury due to proposed action or omission, in the course of their duties or within their everyday lives. An ancillary mission of the FGF is to educate elected officials and private entities on the various problems, concerns and issues faced by First Responders in their everyday duties. The FGF is therefore dedicated to advocating for First Responder rights and illuminating, to proper authorities, the serious issues they encounter. In order to assist these individuals the FGF may, but is not limited to, provide financial assistance; place the individual in contact with medical professionals where possible and appropriate; place the individual in contact with legal professionals where possible and appropriate; advocate on behalf of the individual before appropriate authorities, both private and public and provide any other assistance that the FGF Executive Board deems necessary and proper in a particular circumstance. The FGF reserves the right to determine on a case by case basis what assistance to provide in each particular case

(continued)

Appendix 5.1 (continued)

Association	Founding year	Mission at founding	Mission at present or at last update
WTC United Family Group -> September 11th Education Trust	2001	(2008) The September 11th Education Trust World Class 9/11 and Civic Literacy Education Programming: Evolving from its genesis as the WTC United Family Group—one of the original and largest of the 9/11 community organizations—the September 11th Education Trust produces comprehensive, flexible, and engaging 9/11 and civic literacy education programs that protect the legacy and memory of the victims of the terrorist attacks, preserve and harness the lessons of 9/11 and its aftermath, unify and direct our nation's youth toward informed and effective civic participation. Our lesson plans are personalized and enriched through first-hand accounts, filmed oral histories, and authentic, primary archival materials to permanently record this shared historic event in a way that is not stagnant, but inspiring and relevant to the nation's youth. World Trade Center United Family Group 9/11 Victims' Support Services…An Empowered 9/11 community of Trust and Shared Experience In an effort to meet the ongoing and evolving needs of those directly impacted by the 9/11 terrorist attacks, the September 11th Education Trust—through its WTC United Family Group program offerings—provides comprehensive year-round services for our 9/11community members—victims' families, survivors and rescue workers across the nation—through innovative peer support programs including our September 11th/Oklahoma City Family Exchange, annual holiday gathering, advocacy on 9/11 issues, coordinated philanthropic projects to empower our community, publications and outreach, and other means of healing	Present: Same

Chapter 6
The Relationship Between the International Criminal Court (ICC) and Truth Commissions

Kate Louise Mc Eleney

An Interpretation of the Rome Statute

Admissibility, Complementarity, and Prosecutorial Discretion Within the Rome Statute

Since its inception, the Rome Statute has been subjected to much scrutiny and interpretation. Judicial determination, however, has directed that ultimately, the Statute and its aims shall be deduced in light of the "wider aims of the law as may be gathered from its preamble and general tenor of the treaty" (*Situation in the Democratic Republic of the Congo* 2006). Thus, in deducing the intent behind the Rome Statute, one must do so vis-á-vis Article 31(1) of the Vienna Convention on the Law of Treaties (1969), affording "good faith in accordance with the ordinary meaning to be given to the terms of the treaty in their context and in the light of its object and purpose." Hence, one must inquire as to what exactly the aims and objectives of the Rome Statute are and, following on from this, how these aims affect the potential for broad and narrow interpretation of Articles 16, 17, and 18 contained therein. To determine the principles of admissibility, complementarity, and prosecutorial discretion contained within these Articles, respectively, each provision must be analyzed and assessed.

K. L. Mc Eleney (✉)
Former McCabe Fellow (2013-2014) at John Jay College of Criminal Justice,
New York, NY, USA
e-mail: kl.mceleney@gmail.com

G. J. Andreopoulos et al. (eds.), *The Rule of Law in an Era of Change*,
Springer Series on International Justice and Human Rights,
https://doi.org/10.1007/978-3-319-89908-4_6

Aims and Objects: Peace and Justice

"Lasting peace requires justice" (Moreno Ocampo[1] 2007) – this short succinct statement by the former Chief Prosecutor at the ICC concisely sums up the aims of the Rome Statute as intended by the drafters. However, counter to this supposition is the argument that peace and justice should not be viewed as interdependent, but rather they should be viewed as separate ideals that remain inherently linked. Commenting on the peace/justice paradigm in the Preamble, Schabas (2010) validly states that lasting peace is attainable without judicial accountability and that the fragility of peace can be shattered even when justice has been served.

Expanding on the interdependence between peace and justice, accountability advocates advanced the idea of an international criminal law system that existed free of the jurisdictional restrictions previously experienced. This vision of the international community as a collective imparts a new conception of a community that exists as an entity separate from the states that constitute it. This entity has become an independent stakeholder in the international criminal law forum that "enjoys the power to criminalize those acts that jeopardize the fundamental values on which it is based" (Olásolo 2005).

The Preamble announces the condemnation of "grave crimes" and alludes to the fact that such crimes can impair and "threaten the peace, security and well-being of the world" (Rome Statute of the International Criminal Court, Preamble 1998). The Preamble appears to infer a strong preference by this independent stakeholder toward fortifying the peace, security, and well-being of the world by applying a system of justice based solely on retributive and deterrent measures (Olásolo 2005). This strengthens the drafters' view that justice of a retributive and deterrent nature is the key to lasting peace. The international community as a separate legal entity, driven to end impunity, is nonetheless composed of 124[2] states whose declared view on ending impunity may not envisage the strict fusion between peace and justice, specifically retributive justice. All too often the multifaceted realm of peace making is condensed into "trite legal formulae" (Schabas 2010). Some analysts have argued that the aims and objectives of the Rome Statute focus too much on the union of peace and justice by means of invoking strict retributive justice. Others have argued that both ideals should be envisaged separately and looked upon by the international community in a manner which aims to bring as much of "each as possible in the circumstances of a particular conflict" (Schabas 2010). As will be further discussed in more detail, the drafters of the Statute provided an element of ambiguity in determining the role of complementarity. In light of this, should the object and purpose of the Rome Statute be so rigidly interpreted so as to exclude all other forms of justice and save retributive/deterrent ones?

[1] Luis Moreno Ocampo, first Chief Prosecutor of the ICC, 2003–2012.

[2] The State Parties to the Rome Statute as of 31 August 2017, taken from https://asp.icc-cpi.int/en_menus/asp/states%20parties/pages/the%20states%20parties%20to%20the%20rome%20statute.aspx El Salvador, are the most recent State Party as of 3 March 2016.

The Principle of Complementarity: The Cornerstone of the ICC

The Preamble

The Preamble of the Rome Statute has received scant attention in judicial rulings on the interpretation of the Statute (Schabas 2010), despite having been described as "the marching orders" given to the ICC by the international community (Robinson 2003). This realization is alarming considering the wealth of interpretative assistance that the Preamble provides in accordance with Article 31(2) of the Vienna Convention on the Law of Treaties (1969). In particular, the Preamble significantly reinforces both principles of complementarity and admissibility, which remain hugely important in the relationship between the ICC and truth commissions. The lack of judicial reference is arguably an erroneous development of the jurisprudence of the Court as it has diminished the weight of clarity that the Preamble can offer in interpreting the Statute. This strand of thought is a direct result of the contents of the Informal Expert Paper commissioned by the Office of the Prosecutor in 2003. The most consequential aspect of this paper is undoubtedly that although "the preamble does not as such create legal obligations, the provisions of the Statute may be interpreted in the light of the preamble" (Schabas 2010). This is arguably incorrect as a teleological interpretation of the Preamble invokes a requirement upon State Parties to take action against impunity or, failing their inability or unwillingness, forgo their sovereignty and succumb to the jurisdictional reach of the Court providing *ipso facto* a legal obligation.

The lack of utilization of the Preamble in judicial determinations of the Rome Statute is a consequence of the highly politicized nature of the drafting of the Statute. This is evident in the evolution of the Preamble from nonexistence in the 1993 Draft Statute prepared by the International Law Commission to the 11-paragraph Preamble that was ultimately adopted in 1998. The highly politicized journey of the drafting of the Rome Statute is specific in terms of reference to complementarity which features solely in the Preamble and Article 1. Two reasons exist for this lack of reference: the first being that the position of the principle of complementarity in the Rome Statute should remain an "underlying principle" without cause for specific recognition (Schabas 2010) and the second being that the highly politicized and often conflicting views of the participants led to a realization that an overtly explicit use of the principle would, in practical terms, result in an ill-advised codification of terms of reference for national justice measures (Robinson 2003). The latter is by far the most persuasive, given that the drafters of the Rome Statute had the foresight and wisdom to use a degree of ambiguity in order to allow the Court to evolve and develop a non-exhaustive consideration of national programs of justice as it so determines (Robinson 2003).

The succinct wording and use of the verb "emphasize" accredits the Court with enough "creative ambiguity" (Scharf 1999) to cement its role as a complementary mechanism of justice. In addition, it is suggested that the drafters included this principle as an act of compromise between the legal obligation to prosecute and the primacy accorded to state sovereignty (Jurdi 2010). The importance of state sovereignty and the national pursuit of justice cannot be overstressed, and one asserts that the principle of complementarity is, in effect, a safety net to which State Parties may fall when, through various circumstances, they are unable or unwilling to act upon incidences of grave crimes.

Admissibility: Article 17

A comprehensive understanding of complementarity within the Rome Statute must be addressed in conjunction with admissibility, as provided for by Article 17. Article 17 affords concrete means for the Court to act with implicit complementarity toward national jurisdictions (Schabas 2010). The position of the international community as a singular entity in dealing with crimes which fall within its remit is to "complement, not supplant national proceedings" (Roche 2005). This was noted by the former Prosecutor when he stated that "the system of complementarity is principally based on the recognition that exercise of national criminal jurisdiction is not only a right but a duty of States" (Office of the Prosecutor, International Criminal Court 2003b). However, the flipside of this is: that which is triggered by the admissibility principle, and through which the complementarity mechanism actually operates, contradicts what it initially intended to do. As a result of Article 17, State Parties to the Rome Statute relinquish their primacy to the ICC, thus allowing the Court to act when the State has failed or is incapable of addressing the matter in contention (Olásolo 2005). Olásolo (2005) has concluded that complementarity has two primary goals: firstly the promotion of investigation and prosecution by national jurisdictions for "serious crimes of international concern" and secondly through the ultimate action of the ICC, extirpating impunity for the perpetrators of such crimes that prevents investigation and prosecution at a national level.

However, at this point, having not yet examined the intricacies of Article 17, an air of skepticism surrounds Olásolo's views, primarily the fact that State Parties to the Rome Statute have inadvertently renounced a certain aspect of their sovereignty, which has been guised under the realm of apparent complementarity. The loss of such sovereignty is alarming as he alludes to the fact that impunity prevents national jurisdictions from investigating and prosecuting without taking cognizance of the reasons why states may choose not to prosecute in certain circumstances, such as in the case of self-referral to the Court.

Grounds for Inadmissibility Within Article 17

The opening lines of Article 17 echo the proviso of complementarity in the Preamble without explicitly mentioning it. This results in a situation where the ICC, having already presupposed jurisdiction in a given case, has to decide whether or not to exercise this jurisdiction (Ambos et al. 2009). The provisos of admissibility contained within Article 17 are, at best, simplistic, and had the drafters afforded further expansion of the terms contained within, the debates concerning Article 17 would be significantly fewer. However, was this an intended tactic by the drafters to permit the Prosecutor a degree of liberty in his assessment of cases in terms of admissibility? To answer this question, the provisions of Article 17 will be examined below.

The content of Article 17 can be classified into grounds for admissibility under reasons of complementarity, gravity, and the rule of *ne bis in idem*. However, for this chapter, only grounds of admissibility that fall within the ambit of Article 17(1) (a) and (b) will be examined. Admissibility has been categorized into separate instances, and the same is also true of admissibility on complementarity grounds in that the concept may be examined under grounds of "complementarity and activity" or "complementarity and inactivity" (Schabas 2010). It is worth noting that Article 17 refrains from distinguishing between the various triggers for prosecution exemplifying the preference by the drafters of instilling mechanisms with a degree of ambiguity in the text (Lipscomb 2006). In this context, it is argued that the existence of such ambiguities is trivial in that the Preamble makes clear inference to the principle of complementarity being an "intrinsic" characteristic of the Statute (Lipscomb 2006). This approach by the drafters creates an element of flexibility for the court, in its interpretation of state action or inaction in respect of admissibility under the principle of complementarity, in an attempt to further strengthen the principle itself. Such lack of reference can be counterproductive. On the last day of the Rome Conference, a number of broad provisions were adopted in haste with no time to tweak the admissibility definition to make it consistent with the fundamental features of the triggering mechanism, further lending credence to this criticism (Olásolo 2005).

State Action

The admissibility of a case under Article 17(1) (a) and (b) in terms of state action depends on a certain level of action being met. The required threshold in order to render a case inadmissible under grounds of "complementarity and activity" is that a State must be contemporaneously in the process of investigating or prosecuting a case or has previously investigated a case and has decided not to prosecute (Rome Statute, Article 17 1998). However, this threshold is subject to a system of checks and balances provided by Article 17(2) and (3) which affords a strict and narrow determination of unwillingness through the due process criteria in addition to outlining acceptable grounds that render a State "unable" to comply with its obligations. To consider the consequences of this, it is helpful to examine the rationale for inadmissibility under Article 17(1)(a) or (b).

In respect to subsection 1(a), the wording suggests that it relates solely to cases in which a State is actually in the process of investigating or prosecuting a case and admissibility is triggered only when it is apparent that a State is "unwilling or unable genuinely to carry out the investigation or prosecution" (Rome Statute, Article 17 1998). This subsection appears restrictively narrow, as it does not allow for exceptions to retributive justice, such as alternative justice mechanisms that may result in a State not proceeding with already initiated prosecutions. Those drafting the Rome

Statute may have hidden behind their reluctance to embrace such controversial political assertions (Robinson 2003), but it was indeed their foresight that led them to close Article 17(1)(a) with such succinctness that allowed for the expansion of Article 17(1)(b). Thus, an avenue of feasibility for non-prosecutorial mechanisms was created (Robinson 2003).

Article 17(1)(b) serves to permit inadmissibility in respect of a non-prosecution situation based on the definite fulfillment of three required factors: first, that the State must have, in some manner, actually "investigated" the issue; second, a decision must have been made not to prosecute following the investigation; and last, the decision not to prosecute must not have been undertaken as a result of an unwillingness or inability on behalf of the State (Ambos et al. 2009; Robinson 2003). This set of criteria is subject to debate, and it is apparent that the principle of complementarity is further broken down into yet another subdivision. The reach of these conditions may be assessed in both a broad and narrow interpretation using Article 17(2) and 17(3), which shall be discussed further.

"Investigation"

What measures must a State invoke in order to satisfy the requirements of the term "investigation"? Throughout the negotiations in the lead up to the adoption of the Statute, a number of delegates,[3] notably South Africa (who raised the point no doubt with conviction from experience), sought unequivocal recognition of alternative justice mechanisms, in particular truth commissions, in the wording of Article 17 (Robinson 2003). The "politically controversial" nature of this proposition ensured that it never found its way into the text of the Statute (Robinson 2003). Records of the Preparatory Committee on the establishment of the ICC indicate that State delegates had differing views on determining admissibility in the context of national investigations (United Nations Preparatory Committee 1997). In fact, the issue of amnesties was mooted as a determining factor in admissibility with one delegation stating that amnesties (as opposed to retributive justice) could provide a mechanism in the facilitation of the restoration of the rule of law following conflict (United Nations Preparatory Committee 1997).[4]

Is one left with a narrow interpretation of an "investigation" – envisaged as one with the core objective of attaining "criminal prosecution or adjudication" (Ambos et al. 2009) – which requires a minimum standard of investigative techniques most associated with that of a criminal investigation seeking to obtain a certain standard in terms of attaining and presenting evidentiary material? If this is indeed the case, then what remains is a stringent legalistic determination that perceives justice as exclusively retributive. On this basis, any investigative measures that do not comply with this concept will be inadvertently deemed null and void, rendering the State in

[3] Including the United States of America.

[4] Unfortunately the records of the Preparatory Committee do not indicate which delegations were in favor of such measures.

question subject to the jurisdiction of the Court. This view does not sit well with those who argue in favor of alternative mechanisms of investigation, such as truth commissions. Investigations of a broad disposition, which establish facts without imparting criminal responsibility on any one particular individual, do not match the rigorous conditions attached to a criminal investigation that ultimately ends in an adjudication of sorts (Ambos et al. 2009).

One could argue that the lack of "criminal" adjacent to the term "investigation" suggests an investigation does not have to meet the rigorous threshold of a criminal investigation. This infers that an investigation that is not primarily concerned with criminal prosecution may be acceptable under Article 17, provided that there is provision for the possibility of referral to a criminal prosecution, if the facts so warrant it. Stahn reinforces this claim in that he suggests "it is more convincing to argue that Article 17(1)(a) and (b) allows not only typical criminal investigations, but also applies to other forms of investigation" (Stahn 2005), thus permitting alternative justice mechanisms, such as truth commissions, to satisfy the investigative interpretation of Article 17. This would suggest that this broad interpretation of "investigation" is in line with the aims and objects of the Rome Statute and the Court should take cognizance of such. Ambos et al. (2009) considers this notion of investigation to be untrue as he interprets the notion of prosecution to infer strict criminal prosecution which is presupposed by a "criminal or at least individualized investigation which precedes and prepares" for the said prosecution. Thus, investigations not conducted in the pursuit of retributive justice would only be possible under Article 53 (Ambos et al. 2009) – a view that is too restrictive. However as discussed below, the provisions of Article 17(2) and (3) do considerably narrow the range for such a broad interpretation.

Article 17(2): "Unwillingness"

Article 17(2) explicitly refers to due process principles under the auspices of international criminal law in the determination of "unwillingness" based on three separate criteria, the importance of which has been highlighted by Pre-Trial Chamber I in *Prosecutor v. Thomas Lubanga Dyilo* (2006).[5,6] An examination of the provision of Article 17(2) when read in light of Rule 51 of the Rules of Procedure and Evidence (hereafter referred to as RPE) of the ICC infers that an investigation/prosecution

[5] 32: The Chamber also notes that when a State with jurisdiction over a case is investigating, prosecuting, or trying it, or has done so, it is not sufficient to declare such a case inadmissible. The Chamber observes on the contrary that a declaration of inadmissibility is subject to a finding that the relevant State is not unwilling or unable to genuinely conduct its national proceedings in relation to that case within the meaning of Article 17(1)(a) to (c), (2), and (3) of the Statute.

[6] The decision does not include the word "criminal" adjacent in its reference to prosecution, investigation, or trial. Of equal importance is the explicit use of "or" as opposed to "and" at this juncture as this would imply that the Chamber does not recognize that an investigation should be means to or automatically infer a criminal prosecution – providing further support for one's argument in favor of a broad interpretation in Section (a)(ii).

submitted as grounds for admissibility under Article 17(1)(a) is required to meet a standard of proof to exemplify that the grounds for admissibility sought did not arise through the defined "unwillingness"(Schabas 2010).

Ambos et al. (2009) argues that an interpretation of Article 17(2) should be afforded a strict "literal and teleological interpretation" which would render the phrase "whether one or more of the following exist" (Rome Statute, Article 17(2) 1998) as an unambiguous and exhaustive list. This observation is excessively restrictive as it provides a three-way exhaustive list, which is contrary to the overall object of the provision. In support of this interpretation, Robinson confirms that the overall object was not to impart an exhaustive list on the Court, but rather the Court should take into account the significance of the textual choice "shall consider whether" which reflects a degree of openness, thus imposing certain flexibility on the Court in its interpretation of "unwillingness" (Robinson 2003). Thus one could argue that the realm of "unwillingness" has the potential to extend further than the three factors illustrated in Article 17(2): the investigation/proceedings were or are being undertaken for the purpose of protecting the person subject to same from criminal responsibility; the adage "justice delayed is justice denied" is apparent; or the proceedings/investigations lack a required degree of independence or impartiality in a fashion that is contrary to the intent of bringing a person to justice. Thus, the employment of a non-criminal investigation, with or without retributive consequences, can fall within the remit of unwillingness under this Article, as it does not meet the required criteria set forth in Article 17(2).

State Inaction and "Inability"

A State's "inability," as construed in Article 17(3), may be viewed in light of inaction under the principle of complementarity. Schabas (2010) notes that, territorial and active personality jurisdiction aside, the real issue at hand in terms of State inactivity is whether or not "any proceedings have taken place anywhere." This view is correctly supported once again by the jurisprudence of the Court, as provided by Pre-Trial Chamber I, when case admissibility is alluded to as being acceptable only when "those States with jurisdiction over it have remained inactive in relation to that case or are unwilling or unable within the meaning of Article 17(1)(a) to (c), 2 and 3 of the Statute" (*Prosecutor v. Thomas Lubanga Dyilo* 2006). One considers that the Pre-Trial Chamber I's use of "or" as opposed to "and" in this statement indicates that it is not fully satisfied that inaction and inability are considered as one condition but rather that they remain mutually exclusive of one another. However, inaction and inability are, in certain circumstances, interrelated, for example, a state that is debilitated by mass crimes to such an extent that render it unable to prosecute in that it cannot effectively exercise jurisdiction. In such circumstances, "inability" to prosecute may prevent a State from exercising jurisdiction and "inaction" by a State is in fact the most appropriate form of action (Office of the Prosecutor, International

Criminal Court 2003a). Thus, this stance taken by a State with jurisdiction due to its incapacitation and resultant inability is inherently linked to inaction contrary to the Pre-Trial Chamber I's apparent interpretation. One criticism of this interpretation of inactivity through inability is that States may misconstrue the principle of complementarity and view the ICC as a "Band-Aid" to fix all wounds – going completely against the grain of the object of the Statute, which is essentially to spurn States to deal appropriately with such crimes themselves. Such misconstrued ideals could inhibit the Court's functionality as States become languid. The flipside of such criticism is, however, that the Court's interpretation of inability may render a State's sovereign efforts at dealing with situations under the Court's jurisdiction through transitional justice mechanisms as an inability on the part of the State, thus establishing grounds for admissibility under the principle of complementarity. Transitional justice mechanisms, once operational, should be considered carefully by the Court when assessing potential exercise of jurisdiction through unwillingness or inactivity.

Articles 18 and 19: Challenges to Admissibility and Jurisdiction

The drafters of the Rome Statute clearly had the premise of accountability in mind when they installed a system of checks and balances in the Rome Statute (Articles 18 and 19). Deferral of an investigation through Article 18 by the Prosecutor to a State with jurisdiction, after that State claims inadmissibility under Article 17, is permitted subject to a number of conditions. First, the Prosecutor may refer such a claim to the Pre-Trial Chamber in an application to continue his/her investigation contrary to the claims of inadmissibility by the State (Rome Statute, Article 18(2) 1998). Second, such deferral shall be subject to review by the Prosecutor up to 6 months post the date of deferral or at any other time if it becomes apparent that the State is unwilling or unable to conduct the investigation (Rome Statute, Article 18(3) 1998). Third, having deferred an investigation, the Prosecutor may at any time require the State concerned to report and inform the Prosecutor periodically on the status and advancement of its investigations (Rome Statute, Article 18(5) 1998). The cumulative effect of these conditional provisions is that a State's jurisdictional approach is continually under the scrutiny of the Office of the Prosecutor even in the event of a deferral. Of what consequence is this to a State, which undertakes investigative measures under the auspices of non-retributive justice? The subjectivity of the Prosecutor and, indeed of the Pre-Trial Chamber, will undoubtedly play a part in their decisions on this front.

Following from this, the Prosecutor may still find his/her actions subject to challenge. Having established jurisdiction over an investigation, provision for challenges to the jurisdiction of the Court is addressed in Article 19. However, the likelihood of the invocation of the provisions of Article 19 by a State is slim given the jurisdictional, as opposed to admissibility, nature of its contents.

Article 16: Deferral Upon Request from Security Council

Should a case or situation qualify jurisdictionally, and in line with the requisite principles of complementarity and admissibility, deferral may in fact be sought by an entity other than the individual subject to the proceedings or by the state that has declared jurisdiction over an investigation. The United Nations Security Council can, under Article 16 and acting under the auspices of Chapter VII of the UN Charter, request temporary deferral of an investigation by the Prosecutor for a period of 12 months, subject to renewal. Essentially, such an undertaking by the Security Council is permitted only if and when it determines the existence of "threats to the peace, breaches of the peace, and acts of aggression."

The overarching aim of any action taken under Chapter VII is the restoration or maintenance of international peace and security (United Nations Charter, Article 39 1945). The notion of why and how the Security Council might undertake an application to request a deferral of an investigation can be quite troublesome to comprehend as the very object of the Rome Statute is the ending of impunity for those who commit the most heinous crimes. Destabilization of international peace and security based on the initiation of an investigation by the Office of the Prosecutor can be difficult to comprehend at first, in an ideal context that is "conflict simpliciter" – how can an action, which aims to resolve impunity, create further conflict? However conflict is rarely, if ever, simple, and all too often instances of fragility do exist in which the cessation of armed conflict may be harmed by interference from the ICC, notwithstanding a duty upon States and the international community as a whole to prosecute (Keller 2008).

It is plausible that this means of deferral is a "viable means to allow alternatives" to criminal prosecution by the Court (Keller 2008). This means of deferral undoubtedly reflects the recognition of the unsuitability of interference from the Court when a fragile "non prosecutorial truth and reconciliation process is underway" (Robinson 2003).

In safeguarding the principles of the United Nations, the deviation by the Security Council from the general consensus to end impunity will result in an amount of furor that will only be quelled by exemplary justification of the conditions that required it, such as "necessity, peacebuilding, reconciliation, conflict prevention, threats to democracy, and risks of future mass atrocities" (Robinson 2003).

How deferring an investigation or prosecution under this Article for the purposes of allowing a truth commission to proceed over intervention by the Court, based on one of the above grounds provided by Robinson, remains to be seen. One strict and conclusive rule of thumb will not by any means fit appropriately in this situation. A flipside of the Court objectivity in permitting such a deferral is that the Security Council must also act with a degree of caution when submitting an application to defer, as an "indiscriminate exercise of this power in purported dispute of peace will emasculate the ICC, and undermine efforts to strengthen deterrence and institutionalize human rights norms" (Grono 2007).

"Interests of Justice" and Article 53

> "The point where many of the philosophical and operational challenges in the pursuit of international criminal justice coincide" (Office of the Prosecutor, International Criminal Court 2007).

Article 53 undoubtedly contains one of the most contentious and controversial provisions of the Statute. Having established jurisdiction and admissibility and having overcome any challenges to same (if any), the Prosecutor is afforded an opportunity to place a stay on his/her investigation that is based wholly on his/her interpretation of the concept of the "interests of justice," having regard of course for the degree of gravity of the crime and the interests of the victims (Rome Statute, Article 53 1998). The "interests of justice" concept finds itself the subject of two junctures within Article 53 – in respect of the initiation of an investigation at Article 53(1)(c) and in respect of the initiation of a prosecution at Article 53(2)(c).

In analyzing the contents of Article 53, one must first determine the exact meaning of the term "justice" here – shall it be subject to a narrow retributive interpretation or should one bestow a broad interpretation upon it? A major flaw in the drafting of not only this provision but also the Statute as a whole is the lack of elaboration of the term "justice." This may have been a formulation employed to avoid the Prosecutor from being restricted by the intrinsic legal technicalities of Article 17 in the exercise of his discretion (Ambos et al. 2009). However, without even the slightest degree of elucidation as to what in fact "justice" entails, it is arguable that the "interests of justice" clause was merely the result of political motivation. Whether or not the inclusion of such a clause was politically motivated, the fact remains that its very inclusion "provides the Prosecutor with an enormous scope for what amounts to a highly discretionary determination" (Schabas 2010).

Thus, based on this inference of far-reaching discretionary determination, it solidly supports a broad interpretation of what "interests of justice" incorporates, *id est.*, justice of an all-inclusive nature (Stahn 2005). However, the employment of such a broad view will depend on the very discretionary nature of the provision in that its span will only reach as far as that of the individual Prosecutor. The subjectivity of the Prosecutor will have enormous bearing on such decisions; however, one hopes that current and future holders of this office will not be swayed by political connotations attached to Article 53. This view is in line with that of Ambos et al. (2009) who supports the notion that justice ought to be perceived in light of "an overall assessment of the situation taking into account peace and recognition as the ultimate goals."[7] Despite this, individual subjectivity and interpretation of the assertions of Ambos could lead, in theory, to Prosecutors reaching opposite conclusions having utilized identical principles.

---

[7] See also for a contrary view: Human Rights Watch, Policy Paper (2005, p.4):

> Human Rights Watch believes that the construction of the phrase "in the interests of justice" that would be consistent with the object and purpose of the Rome Statute as shown in the preamble would be a narrow one.

The "interests of justice" clause consequently provides the least limitative avenue for alternative justice mechanisms to exist as an alternative to criminal prosecution by the Court (Ambos et al. 2009). Robinson (2003) considers that when the ordinary meaning of the text within the Article is examined under the auspices of object and purposes, it concurs with this broad notion of justice. Thus, justice should not be preoccupied with the singularity of a particular case, but rather the notion of justice should encapsulate "alternative forms of justice" (Ambos et al. 2009). However, looking above and beyond this is the consideration of the Article in light of the overall object and purposes of the Statute. It would seem that such a broad view would be contradictory to the Statute insofar as a discretionary decision not to proceed with a case that is otherwise admissible, in light of the argument that prosecution *per se*, is in the interests of justice (Seibert-Fohr 2003). Despite this opinion, both Ambos and Robinson make a strong case in favor of a broad deduction of the concept of what constitutes "justice" in terms of the "interests of justice"; this combination of opinions is more in line with the overall hypothesis of ending impunity by incorporating all aspects of justice, not solely criminal punitive justice through trials.

Supplementary to the above-established broad interpretation of "justice" is the explicit reference to the "interests of victims" which appears in respect of non-initiation of an investigation and non-initiation of a prosecution. The Office of the Prosecutor has stated that it considers the "interests of victims will generally weigh in favour of prosecution" despite the fact that it will afford "due consideration" to the various views of victims and their communities and a composite of society in general (Office of the Prosecutor, International Criminal Court 2007). Nevertheless, as noted above, the degree of discretion exercised by the Prosecutor will be fundamentally subjective, a consequence of which may be a divergence in the factoring of "due consideration" afforded to the views of the victims.

Finally, the "interests of justice" paradigm may have variable effects on the non-initiation of an investigation and a prosecution given the distinct wording used to infer employment of the clause in Article 53(1) and (2). The former is construed using the term "reasonable basis" in determining whether or not to proceed with an investigation. Given the discretionary nature of Article 53, "reasonable basis" has the potential to fluctuate based on the subjective opinion of the Prosecutor or indeed on the basis of political intervention, which could narrow the interpretation of justice. The latter is termed "sufficient basis," which may be considered as being a strictly legalistic and pragmatic consideration based on the circumstances of the case, including the stipulated requirements in Article 53(2)(c). In light of this observation, in terms of prosecutorial discretion and its implications for the consideration of alternative justice mechanisms, there are certainly greater grounds for consideration when the Office of the Prosecutor is deciding for or against the initiation of an investigation as opposed to a prosecution.

Transitions and Truth Commissions

> "...from dictatorship to a transitional period before at last entering into the democratic Eden" (Hazan 2010).

The Transitional Society

The definition of transition and its temporal status in society is subject to constant debate and scrutiny. When does a society commence its transitional phase? When does that same society cease to be in "transition"?

A simple attempt at defining a transitional society is a society that is experiencing "change in a liberalizing direction" (Teitel 2000). This unadorned deconstruction of a society in transition is supplemented and fortified by quoting Ariel Colonomos (2005), who states, "the congenital evangelism of liberalism gets the upper-hand of the negative anthropology of realism." The concept of "transitional justice" that flows from this supposition can be defined as a "conception of justice associated with periods of political change, characterized by legal responses to confront the wrongdoings of repressive predecessor regimes" (Teitel 2003). However, one criticism of this conception is that it does not define the temporal dimension of when society begins its transitional phase and when this phase ends. One possible reason for this is that a transitional milieu could vary quite substantially as turmoil may have ceased before transition occurs; the society may have endured turmoil up to the point of transition; or indeed the society may well be undergoing transition even though crimes are still being committed (Đukić 2007). Though potentially problematic, a lack of temporal specificity does not undermine the aims of transitional justice as one trait is common in all of these circumstances that serves to unite all of the above variations – "the legacy of widespread violence and repression" (Freeman 2006).

Therefore, how does one address this legacy of violence and repression? Transitional justice seeks to apply a holistic and comprehensive approach in addressing such by virtue of the employment of four main mechanisms: first, judicial trials, both civil and criminal in nature, which may be conducted on a national or international level, permanently established or established on an ad hoc basis; second, fact-finding bodies, such as truth and reconciliation commissions; third, reparations; and last, judicial reform which can often result from recommendations made by trials or fact-finding bodies (Freeman 2006). It has been stated that a consequence of transitional justice is the elaboration of "concrete solutions" that determine "a compromise between the ideal of justice and political realism" (Hazan 2010).

The ICC, in accordance with the above understanding of transitional justice, is one component of the overarching goals of what transitional justice seeks to address. However, as Hazan points out, transitional justice is in actuality a "compromise" between the drive for justice and the force of political realism which in light of the interpretation afforded to "justice" under the auspices of the Rome Statute could be a rather unsettling conceptualization. Does this conceptualization of transitional justice infer that it can be easily manipulated by the strings of politics? It can be argued that this understanding is incorrect given the aforementioned interpretation of the concept of justice.

Definition of a Truth Commission

> "... official, temporary, non-judicial fact-finding bodies that investigate a pattern of abuses of human rights or humanitarian law committed over a number of years". (United Nations Security Council Report, Part XIV, 17 2004).

What are the requirements that a body purporting to be a truth commission must fulfill? According to Priscilla Hayner, these requirements include the following:

Truth commissions focus on the *past,*[8] specifically the recent past*;* they investigate a pattern of abuses over a period of time, rather than a specific event; a truth commission is a temporary body, typically in operation for 6 months to 2 years, and completing its work with the submission of a report; and these commissions are officially sanctioned, authorized, or empowered by the state (and sometimes also by armed opposition, as in a peace accord) (Hayner 2002).

In tandem with state authorization, a truth commission by definition must concentrate on violations that have been committed in the sponsoring state (Freeman 2006). However, violations considered by a truth commission do not necessarily have to be committed under the auspices of the sponsoring state; non-state actors or indeed an occupying power may commit them (Freeman 2006). Truth commissions must stand alone, in relative independence from the state concerned (Freeman 2006).

How can one assess the independence of a state sanctioned "non-judicial" body? The value given to such impartiality should be measured against other contributing factors (Freeman 2006). It is difficult to quantify impartiality, as a veil of political influence often obscures its vision. Such political input is the crux of the measure of impartiality – a body that engages with the State but, does not answer to the State, appears to set the standard. Bodies that act as "interfaces" between State authorities and the public do not meet the requisite threshold (Freeman 2006).

Hayner (2002) states that previous truth commissions were created "to be the central component of a transition from one government to another or from civil war to peace." To be recognized as such, a truth commission must satisfy the aforementioned criteria, and although those suggested by Hayner are contextually quite broad, it is argued that they require further expansion (Freeman 2006). In doing so

[8]This temporal stipulation would appear to be in direct conflict with the overall demarcation and concept of transitional justice, which may be concerned with post-conflict periods, periods immediately preceding the ceasing of conflict, and periods during which conflict is still in existence.

Freeman (2006) alludes to the evolutive nature of the truth commission and argues that further attributable qualities of the truth commission are derived from "past and present truth commission experiences." He asserts that Hayner's definition makes implicit reference to these further requirements and that their existence is necessary to fully grasp the concept of the truth commission.

Traits of Distinction

First, the distinction is made between truth commissions and courts or administrative tribunals in that truth commissions, by the mandate upon which they are established, are commissions of inquiry that have the primary aim of investigation as opposed to adjudication (Freeman 2006). Thus, truth commissions should never be viewed as an equivalent of courts and tribunals. Second, truth commissions concentrate on "severe acts of violence or repression" that may constitute violations of criminal law but also human rights and/or humanitarian law (Freeman 2006). Parallel to this thought is that truth commissions are designed to concentrate on violations that occurred "during recent periods of abusive rule or armed conflict" and that more often than not, these periods have ceased (Freeman 2006). Freeman (2006) validly states that truth commissions are not only for the sole purpose of establishing the facts of individual and separate cases but that part of their mandate includes the requirement to establish the "broad causes and consequences" of the events that are being examined. Thus, truth commissions are intended to be victim-centered, and they should strive to achieve comprehensive understanding of the atrocities in the widest sense possible.

An Alternative Definition

Having primarily considered the definition of a truth commission according to Hayner, it is nonetheless worth noting Freeman's attempt at defining it:

> A truth commission is an ad hoc, autonomous, and victim-centered commission of inquiry set up in and authorized by the state for the primary purposes of (1) investigating and reporting on the principal causes and consequences of broad and relatively recent patterns of severe violence or repression that occurred in the state during determinate periods of abusive rule or conflict, and (2) making recommendations for their redress and future prevention (Freeman 2006).

Neither of the aforementioned definitions make any reference to criminal justice; nor do they refer to any interaction between criminal justice and restorative justice, and this omission constitutes a fundamental flaw of both definitions.[9] However, based on an examination of both definitions, for the purposes of this chapter, Freeman's definition is deemed preferable. His understanding seeks to embody the

[9] Freeman's use of the term "redress" makes implicit reference to the possibility of referral of certain cases to a criminal justice system.

very nature of transitional justice and acknowledges the ever-changing and evolutive nature of same.[10]

Truth Commissions: A Tenuous Relationship with International Criminal Law?

The relationship between international criminal law and truth commissions will be assessed in light of grounds for deferral of an ICC investigation to a truth commission under Articles 16, 17, and 53. This section will critically examine how a truth commission may be considered in determining grounds for deferral.

Article 16

Arguably the provision with the most "clout" for deferral, Article 16, may, in theory, request the deferral of an investigation/prosecution if the undertaking of such by the ICC would constitute "a genuine obstacle to peace" (Keller 2008). The inclusion of Article 16 reflects the tenuous relationship between the highly political Security Council and the ICC. The essence of the Article is a compromise – between those who sought the Court's complete independence and those who were in favor of a Court controlled by the Security Council (Schabas 2010; Robinson 2003). Initially, political abuse of this provision was presumed to be highly unlikely (Robinson 2003). However, such a presumption exemplified a high degree of naiveté considering that the first time the Security Council engaged the provision (United Nations Security Council Resolution 1422 2002), it did so on grounds that flew in the face of the maintenance or restoration of international peace and security (Robinson 2003). The remoteness of the Security Council resolution to the apparent goal held in Chapter VII of the United Nations Charter portrayed a troubling disregard for the Court. As a result, the case for the Security Council using the provision to request deferral of prosecution in order to promote and facilitate the achievement of peace through a truth commission is highly unlikely. Having said that, such an occurrence is not inconceivable, if a truth commission is underway (Robinson 2003). A lack of judicial interpretation in respect of this Article has rendered its use problematic, and the Security Council has not pursued use of the provision with any degree of consistency.

For example, the Security Council deviated from its stance on Article 16 deferral during the case of the arrest warrant issued for President Al-Bashir of Sudan despite calls by the African Union to apply the provision (Schabas 2010). The Security

[10] Freeman (2006) comments on his definition:

> …the definition is not normative in character. It is not a description of what truth commissions *should* be. It is descriptive only. Its singular aim is to improve …our collective understanding of the truth commission phenomenon.

Council did not reject requests made by the African Union and others; however, its failure to act was tantamount to refusal. Once again, this inaction was politically driven. Although quite critically in this case, one of the Council's permanent members declined to make explicit reference to Article 16 during the debates; instead they opted for statements that inferred their opposition to a deferral (Schabas 2010).[11]

The above examples of Security Council engagement with Article 16 evidently do not bode well for prosecutorial deferral on grounds of a truth commission aiding the restoration or maintenance of international peace and security. They exemplify inconsistency and political motivation for action or inaction in respect of Article 16 and the use of Article 16 by the Council shall always be subject to the political context of the situation, which echoes the compromise upon which this provision is built. Therefore, deferral to a truth commission by virtue of the use of Article 16 is possible but unlikely, given the politicization of the context, the lack of adjudication, and the Security Council's inconsistent use of the provision.

Article 17

In contrast to Article 16, the jurisprudence that has stemmed from Article 17 has not contributed to the case for ICC prosecutorial deferral to a truth commission. The former Prosecutor has stated that, in his view, he does not consider alternative justice mechanisms to fit within the realm of admissibility under Article 17 *per se* as, for the purposes of complementarity, they do not constitute "criminal proceedings" (United Nations Security Council Report 2006). Contrary to this is the view that the court may in fact consider a "sincere" truth commission to constitute an investigation under Article 17 that negates a suggestion of unwillingness on behalf of the State in question – thus permitting grounds for deferral to such mechanism under the principle of complementarity (Schabas 2010). In commenting on this possibility, Schabas (2010) asserts an air of doubt when stating that even though such a possibility exists, the likelihood of the Court affording such consideration to a truth commission is slim. Such considerations remain problematic without judicial interpretation on the matter. The earlier deconstruction of Article 17 provides an insight to how such matters may be handled by the Court should they arise.

The views of the Prosecutor have an insurmountable bearing upon the interpretation of complementarity by the court. However, leaving this factor aside, one must assess how the definitive truth commission aspires to be considered grounds for deferral under Article 17. As noted, Article 17 refers to an "investigation" but does not refer to a "criminal investigation," strongly suggesting that a broad and somewhat literal interpretation of the term alludes to an acceptance of justice that is not solely retributive. Freeman's definition would satisfy the investigative requirements

[11] Citing United Nations Security Council Report (2008b) in reference to the US abstinence rationale that acceptance of such an application would "send the wrong signal to Sudanese President Al-Bashir and undermine efforts to bring him and others to justice."

given remit for broad interpretation, as his assertion clearly constitutes a body which primarily purports to investigate and report. This definition, combined with the aforementioned broad interpretation afforded to "investigation" as supported by Stahn (2005),[12] infers that truth commissions do comply with the potentially self-restrictive provisions of Article 17. In addition, there are concrete grounds to state that such a body does fulfill the requirements of the principle of complementarity – in terms of positively identifying it as an "investigative" body. Moreover, it has already been stressed that, had the drafters of the Statute sought to encapsulate retributive justice only under Article 17, they would have acted purposely and inserted an explicit reference to a criminal investigation. Instead, the word "criminal" was omitted.

An examination of Freeman's definition under Article 17(2) supports prosecutorial deferral. Firstly, in terms of "unwillingness," contrary to the literal and teleological interpretation advanced by some analysts (Ambos et al. 2009), the application of the criteria set forth in Article 17(2) should not be taken as an exhaustive list. Although one may deem the wording of the provision to infer open-endedness, the definition of a truth commission must be examined under the existing criteria to determine how it could perform in the instance of judicial interpretation on the issue. Freeman's definition when examined under Article 17(2)(a) could be considered by some to fall short of the provisional requirements as it does not make explicit reference to criminal responsibility for crimes committed that are within the remit of the Court's jurisdiction. However, a broad interpretation of the last definitional sentence supports the suggestion that "recommendations" made by truth commissions may encompass recommendations for criminally prosecuting individuals by a judicial criminal justice body based on its findings. Fortifying this is his use of the term "redress" adjacent to recommendation – inference to possible retributive justice[13] when appropriate. Thus, given a broad interpretation, Freeman's definition satisfies the first condition of Article 17(2).

In fulfilling the requirement set forth in Article 17(2)(b), Freeman's definition critically falls short of the mark as no reference is made to any temporal aspect with the exception of the use of "recently." The engagement of "recent" makes implicit reference to an investigation that is conducted quite soon after the examinable crimes have been committed. Having refrained from using "immediate," Freeman echoes Hayner and maintains the view that truth commissions need not necessarily occur in the direct aftermath of turmoil. Therefore, and on the basis of these interpretations, the decision to take the route of a truth commission over the prosecutorial route does not necessarily mean "justice delayed is justice denied." In the context of this study, prosecutorial deferral is examined in situations when a truth commission is underway or is proposed, thus negating the supposition of delayed

[12] "It is more convincing to argue that Article 17(1)(a) and (b) allows not only typical criminal investigations, but also applies to other forms of investigation."

[13] This aspect of truth commissions interacting with criminal and retributive justice warrants further discussion.

justice. This substantially strengthens support for Freeman's definition in fulfilling the condition set out in Article 17(2)(b).

The last criterion of Article 17(2) relates to the independence and impartiality of proceedings that, if negated, allows an investigation or prosecution to continue. Freeman has chosen "autonomous" to infer to the independent nature of the body. As already highlighted, a truth commission may exist and function with the sanction of the state concerned, but sanction does not imply that the body acts as the State's bidding agent. Thus, the autonomous character of the said body unquestionably reaches the threshold of independence and impartiality set by the provision.

The conclusive condition of Article 17(2) is that the truth commission must not act to contravene justice. Justice, as discussed earlier, should be afforded a wide reach and broad interpretation so as to scrutinize the Article in light of how it was intended. This holistic conception of justice is the underlying tone in Freeman's definition, which promotes a "victim-centered" purpose to achieve redress and the future prevention of conflict.

In respect of Article 17(3), Freeman's definition is rather unproblematic in the consideration of inability under the principle of complementarity, as the establishment of a definitive truth commission should not be construed as an omission by the State to fulfill its obligations under the Rome Statute. Hence, deferral to a truth commission cannot be negated by arguing that the truth commission engagement denotes that the State's legal system has gone asunder or that retributive means of justice are unavailable. Counter to this is the fact that prosecutorial subjectivity may adversely discriminate against alternative justice mechanisms and, consequently, translate such instances as an inability by a State to act, thus allowing the Prosecutor to continue with his/her investigation or prosecution.

This consideration of deferral by the Prosecutor to a truth commission under Article 17 is undoubtedly contentious, and persuasive arguments can be employed both for and against deferral. Nonetheless, the definition afforded by Freeman facilitates a convincing rationale for allowing deferral as it negates both the unwillingness and inability criteria set forth in the Article. In spite of this, the subjectivity of the former Prosecutor, and his previous comments, do not conjure up much hope for deferral under Article 17 to a truth commission in the near future. This is a pessimistic view given the concrete potential of such a deferral based on the interpretation of the Article in light of Freeman's definition. Consequently, it leads one to concur with the aforementioned skepticism of Schabas (2010) on the matter.

Article 53

The core objective of Article 53 is the codification of permission afforded to the Prosecutor to refrain from investigating by virtue of the justification that serves in the "interests of justice;" this provision clearly supports the notion that justice under the Rome Statute is justice that reaches far beyond criminal justice only (Freeman 2009). Article 53 fails to make explicit reference to deference to truth commissions in pursuit of acting in the interests of justice. However, this does afford a high degree of discretion to the Prosecutor in applying the clause (Đukić 2007), thus providing the Prosecutor with a wide margin in making a decision based on the interests of justice without the restriction of a codified and exhaustive list of other justice mechanisms that he/she may defer to.

In examining how Freeman's definition of a truth commission fits within the contents of the interests of justice clause, the first striking similarity between them is the explicit reference to the victims' interests. Freeman states that a truth commission is an inherently victim-centered body which fits seamlessly into the conditional criterion of Article 53(1)(c) and (2)(c). Therefore, one can adduce that a body that asserts itself under Freeman's definition has substantial grounds for consideration of deference to by the Prosecutor under Article 53. The subjective nature of the Prosecutor and the political influence held over this office has weakened the preference of Article 53 as a means for deferral to a truth commission. The most likely cause of this weakening is the obstacle faced by the Court of "articulating in a persuasive manner the dividing line between its judicial function and the political ramifications of its decisions" (Goldston 2010). However, this perceived weakness could actually be used as leverage by the Prosecutor to strengthen the case for deferral to a truth commission in the "interests of justice." The Prosecutor, when succumbing to political pressure to pursue an investigation or prosecution through the avenues provided by the Rome Statute, should, when appropriate, highlight the often-fragile nature of situations that find their way under the radar of the Court by referral.

The positive argument in favor of the Prosecutor stepping back from political assertions and assessing each individual case under the interests of justice clause is best supported by Carlos Nino. Nino (1991) states that although:

> It is true that many people approach the issue of human rights violations with a strong retributive impulse, almost all who think momentarily about the issue are not prepared to defend a policy of punishing those abuses once it becomes clear that such a policy would probably provoke, by a casual chain, similar or even worse abuses....

Acknowledgment of this fragility referred to by Nino, and an increased awareness of such, can only work to strengthen grounds for deferral under Article 53 to truth commissions when criminal prosecution would serve only to cause further strife and turmoil (Schabas 2004) – fulfilling the conditional requirements of Article 53. In rationalizing his definition, Freeman states that it is not intended to convey any sense of superiority (Freeman 2006) and, in light of this, prosecutorial discretion under Article 53 should be based solely on the merits of each individual case.

One final element of deferral under Article 53 to be examined is the reference to the condition of the individuals' role in the crime in terms of prosecution under Article 53(2)(c). The ICC is concerned with ending "impunity for the perpetrators" (Rome Statute, Preamble 1998) of crimes that fall within the remit of the Court's jurisdiction, *id est*, endeavoring to end impunity for those most responsible. Therefore, truth commissions play a major part in the determination of prosecutorial discretion under Article 53(2)(c). An interpretation of the interests of justice clause can therefore amount to grounds for deferral to a truth commission based on the very objective of the Rome Statute in the non-prosecution of low-level offenders, leaving the Court to remain concerned with high-level offenders if the case requires. This assertion in favor of deferral is not as robust as that of the immediate previous assertion regarding state fragility in a post-crisis situation.

Consequently, the broadness of the clause contained within Article 53 should be read in conjunction with the views of Nino for two reasons. Firstly, such reading would serve to allay adverse political concerns and consequent influences over the subjective nature of the Office of the Prosecutor. Secondly, Nino's views provide a measure of accountability through foresight that could be used by the Pre-Trial Chamber as a guide, if it is called upon to consider requesting that the Prosecutor review his/her decision not to prosecute.

Having afforded a critical analysis to all three provisions within the Rome Statute concerning deferral of an investigation or prosecution in light of the definition provided by Freeman, it is clear which provision holds most favor for deferral to a truth commission – Article 53 through the interests of justice clause. Each provision – Article 16, Article 17, and Article 53 – has redeeming features in terms of deferral; however, Article 53 is clearly the most deferral-sensitive.

Article 16 is tinged with inconsistency and undue influence from political motivations – motivations that are an inherent component of the provision given its label as a "compromise" in the drafting stages of the Statute. The high threshold of Chapter VII requirements also inhibit the potential of such deferral. Article 17 is, upon initial examination, quite promising as Freeman's definition of a truth commission negates both the unwillingness and inability precursors to state fulfillment of the provision. Nonetheless, academic commentators remain skeptical of the real potential of the provision. As a result, Article 53 provides those in favor of deferral to a truth commission with significant prosecutorial discretion and a far-reaching discretionary clause, thus allowing a higher chance of deferral in light of this latitude. State Parties to the Statute, in addition to other relevant stakeholders (members of the United Nations Security Council), should be sensitive to the potential ramifications of pursuing a robust criminal prosecution, and awareness of alternatives is undoubtedly necessary for the correct and successful engagement of Article 53.

Conclusion

> ...when the International Criminal Court comes into being, it will not, either by definition or by approach, discourage attempts by national states to come to terms with their past... It would be regrettable if the only approach to gross human rights violations comes in the form of trials and punishment. Every attempt should be made to assist countries to find their own solutions provided there is no blatant disregard of fundamental human rights. (Boraine 2000).

The above excerpt echoes with certainty the true sentiments of those who conceived the Rome Statute through a common desire to end impunity. The end of impunity and the restoration of the rule of law are inherently linked to the establishment of peace and reconciliation. The status of truth commissions is not afforded explicit reference in the Rome Statute, something that has been condemned because it asserts non-recognition by the ICC of truth commissions. However, this assertion is fundamentally incorrect as the very lack of explicit reference allows transitional justice, and, in turn, truth commissions, to evolve and adapt alongside the ICC without the restrictions of an exhaustive codification. This is reinforced by the broad interpretation of "justice" contained in the Rome Statute. The essence of the principle of complementarity richly fortifies this assertion as its very inclusion in the Rome Statute emphasizes the importance of national criminal jurisdictions in the drive to end impunity. This sentiment is echoed in the early records of the United Nations Preparatory Committee, which demonstrate the recognition by state delegates of the significance of the restoration of the rule of law through varying measures, including those considered to exist beyond strict prosecutorial justice (United Nations Preparatory Committee 1997).

By definition, the independence of truth commissions from state interference could infer that they lie outside the realm of national criminal justice systems. However, the vital role of truth commissions to date in advancing the cause of justice in transitional states negates such assertions; such recognition has been endorsed by both the Security Council and the Prosecutor of the ICC (Annan, letter to the President of the Security Council 2001 and; Moreno Ocampo 2007).

The relationship that currently exists between the ICC and truth commissions is still in the tender stages of its infancy, so how should one define this relationship? As one which is defined by strict separation of the two or one that reflects the amelioration of peace through joined efforts?

Arguably a relationship based upon strict separation could serve to enhance the integrity of each entity (Shriver 2001), integrity that is further enhanced by the establishment of a permanent truth commission (Eisnaugle 2003). One can legitimately disagree with this assertion, as the relationship between the ICC and truth commissions is one based upon complementarity and their acceptance of each other's relevant role in transitional justice. One posits that this relationship, although one of mutual exclusivity, is one that requires input from both entities. A strict retributive approach by the ICC will incur shortcomings for victims and perpetrators, most notably regarding the establishment of a "contested truth" (*Prosecutor v. Plavšić*, Trial Chamber III Sentencing Judgement 2003) and the lack of cathartic self-reconciliation achieved by a criminal court, respectively. The sole engagement of truth commissions can result in impunity for those most responsible while allowing witnesses to testify without the procedural safeguards of evidential rules. The importance of the coexistence of both the ICC and truth commissions, both present and future, must be encouraged through the facilitation of an organic and respectful relationship between both entities. The United Nations (2004) offers a definition of a truth commission that serves to promote the notion that truth commissions are not designed to replace retributive court-based justice, but rather provide a format of accounting for past events.

Reinforcing the importance of the latter is the recognition of the need to give effect to the right to know and the right to truth as espoused by the United Nations in the Updated Set of principles for the protection and promotion of human rights through action to combat impunity (2005). Non-judicial measures such as truth commissions give effect to an "inalienable right to the truth" and a victims' right to the truth by ascertaining the truth and aiding the prevention of the disappearance of evidence, which may be later utilized in judicial processes (United Nations 2005).

One posits that lasting peace can only be achieved through reconciliation, which is in turn inherently dependent upon both entities maintaining transparent and defined relations, thus enabling each body to fill the lacunae left by the other. In addressing all matters pertinent to the establishment of peace, this relationship has the potential to eradicate respective shortcomings of each body when engaged separately. This conclusion is supported by Roche (2005) when he states that this:

> Approach could enhance the legitimacy and effectiveness of both institutions: ICC support would enable truth commissions to hold out a more credible threat of prosecution to those who refuse to confess and make amends for their crimes, while the Court's own legitimacy may be enhanced by its demonstrating a willingness to support states' efforts to address human rights abuses.

Those engaged in the search for lasting peace must consider this relationship as imperative to their aim, bearing in mind that "the quest for justice for yesterday's victims of atrocities should not be pursued in such a manner that it makes today's living the dead of tomorrow" (Goldstone 1998).

References

Ambos, K., Large, J., & Wierda, M. (2009). *Building a future on peace and justice – studies on transitional justice, peace and development, the Nuremburg declaration on peace and justice*. Berlin: Springer.

Annan, K. (2001). Letter dated 12 January 2001 from the Secretary-General addressed to the President of the Security Council. UN Doc. S/2001/40: https://documents-dds-ny.un.org/doc/UNDOC/GEN/N01/211/71/PDF/N0121171.pdf?OpenElement. Accessed 31 Aug 2017.

Boraine, A. (2000). *A country unmasked: Inside South Africa's truth and reconciliation commission*. Oxford: Oxford University Press.

Colonomos, A. (2005). *La morale dans les relations internationales*. Paris: Odile Jacob.

Đukić, D. (2007). Transitional justice and the ICC. *International Review of the Red Cross, 89*(867), 691–718.

Eisnaugle, C. J. N. (2003). An international 'truth commission': Utilising restorative justice as an alternative to retribution. *Vanderbilt Journal of Transnational Law, 36*, 209.

Freeman, M. (2006). *Truth commissions and procedural fairness*. Cambridge: Cambridge University Press.

Freeman, M. (2009). *Necessary evils – amnesties and the search for justice*. Cambridge: Cambridge University Press.

Goldston, J. A. (2010). More candour about criteria - the exercise of discretion by the prosecutor of the ICC. *Journal of International Criminal Justice, 8*, 383–406.

Goldstone, R. (1998). Bringing war criminals to justice during an ongoing war. In J. Moore (Ed.), *Hard choices: Moral dilemmas in humanitarian intervention* (pp. 195–210). Lanham: Rowman and Littlefield.

Grono, N. (2007). Negotiating Peace and Justice: Considering Accountability and Deterrence in Peace Processes. International Crisis Group. http://homepage.univie.ac.at/herbert.preiss/files/ICG-Grono-Negotiating_Peace_and_Justice.pdf. Accessed 9 May 2018

Hayner, P. (2002). *Unspeakable truths – facing the challenge of truth commissions*. London: Routledge.
Hazan, P. (2010). *Judging war, judging history*. Stanford: Stanford University Press.
Human Rights Watch. (2005). Policy paper: The meaning of 'the Interests of Justice" in Article 53 of the Rome Statute. https://www.hrw.org/news/2005/06/01/meaning-interests-justice-article-53-rome-statute. Accessed 31 Aug 2017.
International Criminal Court. (2003a). Informal expert paper: The principle of complementarity in practice. https://www.icc-cpi.int/NR/rdonlyres/20BB4494-70F9-4698-8E30-907F631453ED/281984/complementarity.pdf. Accessed 31 Aug 2017.
International Criminal Court. (2003b). Paper on some policy issues before the Office of the Prosecutor. https://www.icc-cpi.int/nr/rdonlyres/1fa7c4c6-de5f-42b7-8b25-60aa962ed8b6/143594/030905_policy_paper.pdf. Accessed 31 Aug 2017.
International Criminal Court. (2007). Policy paper on the Interests of Justice. https://www.icc-cpi.int/NR/rdonlyres/772C95C9-F54D-4321-BF09-73422BB23528/143640/ICCOTPInterestsOfJustice.pdf. Accessed 31 Aug 2017.
Jurdi, N. N. (2010). The prosecutorial interpretation of the complementarity principle: Does it really contribute to ending impunity on the national level? *International Criminal Law Review, 10*, 73–96.
Keller, L. M. (2008). Achieving peace with justice: The ICC and Ugandan alternative justice mechanisms. *Connecticut Journal of International Law, 23*, 209–279.
Lipscomb, R. (2006). Restructuring the ICC framework to advance transitional justice: A search for a permanent solution in Sudan. *Columbia Law Review, 106*, 182–212.
Moreno Ocampo, L. (2007). "Building a future on peace and justice" Nuremberg – address by Mr Luis Moreno-Ocampo, prosecutor of the international criminal court. https://www.icc-cpi.int/NR/rdonlyres/4E466EDB-2B38-4BAF-AF5F-005461711149/143825/LMO_nuremberg_20070625_English.pdf. Accessed 31 Aug 2017.
Nino, C. (1991). The duty to punish past abuses of human rights put into context: The case of Argentina. *Yale Law Journal, 100*, 2619.
Olásolo, H. (2005). *The triggering procedure of the ICC*. Leiden: Marinus Nijhoff Publishers.
Prosector v Thomas Lubanga Dyilo. Thomas Lubanga Dyilo, ICC-01/04–01/06–2 (International Criminal Court 24 February 2006).
Prosecutor v Plavšić. Trial chamber III sentencing judgement, IT-00-39&40/1-S (International Criminal Tribunal for the former Yugoslavia (ICTY) 27 February 2003).
Robinson, D. (2003). Serving peace in the interests of justice: Amnesties, truth commissions and the ICC. *European Journal of International Law, 14*(3), 481–505.
Roche, D. (2005). Truth commission amnesties and the ICC. *British Journal of Criminology, 45*, 565–581.
Schabas, W. A. (2004). *An Introduction to the International Criminal Court*. Cambridge: Cambridge University Press.
Schabas, W. A. (2010). *The ICC – a commentary on the Rome Statute*. Oxford: Oxford University Press.
Scharf, M. (1999). The amnesty exception to the Jursidiction of the ICC. *Cornell International Law Journal, 32*, 507–527.
Seibert-Fohr, A. (2003). The relevance of the Rome Statute of the ICC for amnesties and truth commissions. *Max Planck Yearbook of United Nations Law, 7*, 553–590.
Shriver, D. W. (2001). Truth commissions and judicial trials: Complementary or antagonistic servants of public justice? *Journal of Law and Religion, 16*, 1–33.
Situation in the Democratic Republic of the Congo, Judgement on the Prosecutor's application for extraordinary review of the pre-trial chamber 1's 31 march 2006 decision denying leave to appeal, ICC-01/04–168 (International Criminal Court 13 July 2006).
Stahn, C. (2005). Complementarity, amnesties and alternative forms of justice: Some interpretive guidelines for the ICC. *Journal of International Criminal Justice, 3*, 695–720.
Teitel, R. (2000). *Transitional justice*. Oxford: Oxford University Press.

Teitel, R. (2003). Transitional justice genealogy. *Harvard Human Rights Journal, 16*, 69–94.
United Nations. (1945). Charter of the United Nations. 1 UNTS XVI. https://treaties.un.org/doc/source/docs/charter-all-lang.pdf. Accessed 31 Aug 2017.
United Nations. (1969, May 23). Vienna convention on the law of treaties. United Nations, Treaty Series, vol. 1155, p. 331, 8 I.L.M. 679.
United Nations. (2002, July 12). UN Doc.S/RES/1422. Security Council Resolution 1422. http://www.securitycouncilreport.org/atf/cf/%7B65BFCF9B-6D27-4E9C-8CD3-CF6E4FF96FF9%7D/POCSRES%201422.pdf. Accessed 31 Aug 2017.
United Nations. (2006, June 24). UN Doc.S/PV.5459. Security Council Reports of the Secretary-General on the Sudan. http://www.un.org/en/ga/search/view_doc.asp?symbol=S/PV.5459. Accessed 31 Aug 2017.
United Nations, ECOSOC. (2005, February 8). E/CN.4/2005/102/Add.1. Updated Set of principles for the protection and promotion of human rights through action to combat impunity. https://documents-dds-ny.un.org/doc/UNDOC/GEN/G05/109/00/PDF/G0510900.pdf?OpenElement. Accessed 31 Aug 2017.
United Nations General Assembly. (2008). A/CONF.183/9. Rome Statute of the International Criminal Court.
United Nations Preparatory Committee. (1997, August 4–15). Working group 3 on complementarity and trigger mechanisms; Committee on the establishment of an international criminal court. http://www.iccnow.org/documents/4PrepCmtWorkGrp3Summary.pdf. Accessed 31 Aug 2017.
United Nations Security Council. (2004, August 23). UN Doc.S/2004/616. The rule of law and transitional justice in conflict and post-conflict societies. https://www.un.org/ruleoflaw/files/2004%20report.pdf. Accessed 31 Aug 2017.
United Nations Security Council. (2008a, July 7) UN Doc.S/2008/443. Report of the Secretary-General on the deployment of the African Union-United Nations Hybrid Operation in Darfur. http://undocs.org/S/2008/443. Accessed 31 Aug 2017.
United Nations Security Council. (2008b, July 31). UN Doc.S/PV.5947. Security council report. http://www.securitycouncilreport.org/atf/cf/%7B65BFCF9B-6D27-4E9C-8CD3-CF6E4FF96FF9%7D/Sudan%20SPV5947.pdf. Accessed 31 Aug 2017.

Chapter 7
Legal Assumptions and Unintended Meanings Before International and Hybrid Criminal Courts: Effects on Trial Proceedings and Defense Rights

Dragana Spencer

Multilayered Interpretation and Translation in International Criminal Law

The relationship between linguistics and international criminal justice procedure is largely unexplored. Pretrial and trial interpretation and translation errors and omissions, which derive from differences between first/original languages and official court languages into which they are translated, can result in inaccurate interpretations and unintended meanings. This could amount to distortions of the truth and ultimately historical records produced by international criminal courts. Most importantly, it could also alter original/intended meanings and lead to misleading interpretations of probative evidence, threatening defense rights, and the fact-finding aims of international criminal justice mechanisms.

Furthermore, as nonverbal messages of testimonies often carry with them sociocultural connotations that cannot always be easily or accurately translated, the aim in this context is to also observe the extent to which court interpreters do and to what extent they should convey such messages to other trial participants. Under examination are therefore the degree of understanding of those diverse messages in multinational contexts and the type and level of paralinguistic training received by court interpreters and other trial participants but most importantly the judges. While it is difficult to establish a direct connection between interpretation/translation errors and corresponding detrimental trial outcomes other than as a sentencing mitigating factor in already decided war crimes cases, it is possible to demonstrate and qualify these for the purpose of quantifying their impact on equality of arms and defense rights, particularly within the legal framework of the ICC.

D. Spencer (✉)
University of Greenwich, School of Law, London, UK
e-mail: Dragana.Spencer@gre.ac.uk

G. J. Andreopoulos et al. (eds.), *The Rule of Law in an Era of Change*, Springer Series on International Justice and Human Rights,
https://doi.org/10.1007/978-3-319-89908-4_7

International criminal justice is predominantly administered in English and French.[1] Courts and tribunals rely greatly on interpretation and translation services to interact with potential witnesses, victims, and defendants. These predominant, official languages are very rarely first/mother tongues languages of the judges and other court personnel. For example, of the 18 current ICC judges, only 3 describe English as their mother/primary language in the ICC Questionnaire for Judicial Appointments,[2] whereas others appear to a have a command which varies from "good"[3] to "fluent" or "excellent." Knowledge of French is not mandatory, and only one judge is a French native speaker, whereas others attest to varying degrees of command, ranging from "none"[4] to "rusty"[5] (writing skills), "limited," "intermediate," "good," and "fluent." Moreover, the jurisdictional scope of the ICC means that the Court is now involved in investigating situations and trying cases from wide-ranging linguistic (e.g., Arabic, French, Swahili, Sango, Armenian, Bambara, Spanish) and cultural backgrounds. As the International Criminal Court continues to expand its activity and hybrid and regional tribunals are favored for the prosecution of international crimes in post-conflict settings, the interaction between English (and French) and original languages and its influence on criminal procedure will only increase; this has already become apparent in recent ICC cases. As a result, it is important to analyze both the impact and significance of possible ambiguities and inconsistencies in parallel multilingual interpretations, caused by dynamic interpretations grounded in legal conceptualizations, by instances where parts of testimonies were left non-translated or misinterpreted for various reasons.

There exists no formal process of assessing language nor paralinguistic abilities of international and hybrid criminal courts' judges. This is critical since judges have the duty and require competency to evaluate the adequacy of interpretation in order to ensure fairness of trial proceedings and the upholding of defense rights (Arzoz 2007, p. 10). Importantly, attention must also be paid to the presumed and actual neutrality of interpreters as key trial actors and the need for a uniform, standardized model for language accreditation for court and field interpreters within the international justice framework. The premise therefore is that translated versions of oral and written testimonies often neglect to take into account cultural and social connotations, expressed through particular cognitive and language means (Tonkin and Esposito 2010). These, due to linguistic ambiguities and different means of

---

[1] This is the case for the International Criminal Tribunal for the former Yugoslavia (ICTY), the International Criminal Tribunal for Rwanda (ICTR), and the International Criminal Court (ICC). The official language of the Special Court for Sierra Leone (SCSL) is only English.

[2] H. Morrison, Coalition for the International Criminal Court (CICC) Questionnaire for ICC Judicial Candidates, December 2011 Elections; G. A. Henderson (CICC, November 2013 Elections and C. Eboe-Osuji (CICC, 2009 Elections).

[3] C. Chung, (CICC, December 2014 Elections).

[4] See, e.g., R.C. Pangalangan (CICC, June 2015 Elections); G. A. Henderson (CICC, November 2013 Elections); and P. Hofmanski (CICC, December 2014 Elections).

[5] Morrison, supra, note 3.

expressions in both source and target language, are often either lost in translation or misinterpreted. Consequently, translated testimonies can reveal unintended meanings, which serve to persuade international judges to understand evidence in a particular light and to produce verdicts. Such defective interpretations can infringe defense rights and could lead to verdicts based on faulty findings of fact (Namakula 2012); the study of relevant case law reveals legal and trial outcome divergences that can clearly be traced in parallel multilingual legal documents because of varying phenomena of cultural, social, historical, and political nature.[6] The impact of defective or incompetent interpretations and translations bear, therefore, a clear correlation to some key aspects of the right to a fair trial.

Rights to a fair trial by an independent and impartial court and equality before the law in the ICCPR Articles 14 and 26, respectively, are considered minimum procedural standards and, therefore, fundamental rights.[7] Basic international human rights provisions such as ICCPR Art. 14 (3), on which the statutes and rules of procedure and evidence of international courts and tribunals are based, stipulate that in the determination of criminal charges a person must be informed promptly, in detail and in a language that he understands of that nature and cause of the charges against him. In affording these specific rights, neither ICCPR Art. 14 (3) nor ECHR Art. 6 (3)[8] requires that the accused also speaks the language, whereas other international instruments do.[9] For example, Rule 41 (A) of the ICTY and ICTR Rules of Procedure and Evidence require that a suspect be informed of his/her rights during investigation in a language that the suspect both understands and speaks.[10] During trial proceedings though, if the suspect or the accused does not understand or speak the language used in court during proceedings against them, they are entitled to have the free assistance of an interpreter (ICCPR Art. 14 (3) (f), ECHR Art. 6 (3) (e)).[11] These interpreters and translators employed by the courts must be "adequate," but international human rights law does not qualify this

[6] Studies dealing with the permanence, regularity, and systematization of ICC so far (Byrne 2007; Karton 2008, Nettelfield 2010; P&V International Team of the European Commission 2012) have produced valid theoretical assumptions in this field, but none of these have been proved empirically with the exception of Namakula (2013), who analyzed transcripts and conducted semi-structured interviews focusing on conversational analysis of courtroom discourse. She focused on data from the International Crimes Division of the High Court of Uganda. However, she has not compared bilingual versions of "identical" texts and has not undergone scrutiny of linguistic investigation into her data, which would supposedly support existing theoretical assumptions.

[7] UN Doc. GAOR, A/53/40/, pp. 20–21, para.104.

[8] When charged with a criminal offence, Art. 6 (3) (a) provides for a right to be informed promptly, in a language the suspect understands, and in detail, of the nature of cause of the charges against him.

[9] See, e.g., American Convention on Human Rights, Art, 8 (1).

[10] See also Principle 14 of the Body of Principles for the Protection of All Persons under any Form of Detention or Imprisonment 1988.

[11] See also, e.g., American Convention on Human Rights, Art. 8 (2) (a). General Comment No. 13 (Article 14), United Nations Compilation of General Comments, p. 125, para.13 provides that this right is independent on the outcome of the case.

requirement.[12] Accordingly, both "interpretations" and "translations" are language services provided by international criminal courts and tribunals. Within the ICC, both forms appear in the Regulations of the Court (Regulations of the Court, Reg. 40) and the Registry (Regulations of the Registry, Reg. 57); the ICC Registry defines and differentiates between "interpretation" and "translation" where interpretation conveys oral discussions/communication, whereas translation is the reproduction of the languages of documents and transcripts into another language.

Interpreters and Interpretation

One of the first issues to be examined in the context of multilingual and multicultural courts and tribunals is the definition of court interpreters and then their roles and functions. More than engaging in literal, simultaneous interpretations, interpreters in international courts engage in not-necessarily qualified roles of intercultural intermediaries and effectively coordinators of exchanges between prosecution, defense, witnesses, and judges (Dieter 2008, pp. 179–219). This is very significant as studies indicate that through those roles, interpreters can change intended meanings, which in turn shape perceptions of court participants. This can be done through rheme, whereby the interpreter conveys the sense of what is being said, rather than literal meaning or through paralinguistic methods (Chernov and Gelly 2004, p. 46). Here, both verbal and nonverbal nuances expressed by the interpreter convey his/her own reaction or credence in relation to what they are required to interpret, expressing "an attitude…either explicitly or implicitly, on the scale of evaluation from positive through neutral to negative" (Chernov and Gelly 2004, p. 54). In order to understand the literal meaning of the speaker, the interpreter inevitably has to try to understand and then convey implicit meanings and by doing so, the interpreter engages in cognitive intervention that cannot easily or readily be assessed for quality/authenticity (Chernov and Gelly 2004, p. 69; Eades 1995).

Nevertheless, in "international" criminal courts, interpreters are specifically required to convey all aspects of the speech. ICTY's Code of Ethics for Interpreters and Translators 1999 requires them to "convey the whole message…including any nonverbal clue, such as the tone of the voice and emotions of the speaker, which might facilitate the understanding of their listeners" (IT/44, Art.10 (1) (b)) without any embellishing, omitting, or editing (Art. 10 (i) and (c)). Understanding and monitoring this aspect of interpreting is key when the effect of paralinguistic interpretation influences the "reading" of testifying persons, influencing perceptions of their demeanor and that of the defendants, potentially tainting opinions relating to their honesty and credibility as well as their disposition to cooperate with the court. This

[12] United Nations Human Rights Office of the High Commissioner (OHCHR), Human Rights in the Administration of Justice: A Manual on Human Rights for Judges, Prosecutors, and Lawyers (2003), Chapter 6, p. 12.

is essential in multicultural environments as communicative styles vary and can have a significant impact on the construction of meaning (Adler and Rodman 2010, pp. 78–82). Communicative styles (e.g., eye contact, gesticulating, intonation, etc.) vary across cultural groups, and this is documented extensively in sociolinguistic studies, but the question here is whether interpreters are able to recognize and understand these variances and whether they are able, through adequate training, for instance, to convey them accurately to other participants, particularly to judges (Gibbons and Turell 2008, p. 187). In trying to interpret speech, during simultaneous interpretations, the interpreter uses her/his knowledge and experiences of communicative situations and semantic structure, which means that situational components can easily riddle the semantic ones Berg-Seligson (2008, pp. 12–33); Norman 2007, pp. 273–290).

There are also common tendencies among interpreters to often pause and either repeat or rephrase what has just been said, adding nuances to original testimonies (Garces 1996, p. 139). The pausing and repetition can add a sense of greater conviction and credence so that the interpreted testimony ends up more convincing than originally expressed in the source language (Garces 1996, p. 134). Cultural idiosyncrasies, too, leave room for interpretation inaccuracies as the translation of specific terms and notions implies a mutual intellectual knowledge between the speaker and the listener (Combs 2010, p. 75). Therefore, what is assumed and presumed may end up omitted and lost in translation. The crime of genocide and the corresponding burden of proof create here a tight legal spot. In the context of the mental element of inciting genocide and ethnic hatred, Dojcinovic observes that:

> *...there has not been a trial held so far before the ICTY without numerous references to the words or concepts "Ustasha", "Cetnik", "Turk", "Balija" and "Shquiptar" all so complex in their "meaning" and connotations that there is no adequate single interpretation of any of them. They are, in fact, conceptual structures...bearing no direct semantic correspondence.* (Dojcinovic 2012, p. 81)

This can have significant procedural effects as "lawyers tend to take their point of departure in the meaning of words, whereas translators rather take larger textual units like the sentence of the section as their point of departure" (Engberg 2002, p. 376; Villmoare 2008, p. 378). In the Karadzic case, the judge had to explain to the court that without a specific reference, the translators found it impossible to translate a line of a famous national poem the accused was referring to, "The Mountain Wreath".[13] So conceptualization, which is necessary on the part of the interpreters and translators, is inevitable, meaning that in a legal setting, their perceptions and understandings of contexts can modify the meaning of the communications and testimonies (Alexander 2006, p. 219; Moskowitz 2005, p. 9), affecting fact/trial outcomes (Coulthard and Johnson 2007, p. 59). Here, the interpreter too becomes a subject of contextualization by other trial participants, so complete certainty and neutrality cannot simply be presumed. The interpreter may, emotionally, con-

[13] Prosecutor v Karadzic, Case No. IT-95-5/18, Public Transcript, 12 February 2014, p. 46893, at 2.

sciously, or unconsciously, side with the court or the witness/accused (Zimanyi 2009, p. 59).

To minimize the impact court interpreters have on proceedings, it is generally accepted that they should not attempt to decipher paralinguistic gestures (Berk-Seligson 2017, p. 259). Any attempt to do so would be personal and not subject to any qualifying scrutiny, potentially leading to undesired and maybe even "comical effects" (p. 193). Understanding explicit but particularly implicit meanings of testimonies requires extralinguistic contextualization and knowledge as well as excellent ability to read various communicative situations and styles (Ephratt 2011, p. 2292). From this perspective, the authenticity of simultaneous interpretation depends on the skill and ability of the interpreter to convey the sense of the message and the extent to which his or her interference departs from the original meaning. On the other hand, a mechanical and rigid semantic transfer from the source language into target language requires exact parity and coincidence of parameters (grammatical, lexical, and even acoustic ones) between the two that may be difficult to identify.

Moreover, considering the important role demeanor and corresponding cultural communicative styles play in the courtroom and generally in the legal process, any interpretation of the same can influence perceptions of accuracy and credibility (Eades 2010, p. 93). Just to give a few examples of non-semantic messages, exaggerated hand gestures common in some cultures are used to emphasize a point but could be easily interpreted as indications of aggression in others. Likewise, silence is very common in Native American communication, but this could be interpreted in the Western culture as an avoidance tactic or indication that a person is not willing to cooperate or that they are hiding something (Eades 2010, p. 92). Talking too fast may also result in the interpreter not being able to follow quickly enough the testimony, which can create tension between the witness/accused and the judge. This is clear from the following example in the Karadzic case: the accused is asked by the judge to speak more slowly when the interpreter informs the court that they find it impossible to follow the testimony.[14] The judge then asks Karadzic to repeat a point by speaking very slowly, to which he replies "Your Honour, listen and understand what I'm saying…" The judge replies:

> *You probably don't understand. Unfortunately I do not understand your language. I hear from the interpreter's interpretation. If you speak so fast, it's impossible for them to interpret. (at 17–20)*

The issue is further complicated by indications that witness memory may be different in different languages (Filipovic 2013, pp. 1–19). The results of a recently conducted experiment on witness memories presented in English and Spanish, with the focus on expression of causal intentionality, point to ambiguities of English constructions which detract "from memory of intentionality in causation events, while the consistent tendency to differentiate intentional from non-intentional events in Spanish can result in an advantage of memory" (Filipovic 2013, 4). Hesitancy is also an interesting factor that can erroneously indicate uncertainty in what is communicated, as well

[14] Ibid. Public Transcript, 09 December 2013, p. 44785, at 11.

as evasive eye contact. Addressing the issues surrounding the interpretation of forcefulness of rape victims before the ICTY an observer concludes in fact that:

> *[i]nterruptions and errors focus attention on the linguistic mode of production rather than on the testimony itself. Undoubtedly, interpretation and translation problems have at times interfered with the overall impact of rape victim testimony and the presentation of evidence of rape. However, no feasible alternative exists.* (Coan 2000, p. 203)

While it is desirable that the interpreter conveys the meaning of the speech, such inferences alongside other paralinguistic methods can alter or undermine the precision of a testimony (Coan 2000, p. 203). Interpreters frequently use substitutions that undermine the fidelity of phonetic standards (Moosmuller 2011, pp. 179–205). Under the ICTY Code, for example, interpreters are required "to convey with greatest fidelity and accuracy, and with complete neutrality, the wording used by the persons they interpret or translate" (1999, IT/44, Art. 10 (1) (a)) and in cases of ambiguities they should request repetition, rephrasing, or explanation (Art. 10 (2)). Neutrality here is presumed, but it is not necessarily simple to maintain during prolonged trials. Studies have shown that when the interpreter is the only person to fully understand the accused or a witness, the risk of developing and establishing an emotional relationship is increased given that they share "the language…and culture, country of origin, the traditions, the ethnic group or even certain characteristics such as sex, age, experience" (Valero-Garces 2005; Morris 1999). Long war crime trials also produce environments where vicarious trauma affecting interpreters can occur. In a study of translation students, over sixty percent of participants reported experiencing some form of distress because of the subject matter they were involved with, and for that reason, over sixty-five percent felt unable to maintain neutrality (Valero-Garces 2005). Naturalistic studies of professional court interpretations indicate that:

> *faithful rendition of original utterances is highly demanding and the translatability of the stylistic features of spoken discourse may be limited under time pressures and cross-linguistic constraints* (Lee 2011, p. 2)

and that "interpreted renditions are inevitably interpreters' products based on their interpretation of the meaning and style of the original" (Lee 2011, p. 2). In order to facilitate and ensure that interpreters are adequately focused during difficult, often emotionally and technically demanding hearings (Heanel 1997, pp. 68–71), ICTY Code of Ethics for Interpreters provides that, and this is common to other multilingual court settings, there is a bank of backup interpreters who observe interpretations and alternate at regular intervals.However, the taking of breaks and alternating of interpreters is not straightforward. Factual and legal points identified during a hearing are likely to be raised during cross-examination, and from the perspective of persons testifying, it is imperative that there is lexical consistency, as well as continuity in conveying nonverbal messages and intention between alternating interpreters (Elias-Bursac 2015). This is crucial as the judges will, through these aspects of communication, measure the credibility of the witness and the veracity of their statements. When different interpreters adopt different styles in describing the same message, this potentially undermines the perceived reliability of the witness. The paralinguistic aspects of interpretation, as well as lexical ones, are important here as the aspects of speakers' communication such as expressions, tone, intonations, hesitations, and emotional displays need to be conveyed to the audience so the interpreter needs to adjust their voice and tone to convey meaning (Buring 2016, p. 17). To that end ICTR interpreters are specifically trained in Rwandan language, culture, and history, but this policy is not uniform among international criminal courts. This gap in uniformity is significant:

> *in legal translation, certain changes due to the role of the interpreter are produced which can lead to the witness's testimony being less convincing, too correct, lacking in veracity, or full of doubts, all of which proves that interpretation is not always innocent.* (Garces 1996, p. 139)

From this perspective, the understanding and conveying of non-semantic information becomes somewhat problematic, so it remains imperative that interpreters are qualified and adequately trained in paralinguistics and in the culturally specific communicative styles. For example, Article 9 (1) (a) of the ICTY Code for Interpreters and Translators states that interpreters and translators shall only accept assignments that they are competent to perform. This seems to imply that under the ICTY model (which is followed in other jurisdictions), there is no uniform or accepted method of assessing the competence of interpreters and translators; rather, they themselves, instead of the Tribunal, have the responsibility of making sure that they are able and skilled to undertake particular assignments. As such, this framework is uncertain and potentially, from the point of view of the defense, legally unsound. The ECtHR jurisprudence clearly indicates that the obligation ultimately rests with the presiding judge to ensure that interpreters are appointed and that those supervising them during proceedings are adequately monitored and, significantly, that it is therefore the role of the judge to have control over the adequacy of the interpretation provided.[15] The provision of services on the part of a court must be "effective"[16] – it cannot be procedurally safe that the court merely nominates/appoints interpreters without the competence, but more importantly, without the responsibility, to assess the adequacy and quality of their work. The duty to ensure a fair trial cannot be delegated to other trial actors. It must be firmly imposed on the judges. However, if the judges have not received specific linguistic and paralinguistic training, they are not in a position to adequately assess the quality of interpretation, which could mean that neither the accused nor the judges appreciate the potential poor quality of interpretation (Nakane 2013, p. 314). One possible, limited solution, limited because it would be ex post facto, would be to pass on the verification task to a court's Registry, as is the practice at the International Court of Justice.[17] The frequent delegation of the verification and authentication functions to third, out of court parties, is in fact unregulated and for that reason questionable. In a cost-

[15] Kamasinski v Austria, No. 9783/82, Judgment, 19 December 1989, para. 74.

[16] In relation to "effective legal assistance" under ECHR Art. 6 (3) (e), see supra note 11, Chap. 7, p. 17.

[17] ICJ Statute, Art 70 (2) of the Rules provides that the *Registrar shall make arrangements for the verification of the interpretation provided by a party of evidence given on the party's behalf. In the case of witnesses or experts who appear at the instance of the Court, arrangements for interpretation shall be made by the Registry.*

saving exercise, the ICTY used to outsource translations for the Office of the Prosecutor to nonqualified staff, such as data entry clerks.[18]

The issue is further compounded by the fact that the ICTY Code imposes an additional responsibility on interpreters and translators to:

> *ensure that the conditions under which they operate facilitates communication. In the event that an external element including technical hindrances...interferes with the accuracy or the completeness of their interpretation or translation, they shall inform their listeners or readers promptly. (ICTY Code, Art. 9 (1) (c))*

As already mentioned, there is no uniform or single procedure in international criminal law for the appointment of interpreters and translators. Their qualifications, level of competence, professionalism, and status therefore vary significantly across jurisdictions. ICTY and ICTR, as UN courts, are parties to the AIIC (International Association of Conference Interpreters) – United Nations Agreement 2012–2017, which regulates the appointment of short-term conference interpretation services to UN organizations. The Agreement specifies terms and conditions of employment of conference interpreters and stipulates some minimum professional standards that should be met by the host organization such as, for example, the type of simultaneous interpretation facilities that should be installed according to internationally set standards. The Agreement also provides for various privileges and immunities for those employed under the Agreement (Sec. 2 (10) (a) – interpreters shall have the status of officials, pursuant to the Convention on Privileges and Immunities of the United Nations), social security (Sec. 28), terms over loss of earnings, sickness, accident insurance, and sick leave (Ss.29–30). Alongside competitive remuneration, these conditions offer incentives and benefits that are often not available to field interpreters and generally courts outside the UN structure that are often involved at domestic levels' pretrial proceedings. Because field interpreters are often not professional linguists, but nevertheless play a key role in investigations and more often than not need to work in conflict zones,[19] the ICC specifically provides that during suspect questioning, a competent, rather than a civilian, interpreter must be present. However, competency is not defined in the Statute even though investigative stages are particularly difficult as the rules governing these vary significantly at domestic levels too; an example would be Japan where police interviews may not even be recorded (Nakane 2013, p. 310). In Tadic, the ICTY recognized that "[t]here is no statement taken during the course of the investigation that will be a verbatim report of what the witnesses say".[20] Identifying inadequate interpretation and then quantifying the inaccuracies in order to determine their impact on proceedings are problematic, but at the domestic level, there are a number of cases that attempt to set a threshold beyond which proceedings may be invalidated. For example, in Tran, the

[18] Report of the Court on options for outsourcing translation work, ICC-ASP/7/5, 26 May 2008, para. 13.

[19] See, e.g., Conflict Zone Field Guide for Civilian Translators/Interpreters and Users of their Services 2012. www.fit-ift.org/wp-content/uploads.2013/03/T-I_Field_Guide_2012.pdf. Accessed 24 August 2017.

[20] Prosecutor v Tadic, Case No. IT-94-1-T, Transcript, May 7, 1996, at 47.

Canadian Supreme Court held that interpretation mistakes and omissions violate the right to interpretation only when they affect "vital interests of the accused" rather than "collateral or extrinsic" matters.[21] In Begum, the British Court of Appeal ruled that interpretation was inadequate when the interpreter did not have "full competency" in Punjabi, the native language of the accused.[22] This case prompted numerous changes in the British Criminal Justice System in relation to standards and policies regarding interpretation services. A framework was therefore created, under the National Agreement on Arrangements for the Use of Interpreters and Language Service Professionals in Investigations and Proceedings within the Criminal Justice System, which was last revised in 2011 (Ministry of Justice (MoJ), August 2011). The resulting framework provides for the exclusive use of NRPSI interpreters when selecting face-to-face interpreters for criminal investigations working in police stations as well as courts, and the Chartered Institute of Linguists (CIOL) developed other specific and accredited qualifications, including a Diploma in Translating and a Certificate in Bilingual Skills.

From a strictly lexical viewpoint, international criminal courts deal with multi-ethnic conflicts where defendants and witnesses predictably speak a variety of languages, local dialects which are then normally translated into English, whereby English is more often than not a second language for judges (Karton 2008, p. 718). Dialects too pose a great challenge as the interpreter needs additional training, and in some contexts, especially within the ICTR, defendants and witnesses speak different dialects, which can be "stigmatized and denigrated in the society generally" (Gibson and Turrel 2008, p. 184; see also Brown 2006; Candlin and Gotti 2007). In Akayesu, the ICTR acknowledged that interpreting some of the oral testimony of the witnesses into one of the working languages of the Tribunals has been a "particularly great challenge due to the fact that the syntax and everyday modes of expression in the Kinyarwanda language are complex and difficult to translate into French or English" (Akayesu, Judgment, para. 145). Knowledge of colloquial expressions in two or more languages is critical in the context of any trial but particularly in hybrid and multilingual and multicultural criminal trials. Interpreters are responsible for maintaining the fidelity from the source to the target language and vice versa. The East Timor Special Panels, for example, work in four official languages; the majority of defendants and their lawyers speak Indonesian, prosecutors and international lawyers generally speak English, and the judges tend to use English and Portuguese. Defendants and witnesses also speak local dialects, such as Bunak and Fataluku. On observation of proceedings, a report produced by the Judicial Systems Monitoring Report (JSMP) back in 2001 concluded that in one particular case, "the defendant's credibility was impugned because of apparent inconsistencies in his testimony… [the] possibility cannot be discounted that the alleged inconsistencies were simply the product of language difficulties between the participants in court".[23] In the context of hybrid/internationalized systems and

[21] R v Tran (1994) 117 DLR 7, p. 40.

[22] R v Iqbal Begum (1991) 93 Cr App R 96, p. 100.

[23] Judicial Systems Monitoring Programme (JSMP), Justice in Practice: Human Rights in Court Administration – JSMP Thematic Report 1(Dili: JSMP), 2001.

deferred and referred cases from international criminal courts and tribunals to domestic ones (e.g.,, under the ICC Art. 17 complementarity model), this also raises the question of capacity and resources. Locally, defendants are less likely to have access to resources, adequate interpretation, and translation that is comparable to those provided at the ICC, for example, access to documents and generally to international expertise such as qualified interpreters and translators. As a case in point, UNTAET Regulation 2000/64 did not provide provisions for overseas defenders, nor for a specialized hybrid defense office. This vacuum creates procedural settings that can seriously undermine the rights of the accused in terms of free interpretation and translations of documents in a language he/she speaks and understands as protected under ICCPR Article 14 (3) (f) and the right of the accused to have adequate time and facilities to prepare a defense under Article 14 (3) (b).

Likewise in Kosovo, the UNMIK established panels also suffered from understaffing of adequately qualified interpreters and translators to the point of being described as "fundamentally flawed"[24] because proceedings, particularly before 2005, were often conducted in a language that neither the accused nor their defense team understood and were not simultaneously translated but merely summarized (Villmoare 2008, p. 378). This is significant in the context of minimum ICCPR guarantees. While Articles 14 (3) (b) and (f) do not provide for an explicit right for the accused to be furnished with copies of all relevant documents in a criminal investigation in a language that he understands, relevant documents must be made available to his counsel.[25]

Considering the great cultural divergences in multilingual and multicultural judicial settings, it is imperative that not only interpreters, (including field interpreters) and translators but particularly those responsible for determining probative value of evidence as well as the determination and mitigation of sentences receive adequate training in paralinguistics and sociolinguistics. At the ICC, the Language Services Unit of the Office of the Prosecutor recognized early on the crucial need to develop an accreditation system for permanent and field interpreters.[26] The need for training should also be promoted among lawyers, advocates, and domestically those collecting evidence and those responsible for investigative interviews and pretrial detention.

Interpreter as Witness in International Criminal Proceedings

According to numerous domestic criminal rules, during investigative stages, when police or competent authority interview a suspect through an interpreter, and what has been said is challenged, the interpreter becomes a witness to proceedings and

[24] Amnesty International 2008. Kosovo (Serbia) - The challenge to fix a failed UN justice system arose (January 2008), AI: EUR 70/001/2008, p. 51.

[25] Supra note 11, Chap. 6, pp. 21–23.

[26] See, e.g., Report on programme performance of the International Criminal Court for the year 2007, ICC-ASP/7/8/, p. 39.

may be summoned to give evidence in court under oath. At the international level, however, there has been great reluctance to involve interpreters in proceedings even though the position of the Human Rights Committee is that restrictions imposed on the cross-examination of certain witnesses significantly undermines the right to access to justice and equality of arms.[27]

A good example is provided in the Mucic case at the ICTY. In that case, the Defense submitted that the accused erroneously, and after an unofficial conversation with interviewing police officers during arrest and detention at which an interpreter was present, agreed to forfeit his right to legal representation.[28] Mucic therefore contended that there was an omission in the transcripts of this conversation and that the interpreter was a potential witness of the omission. Mucic also argued that, being an independent party to the proceedings, the interpreter would be the most likely party to provide a truthful account through cross-examination, claiming that the police officers were "not likely to be truthful against their interests" (Decision, 08 July 1997, para. 14) and that such cross-examination was necessary for the conduct of the trial. The Tribunal dismissed the Motion, holding that the interpreter is not responsible for the authentication and that it is procedurally undesirable to involve them in the conflict between the parties (ICTY Rules of Procedure and Evidence, Rule 54).

At a domestic level, the position could not be more different. In the United Kingdom, for instance, where a suspect in detention is interviewed through an interpreter and an issue arises as to the accuracy of proceedings, the interpreter becomes a witness and is required to provide evidence (Archbold, 4–36). Importantly, evidence from interviewing or investigative police officers about what the accused has said during the interview is hearsay, whereby the interpreter is the only valid witness as to what the defendant said.[29] Another feature of the British model is that the interpreter used during investigative stages and in police stations, or in the course of investigations conducted by other agencies, should not be interpreting in court. However, if the language in question is rare (the ICC has already encountered this problem) and it may be difficult to find a fully qualified replacement, all parties as well as the court must be informed of the intention to employ the same interpreter.[30] This may be even harder to comply with when there are more than two defendants as domestic law normally requires that each defendant should have a separate interpreter.[31]

[27] Human Rights Committee, 2007. General Comment No.32, Article 14: Right to equality before courts and tribunals and the fair trial, U.N. Doc. CCPR/C/GC/32 (2007).

[28] Prosecutor v Delalic et al., ex parte Zdravko Mucic, Case No. IT-96-21, Decision on the Motion Ex Parte by the Defense of Zdravko Mucic Concerning the Issue of a Subpoena to an Interpreter, 08 July 1997.

[29] See National Agreement on Arrangements for the Use of Interpreters, Translators and Language Service Professionals in Interrogations and Proceedings within the Criminal Justice System, 2007.

[30] R (Bozturk) v Thames Magistrates' Court, Time Law Reports, 26 June 2001.

[31] See, e.g., Prosecution of Offences Act 1985, Sec. 19 (3) (b).

Development of Language Rights in Recent International Criminal Law Cases

The statutes of the ICC, ICTY, ICTR, and SCSL provide for the right of the accused to interpretation and translation into and from a language he fully understands and speaks.[32] The right under the ICC Statute is broader in that it expressly requires that interpretation be "competent." The general requirement in ICCPR Art. 14 that the courts and tribunals must be competent, independent, and impartial is considered to be an absolute right, relating not only to procedure but also to qualification and appointment of judges.[33]

Within recent ICC proceedings, issues relating to quality of interpretations, translations, and corresponding fairness of trial concerns have been identified frequently.[34] In Lubanga, an originally confidential document revealed that the rotation of four interpreters during the trial was disruptive and detrimental to the quality of proceedings, which in turn led to the production of poor transcripts[35] and that motivation of freelance interpreters, which had an impact on the overall quality of interpretation, did not always match that of court interpreters (Lubanga, 15 July, para. 8). Moreover, due to the shortage of English freelance interpreters, both English and French interpreters worked in the English booth. Within a month it became apparent that non-English interpreters, namely, French ones, had a significant impact on interpretations due to the heavy influence of French syntax, resulting in unusual and confusing sentences (para. 8). Article 6 (2) of the ICTY Code requires that court interpreters inform the judges if they have any doubt about the translation or a lexical lacunae in the source or target language but, as the Lubanga case shows, interpreters themselves may not be aware of these. As a result, in Lubanga the Court underwent a process of transcript reviews (para. 11), but it can be argued that this review is of limited value, as by this point the judges may have already formed opinions regarding the demeanor of the witness and reliability of the evidence (Spears 2003, pp. 126, 131; Gaiba 1998, p. 95). During these reviews, it also became apparent that this issue is further exacerbated by the fact that difficult testimony expressions/words are often omitted, misinterpreted, or misunderstood by the interpreter but identified by court reporters and vice versa (Lubanga, para. 13) and by the fact that, unexpectedly, most ICC witnesses, including politicians, tend to testify in Kinyarwanda rather than French (the latter had normally been the case in the ICTR (para. 16)).

---

[32] ICC Statute (Arts. 55 (1) (c) and 67 (1) (f)), ICTY Statute (Arts. 18 (3) and 21 (4) (f)), ICTR Statute (Arts. 17 (3) and 20 (4) (f)) and the SCSL Statute (Art. 17 (4) (d)).

[33] Human Rights Committee 2007, General Comment No. 32, Article 14: Right to equality before courts and tribunals and for a fair trial, U.N. Doc. CCPR/C/GC/32 (2007). See also Art. 2 (8) EU Directive 2010/64/EU on Fair Trial: suspects' rights to itnerpretation and translation in criminal proceedings which provides that interpretation must of ''sufficient quality to safeguard the fairness of the proceedings."

[34] For example, Ntaganda, Case No. ICC_01/04-02/06, Decision Requesting Observations from the Interpretation and Translation Section, 19 Sept. 2013).

[35] Lubanga, Case No. ICC-01/04-01/06, Registry report on interpretation matters, 15 July 2009, para. 4.

The AIIC-United Nations Agreement (2012–2017) shows examples of good practice that could be followed at the ICC and domestic trials under complementarity. For instance, there shall be at least two interpreters assigned to a booth (Sec. 31 (a)); no single interpreter should be solely responsible for providing relay from a specific working language (Sec. 31 (b)) and, therefore, in two-language settings serviced from one booth at least three interpreters able to work in both languages should be assigned (Sec. 31 (c)). Moreover, interpreters should not be assigned for more than 2.5–3 h per meeting (Sec. 32 (c)), and they should have a break of at least 1.5 h in between sessions (Sec. 32 (b)). However, at the ICC at least, given the workload, this is not always achievable because interpreters whose session has ended[36] are often expected to assist others by cross-referencing legislative provisions, such as the Statute or the Rules of the Court.[37]

Understanding and Speaking the Language of the Court

The right to a fair trial in international human rights law does not imply that an accused be necessarily allowed to use in proceedings his/her mother tongue nor the language that he/she is most competent in, as long as their proficiency in the court's language is "sufficient." Importantly, it appears that the courts do not have the duty to determine whether it would be more desirable for an accused to express himself in a language other than the court's language.[38] International human rights law and jurisprudence indicate varying languages competency thresholds required to trigger the right to free assistance of an interpreter. Some instruments refer to the ability of an accused to both understand and speak the language of the court "adequately,"[39] "fully" (ICC Rule 76), or "sufficiently" (ICCPR Art. 14 (3) (f)). In relation to translation and disclosure of documents, the Human Rights Committee General Comment No. 32 (2007) shows that, if the accused does not understand the language used in court, procedural rights to fairness may be satisfied if relevant documents are made available to his/her counsel who is "familiar" with the official language. The right to a fair trial under the ECHR also includes the right to free interpretation, if the accused cannot understand or speak the language of the court (Article 6 (3) (e)). ICTY and ICTR Rules of Procedure and Evidence qualify this right by providing that when the accused wishes to use a language other than the working languages of the respective courts or the language of the accused, the cost of such interpretation

---

[36] AIIC – United Nations Agreement (2012–2017). Agreement between the United Nations Common System/Chief Executives Board for Coordination and the Association Internationale des Interpretes de Conference, regulating the Conditions of Employment. https://aiic.net/page6394/un-latest-version-of-the-agreement-2012-2017/lang/1. Accessed 24 August 2017.

[37] Ibid.

[38] Supra note 11, Chap. 7, p. 24.

[39] See, e.g., Body of Principles for the Protection of All Persons Under Any Form of Detention or Imprisonment 1988, Principle 14.

should be borne by the Tribunal, unless it is not in the interests of justice to do so (Rule 3 (A)). However, in Boskoski and Tarculovski, the ICTY held that:

> *the fact that the accused, who has chosen to defend himself, does not speak either of the working languages of the Tribunal, does not mean that it is in the interests of justice to assign legal assistance to him free of charge or that it raises a fair trial issue.*[40]

ICC Statute Article 50 (3) allows any party to proceedings (including a State) to request from the Court authorization to use a language other than English or French, and such authorization should be granted if the Court finds that its use is "adequately justified," so additional considerable problems stumbled upon by the ICC relate to interpretation and translation of non-codified languages. For example, in Nourain,[41] the ICC had great difficulties in finding and training of Zaghawa (a non-written language with a vocabulary of around 5000 words) interpreters which led to considerable delays[42] in meeting the obligation of providing the accused with all prosecution witness statements in a language which they could fully understand (ICC Rule 76) as well as the document containing the charges. In 2011, the Registry estimated that the recruitment process would take around 30 months (Nourain, para. 5) which the Defense argued would irreparably jeopardize fair trial rights, starting with the basic right to be informed of the charges against the accused[43] and given that Article 67 (1) (a) of the Statute confirms the right for the accused to be informed of the charges in a language that he or she fully both understands and speaks. This provision further provides for the right to have the assistance of a competent interpreter and all translations as necessary to meet the requirements of fairness should any of the proceedings or documents presented to the Court not be in a language that the accused fully understands and speaks.[44]

This also applies to investigative and pretrial questioning when conducted by the Prosecutor or relevant national authorities (Art. 55 (c)), and during an investigation, all interviews with a suspect should also be audio or video recorded and a copy of the tape(s) given to the suspect (ICC Rule 112; ICTY Rule 43 (iv)). In Katanga, ICC's Appeals Chamber held that the relevant standard used in determining the level of language proficiency and understanding of the accused for the purposes of

---

[40] Decision on the Motions on the Fair Trial and Extensions of Time, Case No. IT-04-82-PT, 19 May 2006, para. 13.

[41] Case No. ICC-02/05-03/09, Order to the Prosecution and the Registry on Translation Issues, 07 September 2011.

[42] According to the Human Rights Committee's General Comment No. 32, what amounts to a considerable delay should be decided objectively but on a case-by-case, taking into account the complexity of the case, the relevant conduct of the accused person and that of the competent authority (Chap. 7, p. 11).

[43] Defense Submission of the Translation of Incriminatory Evidence, Case No. ICC-02/05-03/09-195, 08 August 2011, paras. 2 and 3.

[44] ICC Statute Art. 67 (1) (f) See also The Prosecutor v Bahr Idriss Abu Garda, Decision on the Prosecutor's Request for Extension of Time-Limit, ICC-02/05-02/09-98, 11 September 2009, p. 59. Here the confirmation of charges hearing was postponed so that the suspect with a list of evidence and witness statements in Arabic, the suspect's native language and importantly, one of the Court's official languages.

meeting the requirements of Article 67 is "high, higher, for example, than that applicable to the European Convention of Human Rights and the ICCPR."[45] The affording of ICC rights generally should be "proactive…and of a higher degree than in other courts" (para. 3). This approach is in line with the jurisprudence of the ECtHR where, in the determination of the "interests of justice," the Court should consider the gravity of the alleged offence and the potential severity of the sentence.[46] To apply this higher standard, the language requested by the accused "should be granted unless it is absolutely clear on the record that the person fully understands and speaks one of the working languages of the Court and is abusing his or her right under Article 67 of the Statute."[47]

Yet, one of the problems here is deciding how and who should determine the relevant language competencies of the accused. The ICC Statute, its Rules of Procedure and Evidence, and Regulations of the Court and the Registry are silent on this point, but the Appeals Chamber held in Katanga that "[t]he subject of understanding is exclusively the accused."[48] Therefore, in the absence of clearly developed and established criteria for assessing whether a person is fluent in a particular language in nontechnical conversation, the Chamber "must give credence to the accused's claim that he or she cannot fully understand and speak the language of the Court"[49] and, as the Defense contended, a request for services in a particular language should only be denied if the Court is convinced that such a request is not a genuine one. The Court went on to emphasize that "[t]his is because it is the accused who can most aptly determine his or her own understanding and it should be assumed that he or she will only ask for a language he or she fully understands and speaks."[50] In Katanga, the defendant requested interpretation and translation to and from Lingala. The Court stated that a language that one fully understands and speaks is normally one's mother tongue (ICC-01/04-01/07, 21 January 2008, para. 12), but, given that the Court has not before had to deal with this language or provide language services in Lingala and that the Registry concluded that the defendant had reasonable understanding of French, he was provided with "liaison interpretation."

Under Regulation 61 (d) of the Regulation of the Registry, this type of interpretation is defined as interpretation where interpreters interpret aloud, normally in and out of two or more languages, and interpreting a few sentences at a time. Given the obvious fidelity issues inherent in this type of interpretation, the Court was dubious as to whether liaison interpretation could be adequate and whether its accuracy and

[45] Defense Response to the Report of the Registrar on the Provision of Lingala Interpretation for Germain Katanga at the Trial Stage, ICC-01/04-01/07, 04 February 2009, para. 3.

[46] Supra note 11, Chap. 7, p. 16.

[47] ICC-01/04-01/07-522, paras. 61–62.

[48] Defence Response to the Report of the Registrar on the Provision of Lingala Interpretation for Germain Katanga at the Trial Stage, ICC-01/04-01/07, 04 February 2009, para.6.

[49] Report of The Registrar on the Provision of Lingala Interpretation for Germain Katanga at the Trial Stage, Trial Chamber II, ICC-01/04-01/07, 21 January 2008, para. 23.

[50] Appeals Chamber, "Judgment on the appeal of Mr. Germain Katanga against the decision of PreTrial Chamber I entitled "Decision on the Defence Request Concerning Languages", ICC-01/04-01/07-522, para.59.

quality could at all be equated with simultaneous interpretation.[51] The Court held effectively that liaison interpretation did not significantly benefit the accused and that a reasonable rather than full command of the French was "sufficient" to fulfill the requirements of Article 67 (1) (a) and (f), particularly in view of the fact that the Registrar and the Defense had previously agreed that the accused understood and spoke French to a reasonable standard (ICC-01/04-01/07-175, para. 47). On the basis that the accused was probably able to understand parts or most parts of proceedings against him, the Court indicated that there was no real danger that the accused could miss key elements of the evidence against him. It is for the Trial Chamber dealing with a particular case to determine the language(s) to be used at trial.[52] Even though the ICC established that, in case of doubt as to whether a defendant fully speaks and understands one of the court languages, the language being requested by the person should be accommodated, this request in Katanga was not honored in view of the fact that Lingala was not his mother tongue. The Court made a distinction between mother tongue and a "language of reference," the latter being a language one is exposed to but the command of which is not necessarily full. The Court here concluded that in the context of mixed or bilingual families "speaking different languages to the children does not imply that these children fully understand and speak every language they hear" (Katanga, 21 January 2008, para. 13). It followed therefore in Katanga that he was exposed to a number of languages, but a full command could not be implied in any of them, any more than his command of French could.[53] One of the reasons for this narrow approach to affording language services could be that the Court is facing increasing translation costs, affecting the budget of the Court; requests for judicial cooperation documentation alone have to be produced in over 20 languages. While such rationalization may seem logical, the Human Rights Committee has confirmed on a number of occasions that financial/economic difficulties cannot be used to restrict rights to equality before the law and the right to be tried "without undue delay" or "within reasonable time" as these represent minimum standards.[54]

Right to Review Transcripts

Directly related to the issue of poor interpretations and corresponding translations is that of the right to review translated court transcripts. Yet, judges are often reluctant to allow the review of transcripts unless they relate to the communication of

---

[51] The Prosecutor v Germain Katanga and Mathieu Ngudjolo, Report of The Registrar on the Provision of Lingala Interpretation for Germain Katanga at the Trial Stage, Trial Chamber II, ICC-01/04-01/07, 21 January 2008, para.20.

[52] ICC Statute, Art. 64 (3) (b) and ICC Rule 41 (2).

[53] See also The Prosecutor v William Samoci Ruto et al., Registry's assessment of Mr. Joshua Arap Sang's English Proficiency Level, ICC-01/09-01/11, 31 March 2011.

[54] See, e.g., Lubunto v Zambia, Communication No. 390/1990, U.N. Doc. GAOR, A/51/40 (vol.II), p. 14, para. 7.3. See also Standard Minimum Rules for the Treatment of Prisoners (Nelson Mandela Rules) 2015, Rules 61 and 80.

charges or key evidence. This appears to be particularly the case in hybrid and internationalized courts, and there are numerous examples. In cases before the Kosovo panels, translated transcripts of relevant proceedings are often delayed so much that that time for appeals elapses. This seriously undermines the rights of accused persons and in such cases proceedings should be void. Given the complexity of war crimes trials and the need for expediency, local lawyers are sometimes reluctant to seek translation of documents or ask for review of transcripts as they do not want to be perceived by judges as "an enemy of the court" (Amnesty International, Kosovo (Serbia), p. 52).

In Naletilic and Martinovic, the ICTY held that its Statute, namely, Article 21 and Rule 3 of the Rules of Procedure and Evidence, does not necessarily entitle an accused to obtain all documents from the prosecution in a language that he/she understands and that the procedural and trial guarantees of the Statute (Art. 21 (4)) do not extend to all documents but only to evidence used by the Tribunal to determine charges against the accused (Rule 66 (A).[55] However, a couple of years after this decision, the ECtHR ruled that under ECHR Art. 6 (3):

> *the right...to have free assistance of an interpreter extends to all those documents or statements in the criminal proceedings which it is necessary for the accused to understand or to have rendered into court's language in order to have the benefit of a fair trial.*[56]

In addition, the right to equality of access and equality of arms as guaranteed in ICCPR Art. 14 (1) requires that same procedural rights are to be provided to both the prosecution and the defense. Although this article is not absolute, any procedural or otherwise differentiations between the parties must be based on law and may only reasonably be justified when this does not amount to "actual disadvantage or other unfairness to the defendant" (General Comment No. 32, para. 3).[57] In Prlic et al., the ICTY Appeals Chamber decided that the Tribunal (specifically, the Trial Chamber) has the discretion to determine the scope and extent of language services available without jeopardizing defense rights.[58] Here, a defendant made a request to the Registry for the translation of around 5000–7000 pages of evidence; he was allowed the translation of 1810 UN standard pages and an additional 1500 following the appeal (para. 4). The Appeals Chambers concluded the defendant failed to demonstrate substantial prejudice to his case or rather his ability to prepare a defense (although it was recognized that he would have to reconsider his defense strategy) and that equality of arms does not equate to equality of resources between the prosecution and the defense (para. 30). It was acknowledged, however, that Article 21 of the ICTY Statute allows for individualized assessments of translation resources allocated to the accused (para. 5). This position must be qualified with

---

[55] Case No. IT-98-34-T, Decision on defense's motion concerning translation of all documents, Order, 18 October 2001.

[56] Lagerblom v Sweden, ECtHR (2003), Application No. 26891/95, 14 March 2003, para. 61.

[57] See also Arts. 3(1) and (2) of the African Chapter on Human and Peoples' Rights 1987.

[58] Prosecutor v Prlic et al., Case No. IT-04-74-T, Decision on Slobodan Praljak's Appeal of the Trial Chamber's 13 October 2008 Order Limiting the Translation of Defense Evidence, 05 December 2008, para. 11.

reference to the right to equality of arms under ICCPR Article 14 (1) because affording and depriving of language services must not negate the right of an accused person to participate in proceedings in a "meaningful way" (General Comment No. 32, para. 2).

These competing rights require forensic accuracy in legal translations that must not be underplayed (Dieter et al. 2009, pp. 39–42). In Nikolic M., the ICTY Trial Chamber was influenced by, and decided accordingly to the detriment of the accused, a translation which suggested he was effectively deriding the gravity of his crimes. The Tribunal's language services eventually confirmed that that was an error in the translation which, the accused argued, had a detrimental impact on the assessment of his remorse as a mitigating factor. The Appeals Chamber took into account the damaging outcome of the Trial Chamber's assessment of facts and mitigated the sentence accordingly.[59] Similarly, in Halilovic et al., the Trial Chamber acknowledged receiving two different translations, one reading "directing combat operations," while the other referred to the "control of combat operations."[60] The word "directing" was misleading here because, when translated into English, it implied greater military responsibility.[61]

At the ICTR, the Akayesu case illustrated that there are also fundamental flaws in the translation and interpretation of key documents, such as the actual ICTR Statute; the ICTR evaluated the translation of crimes against humanity in English and French deciding that the French version was more accurate as it implied the required element of premeditation.[62] In view of the fact that translations of key texts often vary, in 2010 the ICC-ASP Bureau proposed the appointment of a Linguistic Drafting Committee with specific powers to make recommendations in relation to linguistic accuracy and constituency across numerous translations of draft amendments to the Rome Statute, particularly in relation to draft elements of crime before these were to be adopted.[63] The ICC routinely outsources translations of key texts and sensitive documents to external translators who normally work for UN agencies, such as the International Court of Justice and the Organization for the Prohibition of Chemical Weapons (ICC-ASP/7/5, para. 2). However, when there is doubt as to the interpretation of legal texts, and by extension, versions of translations of identical texts, the *in dubio pro reo* principle should apply so that a version more favorable to the accused should be adopted. Expediency always plays a part when the court has to make a balancing act between defense rights and effective management of the court's time and resources. Given that the burden of proof rests with the prosecution to prove the case beyond reasonable doubt, it may not always be necessary to allow for the translation of every single document at the expense of

[59] Prosecutor v Momir Nikolic, Case No. IT-02-60/1-A, 08 March 2008, Judgment on Sentencing Appeal.

[60] Prosecutor v Halilovic Sefer, Case No. IT-01-48, Judgment, 16 November 2005, p. 83.

[61] Public Transcript of Hearing, 21 April 2005, p. 64, paras.5–10.

[62] Jean-Paul Akayesu, Case No. ICTR-96-4-T, Judgment, 02 September 1998, para. 589.

[63] Ninth ICC-ASP Bureau Meeting, 29 April 2010.

the court, but the translation of the court's own decisions in other cases, as well as those of other international criminal courts, clearly should be.

In Seselj, the ICTY Registry refused to translate into Serbian (the chosen language of the accused) three relevant Rwandan judgments that dealt with the definition of genocide and burden of proof of *dolus specialis*, as well as one of its own judgments (Limaj). As a result, the defendant, or rather his defense team, had to bear the cost for those translations.[64] The ICC Statute now clearly states in Article 50 (1) that all judgments of the Court should be published in all the official languages of the Court (Arabic, Chinese, English, French, Russian, and Spanish) and under Rule 40 that the Presidency can decide to publish any other decisions in all the official languages, if they relate to any "major issues relating to the interpretation or the implementation of the Statute or concern a major issue of general interest."

Linguistic and Paralinguistic Competence of the Judges

The general inability of judges in international criminal courts and tribunals to speak and understand more than one of the working languages of the court and mother tongues of defendants and witnesses is a significant obstacle in the administration of international criminal justice (Wald 2000, pp. 193–194). In fact, it is very rare that a judge could conduct a trial in more than one language (Wald 2001, p. 92). Equally, judges, although responsible for the conduct of trials and ultimately the protection of trial rights, are not linguists and are not required to have acquired any relevant paralinguistic or sociolinguistic training. Potentially therefore, they can be influenced by the way in which both the defendant and the interpreter express themselves. This likely produces a bias and as a result, a procedural lacuna, the resolution of which is both ambitious and multifaceted.

Linguistic Competence

Generally speaking, when it comes to appointing international judges, the governing rules and procedures are fairly vague and language skills have been largely neglected, the only requirement normally being that one of the working languages of the court or tribunal is spoken fluently. For example, ICTY and ICTR Statutes simply require that both permanent and ad litem judges be of high moral character, are impartial and have integrity, and possess qualifications required in their respective countries for appointment to the highest judicial offices (Articles 13 and 12, respectively). The Report of the Secretary-General on the establishment of a Special Court for Sierra Leone under SC Resolution 1315 (2000) made a clear and

[64] Public Transcript of Hearing 04 July 2007, pp. 1306–1307.

important recommendation that in seeking to appoint qualified personnel to the Court from UN State Members, particular weight should be given to attracting and securing persons from the Commonwealth, who would share the same language[65] and understanding of the common-law legal system.[66] This recommendation was not limited to judges but included prosecutors, Registrar, investigators, and administrative staff.

The need to add language skills into the judicial appointments criteria has also been recognized in the ICC Statute, but this does not extend to mandatory bilingualism. Nevertheless, the Court, through its Statute (Art. 50 (2)) and the Strategic Plan, endeavors to become a truly bilingual court. Under Article 36 (3) (a), the main criteria mirror that of the ad hoc tribunals, but subsections (b) and (c) go further, requiring that "every candidate for the election to the Court shall have an excellent knowledge of and be fluent in at least one of the working languages of the Court" and that during the selection process State Parties need to take into account the need for the representation of the principal legal systems of the world (ss. 8 (a) (i)) as well as equitable geographical representation (ss. 8 (a) (ii)). The Statute also requires States Parties to take into account the need to nominate judges who have specific legal expertise on specific issues, particularly violence against women and children (ss. 8 (b)). In addition, ICC's minimum voting requirements require that potential judges have established competence in criminal law and procedure, and the necessary relevant experience in judicial capacity, in criminal proceedings ("List A" judges under Art. 36 (3) (b) (i)) and that there should be at least two judges with established competence in relevant international law ("List B" judges under Art. 36 (3) (b) (ii)). Given the criticisms of the selection of judges at the ICTY, who often had little or inadequate criminal trial or general judicial experience with complex and often very long criminal cases (Bohlander 2007, p. 326), recent appointments of international criminal courts judges, particularly since the ICC Statute, focus on their qualifications and experience in criminal law, international law, including international humanitarian law and human rights law.

These requirements indicate that the key issue in the appointment of judges is one of capacity and that specific requirements of bilingualism would significantly narrow the pool from which suitable candidates would be nominated and overall compromise the quality of decisions and proceedings. As the Advisory Committee on Nomination of Judges (ACN) highlighted in its 2013 report (29 October 2013, ICC-ASP/12/47, p. 5), now that pretrial and trial proceedings have increased, the ICC must ensure that proceedings are managed effectively while ensuring respect for the rights of defendants. This requires a judicial membership that is very accustomed to the intensity and demands of war crimes trials. However, second-language learning and training opportunities for judges within the ICC framework are also nonmandatory, but the Court does provide courses in practical French for judges on

[65] Article 18 of the Agreement between the UN and Sierra Leone 2002 requires that English be the official language of the Special Court.

[66] Report of the Secretary-General on the establishment of a Special Court for Sierra Leone, 04 October 2000, S/2000/915, para.59.

how to read decisions and legal texts (ICC-ASP/7/5, para. 18). Recently, in the Letter to Foreign Ministers on the Election of Judges to the International Criminal Court (26 March 2014), Human Rights Watch urged states to seriously consider and, more importantly, implement recommendations made by the ACN that their analysis of each candidate's both legal expertise and fluency in one of the ICC's working languages would improve the quality of candidates and promote greater transparency in the election process.

Nonetheless, in domestic jurisdictions too, compulsory bilingualism is uncommon, but here are a couple of examples. In Canada, the Official Languages Act 1985 ensures respect and equality of both English and French as official state languages as well as equality of status and rights as to their use in all federal institutions, particularly courts (Tiersma and Solan 2016, pp.160–162). The Act imposes a duty on every federal court, with the exception of the Supreme Court, to ensure that every judge (and other officers) can conduct and understand proceedings in either or both languages, as requested by the parties, without the assistance of an interpreter (Sec. 16). Similarly, in the United Kingdom the Welsh Language Act 1993 protects the rights of any party to speak Welsh in a Court of Wales and provides that a Welsh-speaking Prosecutor should be provided in such cases (Sec. 22). Although this model would be impractical to impose at the international level, it is worth bearing in mind that these domestic rights coexist with those entrenched in most international criminal statutes, and under the ICC model, should be available to suspects and defendants under complementarity rules.

Paralinguistic Abilities

Behaviorally, judges, just like jurors, are inclined to some extent to hold certain opinions as well as impressions. Potentially, these can be identified and predicted based on aspects of demographic and sociopsychological attributes that can in turn be used to predict behavior. Independence of the judges is therefore imperative, particularly within the scope of key principles of rule of law such as institutional transparency and accountability.[67] In East Timor, UNTAET Regulation 2001/25 goes a little further in qualifying the scope of independence, impartiality, and integrity, but the language skills and requirements are omitted. For instance, Section 2 of the Regulation stipulates that judges shall decide matters on "their impartial assessment of the facts and their understanding of the law, without improper influence, direct or indirect, from any source" (see also Section 2A3). Inevitably, however, perceptions of testimonies will be, quite often

[67] See UN Security Council, "The Rule of Law and Transitional Justice in Conflict and Post-conflict Societies" – Report of the Secretary General, 23 August 2004, UN Doc. No. S/2004/616, at 4, para. 6. See also the recently adopted 17 Sustainable Goals (2015–2030) by the General Assembly, Goal 16 (3) – "Peace and Justice" targets require the promoting of the rule of law at the national and international level to ensure equal access to justice for all.

unintentionally, personal and varied, often motivated by paralinguistic and generally cultural angles and guided by judges' ability and willingness to interpret these (Kelsall 2009, p. 35). Judges, like juries, inevitably carry with them local, regional, and personal characteristics, for example, in the courtroom setting, one study on jury selection based on statistical modeling concluded that ratings of authoritarianism are subject to perceptions that "highly authoritarian persons are more conservative, highly punitive, rigid, sexually repressed and acquiescent to authority" (Frederick 1978, p. 571). Impartiality is, therefore, critical but to some extent dependent on the willingness and ability of judges to socioculturally reference and contextualize witnesses/defendants as well as the messengers, the interpreters, who give away clues and impressions through their own ability to contextualize the message they are trying to convey. Their sonority, gestures, and hesitations add an extra layer to the communication between the defendants and judges, the effects of which cannot easily be detected nor qualified. This puts defendants at a procedural disadvantage that could range from minor (no effect on the quality of trial), moderate where this could amount to a mitigating sentencing factor, or severe, where proceedings may be vitiated.

Conclusions

This chapter tries to raise awareness about the importance of linguistic and paralinguistic analyses in the context of language trial rights including the rights to competent interpretation and translation and to review translated transcripts. It also seeks to demonstrate the need for linguistic counseling of those involved in criminal proceedings, particularly the judges. In this context access to language services and their quality remain subjects that clearly require further development, rationalization, and uniformity.

The lack of an official framework regarding interpreting and translation services within international criminal law models is somewhat surprising, especially within the ad hoc tribunals given that they are UN bodies. The ICTY Code was only created in 1999 and its provisions lack specificity. Recent ICC cases reveal convenient approaches to resolving issues relating to the determination of whether an accused fully understands and speaks a language of the court, ruling that reasonable rather than full understanding may be sufficient to meet the fair trial and equality of arms requirements. To some extent, such pragmatic approach is not unforeseen now that the ICC has to deal with and provide language services for fairly obscure languages, where it becomes challenging to locate and recruit competent interpreters and translators. Although the ICC is working on a system of accreditation, the more prescriptive the requirements of appointment become, the more difficult it will be to deviate from them, but meeting internationally recognized language rights is vital. These should not be regarded nor treated as secondary trial rights, but as fundamental ones. The quality of international trials and overall international justice mechanisms rests on unconditional protection and proactive rather than reactive upholding of these rights. Crucially, the integrity, independence, and transparency of international criminal courts rest in their ability and commitment to promote the rule of law (Nice and Vallieres-Roland 2005, p. 379). Since these courts and tribunals are tasked with developing and refining international criminal norms, it becomes imperative that all aspects of their operations adhere fully and consistently to elevated procedural standards and fundamental human rights.

However, achieving this requires a holistic and dynamic approach where both interpreters and judges engage in the process of quantifiable and verifiable professional development. Judges should be required to continually improve their language skills, including a requirement that they should acquire fluency in all working languages of a court (normally two, English and French). They should also receive training in paralinguistics and sociolinguistics (increasingly though sociolinguists are asked to provide expert evidence) so that they are better able to manage multilingualism and multicultural perspectives by acquiring proficiency to understand and monitor the work of interpreters. Interpreters, on the other hand, should regularly improve their interpreting skills, including sonority, and increase their knowledge of court proceedings, legal/technical vocabulary, as well as relevant language systems that include regionalization, dialects, colloquialism, and relevant cultural differences.

At a normative level, international courts' statutes and rules of procedure and evidence need to undergo a process of standardization where rules regarding access to language services and processes, through which the adequacy and quality of these may be reviewed, are more noticeably and more uniformly followed. The further emancipation of these provisions will have a direct impact on domestic laws (through referral systems, including ICC complementary model), mainly those relating to investigative and pretrial processes. Domestic norms, such as those allowing for the compellability of interpreters as witnesses in court, should on the other hand inform international legislative efforts.

Bibliography

Adler, B. R., & Ronald, B. (2010). *Understanding human communication*. Oxford: Oxford University Press.

Alexander, R. (2006). *Bosnian, Croatian, Serbian: A grammar with sociolinguistic commentary*. Madison: University of Wisconsin Press.

Amnesty International. (2008). Kosovo (Serbia) – The challenge to fix a failed UN justice system. AI: EUR 70/001/2008. https://www.amnesty.org/en/documents/EUR70/001/2008/EN/. Accessed 24 Aug 2017.

Arzoz, X. (2007). The nature of language rights. *Journal of Ethnopolitics and Minority Issues in Europe, 2*, 1–35.

Berk-Seligson, S. (2017). *The bilingual courtroom: Court interpreters in the judicial process*. Chicago/London: The University of Chicago Press.

Berg-Seligson, S. (2008). Judicial systems in contact. Access to justice and the right to interpreting/translating services among the Quichua in Ecuador, *Interpreting, 10*, 9–33.

Bohlander, M. (2007). *International criminal justice: A critical analysis of institutions and procedures*. London: Cameron May.
Brown-Blake, C. (2006). Fair trial, language and the right to interpretation. *International Journal on Minority and Group Rights, 13*, 391–412.
Buring, D. (2016). *Intonation and meaning*. New York: Oxford University Press.
Byrne, R. (2007). Assessing testimonial evidence in asylum proceedings: Guiding standards from the international criminal tribunals. *International Journal of Refugee Law, 19*, 609–638.
Candlin, N. C., & Gotti, M. (2007). *Intercultural aspects of specialized communication*. Bern: Peter Lang AG, International Academic Publishers.
Chernov, V., & Gelly, V. (2004). *Inference and anticipation in simultaneous interpreting: A probability-prediction model*. Amsterdam/Philadelphia: John Benjamins B. V.
Coan, B., & Christian, C. (2000). Rethinking the spoils of war: Prosecuting rape as a war crime in the International Criminal Tribunal for the Former Yugoslavia. *North Carolina Journal of International Law and Commercial Regulation, 26*, 183–237.
Combs, A. N. (2010). *Fact-finding without facts*. New York: Cambridge University Press.
Coulthard, M., & Johnson, A. (2007). *An introduction to forensic linguistics: Language and evidence*. Oxon: Routledge.
Dieter, S., et al. (2008). *Law and language: Theory and society*. Dusseldorf: Dusseldorf University Press.
Dieter, S., Olsen, F., & Lorz, A. (2009). *Translation issues in language and law*. Chippenham and Eastbourne: Palgrave Macmillan.
Dojcinovic, P. (2012). Word scene investigations: Toward a cognitive linguistic approach to the criminal analysis of open source evidence in war crimes trials. In P. Dojcinovic (Ed.), *Propaganda, war crimes trials and international law; from speakers' corner to war crimes* (pp. 71–117). Routledge: Oxon.
Eades, D. (1995). *Language and evidence: Issues confronting aboriginal and multicultural Australia*. Sydney: University of New South Wales Press.
Eades, D. (2010). Sociolinguistics and the legal process. In *Multilingual Matters*.
Elias-Bursac, E. (2015). *Translating evidence and interpreting testimony at a war crimes tribunal*. Basingstoke; New York: Palgrave Macmillan.
Engberg, J. (2002). Legal meaning assumptions – What are the consequences for legal interpretation and legal translation? *International Journal for the Semiotics of Law, 15*, 375–388.
Ephratt, M. (2011). Linguistic, paralinguistic and extralinguistic speech and silence. *Journal of Pragmatics, 43*, 2286–2307.
Filipovic, L. (2013). Constructing causation in language and memory: Implications for access to justice in multilingual interactions. *International Journal of Speech Language and the Law, 20*, 1–19.
Frederick, T. J. (1978). Jury behaviour – A psychologist examines jury selection. *Ohio Northern University Law Review, 5*, 571–585.
Gaiba, F. (1998). *The origins of simultaneous interpretations: The Nuremberg trial*. Ottawa: Ottawa University Press.
Garces, C. V. (1996). Linguistic and paralinguistic aspects in legal interpretation: Some strategies and programs. *Revista de Estudios Ingleses, 9*, 133–142.
Gibbons, J., & Turell, T. M. (2008). *Dimensions of forensic linguistics*. Amsterdam: John Benjamin Publishing Company.
Heanel, F. (1997). Aspects and problems associated with the use of interpreters in psychotherapy of victims of torture. *Torture, 7*, 68–71.
Karton, J. (2008). Lost in translation: International criminal tribunals and the legal implications of interpreted testimony. *Vanderbilt Journal of Transnational Law, 41*, 3–52.
Kelsall, T. (2009). *Culture under cross-examination: International justice and the Special Court for Sierra Leone*. New York: Cambridge University Press.
Lee, J. (2011). Translatability of speech style in courtroom interpreting. *International Journal of Speech Language and the Law, 18*, 1–33.

Moosmuller, S. (2011). Evaluation of the speech behaviour of reference speakers. *International Journal of Speech Language and the Law, 18*, 179–205.
Morris, R. (1999). The gum syndrome: Predicaments in court interpreting. *Forensic Linguistics, 6*, 1350–1771.
Moskowitz, G. B. (2005). *Social cognition: Understanding self and others*. New York: The Guildford Press.
Nakane, I. (2013). Language rights in Japanese criminal courts: Bridging the gap between legal professionals and language professionals. *Asian Studies Review, 37*, 302–318.
Namakula, S. C. (2012). Language rights in the minimum guarantees of fair criminal trials. *International Journal of Speech Language and the Law, 19*, 73–93.
Namakula, S. C. (2013). *Language and the right to fair hearing in international criminal trials*. Switzerland: Springer.
Nettelfield, L. (2010). *Courting democracy in Bosnia and Herzegovina: The Hague tribunal's impact in a post-war state*. New York: Cambridge University Press.
Nice, G., & Vallieres-Roland, P. (2005). Procedural innovations in war crimes trials. *Journal of International Criminal Justice, 3*, 354–380.
Norman, S. (2007). Assessing the credibility of refugee applicants: A judicial perspective. *International Journal of Refugee Law, 19*, 273–292.
Spears, J. (2003). Sitting in the dock of the day: Applying lessons learned from the prosecution of war criminals and other bad actors in post-conflict Iraq and beyond. *Military Law Review, 176*, 96–189.
Tiersma, P. M., & Solan, L. M. (2016). *The Oxford handbook on language and law*. New York: Oxford University Press.
Tonkin, H., & Esposito, M. F. (2010). *The translator as mediator of cultures*. Philadelphia: John Benjamins Publishing Company.
Valero-Garces, C. (2005). Emotional and psychological effects on interpretation in public services. *Translation Journal*. www.translationjournal.net.journal/33ips.htm. Accessed 24 Aug 2017.
Villmoare, E. (2008). Ethnic crimes and UN justice in Kosovo: The trial of Igor Simic. *Texas International Law Journal, 37*, 373–386.
Wald, P. (2000). Judging war crimes. *Chicago International Law Journal, 1*, 189–196.
Wald, P. (2001). International Criminal Tribunal for the Former Yugoslavia comes of age: Some observations on day-to-day dilemmas of an international court. *Washington University Journal of Law & Policy, 5*, 87–118.
Zimanyi, K. (2009). On impartiality and neutrality: A diagrammatic tool as a visual aid. *Interpreting & Translation, 1*, 55–70.

Index

A
Accountability, 73, 74, 77, 94, 126
Administration of justice, 89, 90
AIIC-United Nations Agreement, 164
"Area bombing", 51
Article 16, 134
Article 17
  criminal investigation, 130, 131
  grounds for inadmissibility, 128–130
  ICC, 128
  sovereignty, 128
  state action, 129, 130
  state inaction and "inability", 132
  "unwillingness", 131, 132
Article 53, 135, 136
Articles 18 and 19, 133
Associations
  analytical strategy, 110
  data, 108, 109
  home page banners, 110, 111
  mission statements, 110, 117–124
  non-terrorist crime, 107
  patriotic images, 111
  social support, 113
  Spain, 110, 114, 115
  United States, 109, 110, 114, 115
  Wayback Machine, 109
  WTC Survivors' Network, 114
Associative distance, 20
Asymmetric unfairness
  asymmetric unfairness, 33–36
  drones, 37
  "last resort" principles, 36
  lethal drones, 33
  "war on terror", 36
9/11 attacks, 12
Authority, 80, 81, 108

B
Basque separatist terrorism, 106
Bombardment, 51
British Criminal Justice System, 160

C
Chartered Institute of Linguists (CIOL), 160
Close Combat Tactical Trainer (CCTT), 62
Communicative styles, 155
Complementarity, 127, 128
Concept of emergency, 94, 95
Counter-terrorism, 73
Counter-Terrorism Committee (CTC), 83
  9/11, 92
  administration of justice, 89, 90
  Algeria's definition, 87
  CTED, 93, 95
  databases, 84–85
  draft anti-terror/security laws, 92
  Egypt, 86
  HRC, 85–87, 89, 91
  human rights, 83
  ICCPR, 84
  imprecise/vague legislation, 88
  justice, 88
  NGO, 91, 92
  principle of legality, 84
  Special Rapporteur, 93
  state of emergency, 89
  states of exception, 89

G. J. Andreopoulos et al. (eds.), *The Rule of Law in an Era of Change*,
Springer Series on International Justice and Human Rights,
https://doi.org/10.1007/978-3-319-89908-4

Counter-Terrorism Committee (CTC) (*cont.*)
  UNSC, 92
  UNSC Resolution 1373, 84, 88
Counter-Terrorism Committee Executive Directorate (CTED), 78, 92, 93, 95
Cowardice, 37, 38
  drone warfare, 37
  military drones, 38
  military personnel, 38
  physical courage, 38
  traditional military combat, 39
Criminal investigation, 131
Cultural distance, 20
Cultural divergences, 161

D
Defense rights, 151–153, 168
Deindividuation, 25
Depersonalization, 25–26
  broad commonality, 18
  drones, 25–26
Distance
  associative, 20
  cultural, 20
  epistemic, 19
  ethical concern, 19–21
  geographical, 17
  moral relevance, 18
  moral significance, 17
  and obligation, 21–23
  psychic/emotional, 20
  psychological effects, 28–32
  sensory, 19
  temporal, 20
Distance and obligation, 21–23
Doctrine of double effect, 53
Drone warfare
  complexity, 40
  cost of military combat, 22
  cowardly, 37
  defenders, 30
  indefensible loss, 22
  military actions, 39
  workings, 39
Drones, 55, 64–66
Due process, 167

E
ECtHR, 166, 168
Epistemic distance, 19
Equality of arms, 168
Evidence, 153, 157, 161–163, 166–168
Exacerbates, 34

F
FealGood Foundation, 114
Formalization of legal entitlements, 8
Fragmentation of responsibility
  archetypal war situation, 39
  deflection of, 40
  diffusion of, 40
  drone attack, 39
  drone warfare, 39, 40
  "fixed quantity", 40
  strategic planning, 39
Free market, 8
Future Combat System (FCS), 63

G
"Global terrorism", 59

H
Hegemonic International Law (HIL), 80, 96–98
Human rights, 11, 73
Human Rights Committee (HRC), 85
  counterterrorist measures, 91
  derogable and non-derogable rights, 89
  ICCPR, 85
  security requirements, 86, 88
  terrorism, 86, 87
Human Rights Watch (HRW), 92

I
"Interests of justice", 135, 136
"Interests of victims", 136
International Association of Conference Interpreters, 159
International Atomic Energy Agency (IAEA), 82
International Convention for the Suppression of the Financing of Terrorism (ICSFT), 83
International Covenant on Civil and Political Rights (ICCPR), 84, 85
  Art. 14 (3), 153
International Criminal Court (ICC), 6, 13
  Article 16, 140, 141, 145
  Article 17, 128, 141–143
  Article 53, 143, 144
  legitimacy and effectiveness, 147
  Preparatory Committee, 130
  Rome Statute, 126
  RPE, 131
  transitional justice, 137
  and truth commissions, 146

International criminal justice, 11, 12
International criminal law
ICCPR Articles 14 and 26, 153
interpretation and translation, 151–153
linguistics, 151, 152
outsource translations, 159
paralinguistic abilities, 152
International Criminal Tribunal for Rwanda (ICTR), 160
International laws of war, 69
International rule of law, 10
definition, 6
UNSC, 6
Interpreters
adequacy of the interpretation, 158
agreement, 159
authenticity, 156
communicative styles, 155, 156
cultural idiosyncrasies, 155
distress, 157
fidelity, 160
fidelity of phonetic standards, 157
"fundamentally flawed", 161
ICC, 161
ICTR, 160
ICTY Code of Ethics, 154, 157
"international" criminal courts, 154
international criminal proceedings, 161, 162
neutrality, 157
non-semantic information, 158
NRPSI, 160
paralinguistic methods, 154, 156, 157
roles and functions, 154
silence and talking too fast testimony, 156
witness memory, 156

J
Judicial Systems Monitoring Report (JSMP), 160
Just war theory
area bombing, 51
bombardment, 51
cluster bombs, 52
doctrine of double effect, 53
jus ad bellum, 50
jus in bello, 50
maltreatment of prisoners, 50
mythic form, 50
NATO war, 52
play motive, 50
self-deception, 54
techno-cultural system, 53
traffic system, 52

L
Lack of courage, *see* Cowardice
Language, 151, 152
Article 67 (1) (a), 165
Article 67 (1) (a) and (f), 167
ECtHR, 166
ICC Statute Article 50 (3), 165
ICTY and ICTR Rules of Procedure and Evidence, 164
International human rights law and jurisprudence, 164
interpretation and translation, 166
pretrial questioning, 165
quality of proceedings, 163
Regulation 61 (d), 166
translation costs, 167
two-language settings, 164
Laws of war, 59, 66, 68
Legitimacy, 73, 74, 79–82, 94, 97
Lethal drones, 31, 33
Linguistic Drafting Committee, 169

M
Madrid, 103, 106, 110, 115
Military culture of war, 52
Moral disengagement, 26
Moral sensibilities, 41
Moral trivialization, 26

N
NATO war, 52
New York
attack, 108
9/11 victims' associations, 108, 115

O
Office of the High Commissioner for Human Rights (OHCHR), 91

P
Paralinguistics, 152
abilities, 172, 173
communicative styles, 158
interpretation, 154, 157
linguistic competence, 170–172
protection of trial rights, 170
and sociolinguistics, 161
Play
agonistic form, 48
time and space, 48
virtual reality, 67
work function and human reasoning, 47

Post-Cold War, 79
Post-traumatic stress disorder (PTSD), 66, 67
Preliminary implementation assessments (PIAs), 85
Principle of legality, 84
Psychic/emotional distance, 20

R
Remotely piloted aircraft/vehicles (RPA/Vs), 15
Responsibility to Protect (RtoP), 10
Right to equality of access, 168
Right to review transcripts, 169, 170
Robotics
  nanotechnology, 62
  psychological advantages, 64
  SWORDS, 64
  UAVs, 63
  UGVs, 64
  unmanned vehicles, 63, 64
Rome Statute, 128–132
  accountability, 126
  admissibility, Article 16, 134
  admissibility, Article 17
    complementarity, 128
    grounds for inadmissibility, 128–130
    "investigation", 130, 131
    sovereignty, 128
    state action, 129, 130
    state inaction and "inability", 132
    "unwillingness", 131, 132
  admissibility, Article 18 and 19, 133
  Article 53, 135
  peace and justice, 126
  principle of complementarity, 127, 128
  scrutiny and interpretation, 125
Rule of law (RoL)
  definition, 4
  "formal" and "substantive" versions, 3, 4
  generality, certainty and equality, 3
  human rights, 2, 7, 8
  justiciability, 8
  national and international levels, 4, 5
  predictability and legitimacy, 5, 7
  property rules, 9
  resolution 67/1, 7
  security, 9
  UDHR, 4
  UNSC, 10
Rules of procedure and evidence (RPE), 131

S
Security, 9–11
Security Council Resolution (SCR), 79
Self-deception, 54
Sensory distance, 19
September 11th, 106
  association (*see* Terrorism victims' associations (TVAs))
  Families for Peaceful Tomorrows, 107
  home page banner, 111, 112
  victims of terrorism, 107
September 11th Families for Peaceful Tomorrows, 114
September's Mission, 114
Skyscraper Safety Campaign, 111, 114
Spain, 106
Special Rapporteur (SR), 93
Special Weapons Observation Reconnaissance Detection System (SWORDS), 64

T
Techno-cultural system, 52, 53
Temporal distance, 20
Terrorism, 108
  Basque extremist, 104
  New York City (*see* New York)
  Spain, 106
  United States, 106
  victimization, 105, 107
Terrorism victims' associations (TVAs)
  funding, 106
  political impact, 106
  services and advocating for rights, 105
  United States, 105
  victims and families, 106
Transitional justice, 104, 137
Transitional spaces, 59
Truth commissions, 13, 140–145
  definition, 138, 139, 146
  ICC
    Article 16, 140, 141
    Article 17, 141–143
    Article 53, 143–145
  and international criminal law, 140
  traits of distinction, 139
Tuesday's Children, 111

U
United Nations General Assembly (UNGA), 80
United Nations Security Council (UNSC), 6

Universal Declaration of Human Rights (UDHR), 3
Unmanned aerial vehicles (UAVs), 15, 16, 63
Unmanned ground vehicles (UGVs), 63, 64
Unmanned surface vehicles (USVs), 63
Unmanned underwater vehicles (UUVs), 63
UNSC counter-terrorism, 12
UNSCR 1373, 88
- 9/11, 74–76, 82, 90
- accountability, 77, 78
- anent *vs.* nonpermanent members, 78
- Article 103, 76, 77
- Article 24, 76, 77
- Article 25, 76
- Article 39, 76
- counter-terrorism, 79, 80
- counter-terrorism measures, 75
- CTC (*see* Counter-Terrorism Committee (CTC))
- CTED, 78
- decision-making powers, 81
- human rights, 74, 75, 77
- ICTR, 76
- ICTY, 76, 80
- international peace and security, 76
- jus cogens norms, 75
- legality and legitimacy, 74
- legitimacy, 81, 82, 91
- post-Cold War, 79
- UNGA, 81

UNSC Resolution 1368, 79
UNSC Resolution 1456, 79

V

Victims
- associations, 105, 106
- domestic crimes, 103, 104
- rights movements, 103, 105, 106
- rule of law, 104
- of terrorism, 105
- terrorist victimization, 103
- transitional justice, 104

Victims of terrorism
- victims' associations, 116
- web page-based documents, 107

Visual technologies and robotics, 12
Visual war technologies, 62
- "PlayStation" mentality, 65
- distance factor, 62
- night vision goggles, 61
- robotics (*see* Robotics)
- thermal imaging devices, 61
- virtual reality, 62

Voices of September 11th, 114

W

War
- ancient non-Western cultures, 49
- autonomous robots, 68
- battle of Crécy, 49
- myth of war, 49
- play dimension, 48

War crimes trials, 168
War on terrorism, 54, 55, 57
War video games
- *America's Army*, 56, 58
- *Close Combat Tactical Trainer*, 57
- cost-effective tool, 58
- covert operations, 59
- Defense Department and ICT, partnership, 56, 57
- drone operators, 67
- *Full Spectrum Warfare*, 57
- immersive quality, 67
- "interpellates"/hails, 60
- MIT study, 56
- "transitional space", 58
- virtual identity, 60
- virtual military training, 57, 58
- virtual reality training, 60
- war on terrorism, 57, 58

Weaponized drones, 16, 29
9/11 Widows' and Victims' Families Association, 107

The manufacturer's authorised representative in the EU is Springer Nature Customer Service Centre GmbH, Europaplatz 3, 69115 Heidelberg, Germany. If you have any concerns regarding our products, please contact ProductSafety@springernature.com

Printed and bound by CPI Group (UK) Ltd, Croydon, CR0 4YY
30/09/2026
02225655-0001